THE PROPHETICAL STORIES

PUBLICATIONS OF THE PERRY FOUNDATION FOR BIBLICAL
RESEARCH IN THE HEBREW UNIVERSITY OF JERUSALEM

ALEXANDER ROFÉ

THE PROPHETICAL
STORIES

The Narratives about the Prophets in the Hebrew Bible
Their Literary Types and History

THE MAGNES PRESS, THE HEBREW UNIVERSITY, JERUSALEM

First Published in Hebrew, 1982
Revised Hebrew Edition, 1986
First English Edition, 1988

ISBN 965-223-685-3

Printed in Israel
at Graph Press Ltd., Jerusalem

To the memory of Dr. Raphael Weiss
1940–1974

CONTENTS

Part Three: From *Legenda* to Martyrology

ABBREVIATIONS

1. *Biblical Books*

Gen	Nah
Exod	Hab
Lev	Zeph
Num	Hag
Deut	Zech
Josh	Mal
Judg	Ps
1Sam	Prov
2Sam	Job
1Kgs	Song
2Kgs	Ruth
Isa	Lam
Jer	Eccl
Ezek	Esth
Hos	Dan
Joel	Ezra
Amos	Neh
Obad	1Chr
Jonah	2Chr
Mic	

Unless otherwise noted, the translation of Biblical passages follows the New Jewish Publication Society translation (NJPS): *The Torah*[2] (1967), *The Prophets* (1978); *The Writings* (1982).

2. *Rabbinic Literature*

m *Mishna*
t *Tosefta*
b *Babylonian Talmud*
y *Palestinian Talmud*

3. *Periodicals, Series and Reference Works*

AASF	Annales Academiae Scientiarum Fennicae
AcOr	*Acta Orientalia*
AnOr	Analecta Orientalia
AOF	*Archiv für Orientforschung*
AJSL	*American Journal for Semitic Languages and Literatures*
AsSt	*Assyriological Studies*
ASTI	*Annual of the Swedish Theological Institute*
AUSS	*Andrews University Seminary Studies*
BDB	F. Brown – S.R. Driver – C.A. Briggs, *A Hebrew and English Lexicon of the Old Testament,*Oxford 1907
BibetOr	Biblica et Orientalia
BJRL	*Bulletin of the John Rylands Library*
BK	Biblischer Kommentar
BWANT	Beiträge zur Wissenschaft des Alten und Neuen Testaments
BZ	*Biblische Zeitschrift*
BZAW	Beiheft zur Zeitschrift für die alttestamentliche Wissenschaft
CB	Cambridge Bible for Schools and Colleges
CoBOTS	Coniectanea Biblica, Old Testament Series
CBQ	*Catholic Biblical Quarterly*
DISO	C.-F.Jean – Hoftijzer, *Dictionnaire des Inscriptions Sémitiques de l'Ouest,* Leiden 1965
DJD	*Discoveries in the Judaean Desert,* Oxford 1955 –
EHAT	Exegetisches Handbuch zum Alten Testament
EsB	*Estudios Biblicos*
ExT	*Expository Times*
FRLANT	Forschungen zur Religion und Literatur des Alten und Neuen Testaments
GHAT	Göttinger Handkommentar zum Alten Testament
HbzAT	Handbuch zum Alten Testament
HSM	Harvard Semitic Monographs
HUCA	*Hebrew Union College Annual*
ICC	International Critical Commentary
JBL	*Journal of Biblical Literature*
JBLMS	Journal of Biblical Literature Monograph Series
JJS	*Journal of Jewish Studies*
JNES	*Journal of Near Eastern Studies*
JPOS	*Journal of the Palestine Oriental Society*
JQR	Jewiṣh Quarterly Review
KAI	H. Donner–W. Röllig, *Kanaanäische und Aramäische Inschriften,* Wiesbaden 1962–1964
KB	L. Köhler – W. Baumgartner, *Lexicon in Veteris Testamenti Libros,* Leiden 1953
KEHAT	Kurzgefasstes exegetisches Handbuch zum Alten Testament
KHAT	Kurzer Hand-Commentar zum Alten Testament

Abbreviations

OLZ	*Orientalistische Literaturzeitung*
OrAn	*Oriens Antiquus*
OuTS	*Oudtestamentische Studiën*
OTL	Old Testament Library
PEQ	*Palestine Exploration Quarterly*
RB	*Revue Biblique*
RGG	*Die Religion in Geschichte und Gegenwart*
RiBib	*Rivista Biblica*
RMI	*Rassegna Mensile di Israel*
SATA	Die Schriften des Alten Testaments in Auswahl
SBLMS	Society of Biblical Literature Monograph Series
SBT	Studies in Biblical Theology
SEA	*Svensk Exegetisk Årsbok*
SJT	*Scottish Journal of Theology*
SMSR	*Studi e Materiali di Storia delle Religioni*
StANT	Studien zum Alten und Neuen Testament
SVT	*Supplements to Vetus Testamentum*
ThLZ	*Theologische Literaturzeitung*
ThSK	*Theologische Studien und Kritiken*
ThZ	*Theologische Zeitschrift* (Basel)
VT	*Vetus Testamentum*
WMANT	Wissenschaftliche Monographien zum Alten und Neuen Testament
ZAW	*Zeitschrift für die alttestamentliche Wissenschaft*
ZThK	*Zeitschrift für Theologie und Kirche*

INTRODUCTION

Israelite prophecy has left its impact on biblical literature in two major literary forms: in the words of the prophets, which generally appear in the books bearing their names, and in the narratives about them, extant mainly in the Book of Kings and in the prose section of the Book of Jeremiah (chaps 25–45) but also in short sections in other books. Naturally, the prophetical sayings have been of prime interest, since they present directly the messages of the prophets, their sources of inspiration and their individual personalities. However, the narratives are also extremely valuable for an understanding of Israelite history and religion. They contain information about preclassical Israelite prophecy, about the impression the prophets left on their contemporaries, about the groups of disciples and admirers who surrounded them and how they conceived of their masters. Moreover, these stories – since they describe the prophets' public activities – contain a wealth of information on the kingdoms of Israel and Judah and their relations with the neighboring states. As such, the stories are an important source for the political history of Israel in the monarchial period.

However, before extracting such information from these narratives, one must first establish their character, the exact extent of each story, the author or authors, and the original medium of composition, whether written or oral. In addition, questions concerning the literary genre should be posited: are these stories history, legend, parable, or any other genre? Establishing the date of composition of the stories is also crucial: are they contemporaneous with the narrated events or do they postdate them, and if so by how much? This last point has often been overlooked by readers who ignore the critical gap between the tale and its teller.

It is these points among others, that have been addressed in this book which is first and foremost a historical study of the literary genres of the prophetical narratives, their growth and evolution. The dating of the narratives has been approached primarily through an examination of linguistic evidence: lexical, morphological and syntactical. With this dating, along with the establishment of the literary genre, the stories are put to use as sources for Israelite political and religious history. On the other hand, no historical discussion is complete without an evaluation of the literary achievements of the age discussed. I have therefore at some length gone into the literary aspects of several stories, such as plot and characterization. This is especially important for the chapters dealing with some of the Elisha stories (chaps. 2–4) which reveal greater profundity and a more sophisticated artistic level than the shorter tales discussed in chap. 1. However, our main effort throughout has been devoted to an understanding of the message of the stories, their implicit motive and explicit purpose, as seen against their historical background. Only when this has been elucidated can the specific means of expression chosen by the writer be evaluated. This in turn may provide a more thorough understanding of the story.

In order to analyze the meaning and message of the prophetic narratives, we have classified the literary categories into some twelve distinct genres. This method may be challenged from two opposing standpoints. Biblical form criticism may maintain that only four *gattungen* – *legenda*, historiography, biography, and *exemplum*-parable – actually exist and that their classification should be determined solely according to the circles of authors and their *Sitz im Leben*. Modern literary critics, on the other hand, will undoubtedly claim that assigning stories to distinct categories blurs the distinctive features and originality of any individual literary composition. Our approach seems to fall somewhere in between, and thus is open to criticism from both sides. Nevertheless, it is my firm belief that this approach is valid. Literature is, above all, the creation of the human mind. Therefore, of greater importance than the circle of writers or the situations in public life underlying a particular literary work is determining the questions and issues with which writers wrestle. It was not a specific circle or *Sitz im Leben* which produced the unique stories about Elisha and the Israelite King; rather they originated in the long-standing issue of the prophet's position in relation to the nation's secular leaders. On the other hand, one cannot deny the presence of fixed patterns in intellectual endeavors. Certain issues, such as the origin and end of the Man of God, are repeatedly encountered. Then too, there are set fashions; for example, the method of presenting a problem regarding prophecy in the form of a disputation between a prophet and God occurs several times in the prophetic narratives. It will therefore be proper to speak in terms of a literary category when we have identified a recurring plot pattern. In the final analysis, what will determine the effectiveness of our approach is whether it yields a better understanding of the writings under consideration.

To the best of my knowledge, the general *gattung* of stories about prophets and other holy men has not yet been identified in ancient Near Eastern literatures. And since the writings of Mesopotamia, Anatolia, Syria, and Egypt known at present are much more extensive than biblical literature, we may hazard the conjecture that such stories will not appear in the future either, for these were apparently never written. Thus, though it is probable that in Mesopotamia, too, stories were told about wonders performed by this *ašipu* or that *baru,* they were never recorded in written form or preserved as cherished traditions. This phenomenon is unique to Israel and may be explained by the special status accorded to prophecy by that nation. The Israelite faith was based wholly upon the revelation of a redeeming and legislating God, and the main channel of this revelation was the prophet. For this reason, Israelite prophets achieved a central position in the nation's religious consciousness. This was what distinguished Israelite religion from its ancient Near Eastern contemporaries, and made it phenomenologically related to Judaism, its successor from the Persian period on, and to the two religions which sprang from Judaism – Christianity and Islam. This state of affairs methodologically justifies the elucidation of the stories about the prophets with literary analogies from later periods – including hassidic tales from the eighteenth century up to the present. I have not attempted to elaborate upon these analogies, but merely to indicate possible fertile ground for further research.

This work originally appeared in Hebrew under the title סיפורי הנביאים, (Jerusalem, 1982). The present translation, prepared by Mr. D. Levy, incorporates several corrections, revisions and additions. It has been edited by Ms. E. Cindorf and Ms. S. Deutsch, and repeatedly revised by Ms. J.H. Seeligmann who also saw the volume through the press. The preparation for this book ranged over many years, during the course of which I consulted and received assistance from teachers, students, and colleagues alike at three academic communities where I studied, taught, and worked on this book: Yale University, the University of Pennsylvania, and above all, my alma mater, the Hebrew University of Jerusalem. Limitations of space prevent my mentioning all my mentors, but I wish to assure them of my deep appreciation for their assistance.

The book is dedicated to the memory of a young bible scholar of the Hebrew University, Dr. Raphael Weiss, who died twelve years ago at the age of 34 of an illness contracted in the concentration camp of Bergen Belsen. He was a loyal colleague and a faithful friend, an assiduous student and a brilliant scholar. May his memory be blessed.

Jerusalem
Spring 1987

PART ONE

FROM *LEGENDA* TO *VITA*

Chapter One

THE *LEGENDA*

1. *The Short Legenda*[1]

Six stories about Elisha display several common features: the healing of the spring (2Kgs 2:19–22), the cursing of the youths and their subsequent death (2Kgs 2:23–24), the widow's continuous pouring of the oil (2Kgs 4:1–7), the curing of the stew (2Kgs 4:38–41), the multiplication of the loaves and grain (2Kgs 4:42–44), and the floating of the axehead (2Kgs 6:1–7).

All these stories recount miraculous acts. All of them contain a simple plot: they begin with a description of a crisis requiring supernatural intervention (such as the threatened enslavement of the widow's sons, the famine, the axehead's sinking in the river), usually continue with a plea to Elisha for help, introduce a doubt whether he will indeed succeed in doing so (2Kgs 4:2: "What can I do for you?" 2Kgs 4:43: "How can I set this before a hundred men?"), and conclude with a description of the wondrous deliverance wrought by the Man of God. All these stories involve the circumstances and performance of a single miracle. Each story is independent of those preceding and following it. They contain no references to other stories, and make no attempt to relate the miracle described to any earlier or later incidents in the life of Elisha. The brevity of the stories – two to seven verses each – reflects simplicity. It appears that this length is sufficient to encompass the plot of each of these stories.

The personae who appear in these six stories similarly are neither

1 This chapter is an expanded and revised version of part of my article "The Classification of the Prophetical Stories," *JBL* 89 (1970), pp. 427–440, ad pp. 430–433; earlier literature is discussed there.

complex nor three-dimensional figures. Nothing is told of their origins, histories, physical appearances, opinions, thoughts, desires, or deeds. Not even their names are provided. They are anonymous – ordinary people. These characters are of no interest aside from the particular role they play in each of the stories. When their part has ended, they return to their former anonymity, to the cast of extras. We could say that in these stories there are *roles,* but no *characters.* Elisha is no different in this respect from the others. He knows how to perform miracles and is esteemed by his followers – yet his portrayal, too, never goes beyond the level of a *role.* Nothing more is known of him than of the simple people who surround him. This lack of interest in his character is also discernible in his being referred to, on occasion, not by name but by the title "Man of God" (2Kgs 4:42); the story is concerned only with this aspect of his make-up. For the purpose of these stories, the Man of God, Elisha, is no different from any others who bore this title, and so he, too, lacks distinguishing personal characteristics.[2]

The role of the Man of God is to perform miracles. Those recounted in these stories are all of a similar type: they help ordinary people in their daily lives. They provide food for a day, save a family from the shame of slavery, spare one the harassment of insolent youths, or float a sunken axehead which had been borrowed by a poor man. The greatest miracle of all – the healing of the spring at Jericho – is similarly a local phenomenon. These are not miracles of great national import, such as that of Joshua at Gibeon (Josh 10:12–14) or Samuel at Mizpah (1Sam 7:9–12). They do not affect the history of the nation for coming generations or even for one generation, nor do they possess

---

2 O. Plöger, *Die Prophetengeschichten der Samuel- und Königsbücher* (Diss. Greifswald, 1937), p. 18, has correctly noted that this title is characteristic of Elisha, not of Elijah. This means that the stories recorded in 1Kgs 17:17–24 and 2Kgs 1, in which Elijah is called "Man of God," are among the latest strata of the Elijah cycle, as we will see below. The title expresses the people's admiration for the man who knows secret things and performs wonders (cf. 1Sam 9:6–10). I agree with R. Hallevy, "Man of God," *JNES* 17 (1958), pp. 237–244, that the term should be construed as "Godly Man." This was originally an honorific title conferred on holy men, as suggested by J.A. Holstein, "The Case of *'iš ha'elohim* Reconsidered," *HUCA* 48 (1977), pp. 69–81, ad p. 75. However, unlike Holstein, it seems to me that in post-exilic literature, this title acquired new and different connotations; cf. the convincing observations of P. Joüon, "Locutions hébraïques: איש אלהים homme de Dieu," *Biblica* 3 (1922), pp. 53–55.

religious significance. They are not tests of God's strength, as were the miracles of the desert wanderings, nor do they bring about changes in the religious consciousness of the nation, like the miracle at the Red Sea which induced the people to believe in God and His servant Moses (Exod 14:31). Elisha's miracles are minor deliverances, small acts of salvation, in both scope and effect. They attest merely to the supernatural power of the Man of God who performs them.

The miracles under consideration not only lack national or theological significance, they are also deficient in moral values. In only one of the six stories is it stated that the deceased husband of the recipient of the miracle "revered the Lord" (2Kgs 4:1). On the other hand, did the people of Jericho really deserve the miracle which healed their spring? Was the borrower of the floated axehead worthy of such wondrous aid? Such questions have no answers in these six tales, because they are irrelevant to the aim of the stories. Those benefiting from the miracle are not particularly honest or righteous. They are, however, through some fixed or chance relationship, close to the Man of God. It is this connection with him which makes them worthy. The amorality of these stories is exemplified in the story of Elisha's cursing of the youths. Their punishment is totally disproportionate to their crime. The Rabbis, who also noted this fact, therefore expounded the story in such a way as to find greater fault with the youths and thus to justify Elisha.[3] But according to the literal meaning of the story, the youths are killed not because of any other evil they may have committed, but because of their frivolous insult to Elisha's honor. It is thus evident that not the ethical categories of good and evil are relevant in this and the other stories, but those of

---

3 Cf. Sota 46b: "What means 'little children'? - R. Eleazar said נערים [children] means that they were bare (מנוערים) of precepts; 'little' means that they were little of faith. A Tanna taught: They were youths נערים but they behaved like little children . . . 'And he looked behind him and saw them, and cursed them in the name of the Lord.' What did he see? . . . Samuel said: He saw that their mothers had all become conceived with them on the Day of Atonement. R. Isaac the smith said: He saw that their hair was plaited as with Amorites. R. Johanan said: He saw that there was no sap of the commandments in them. But perhaps there would have been such in their descendants! R. Eleazar said: Neither in them nor in their descendants unto the end of all generations" [trans. A. Cohen, in I. Epstein, ed., *The Babylonian Talmud* (London; Soncino, 1936), Vol. 16, pp. 244–245]. This tendency has been fully outlined by I. Heinemann, דרכי האגדה[2] (Jerusalem, 1955), pp. 87–95.

the sacred and profane. A Man of God is a holy figure (2Kgs 4:9) and as such must be treated with veneration, just as one behaves towards the Divine and the objects associated with the Divine. These youths profaned the Holy Man of God, and like the sons of Aaron (Lev 10:1–3) or Uzza (2Sam 6:6–7), who acted with no intent of malice, their punishment is swift and terrible. Such extreme retribution, even in cases of accidental profanation, is a logical consequence of the conception of the Holy displayed in these tales – the Divine as an awesome, mighty power, which cannot be resisted by mortal men, and whose responses are unfathomable: they cannot be predicted nor can they be comprehended in retrospect.[4] The Man of God performs miracles for those around him without the need for moral justification; his presence brings them blessing. However, it constitutes a danger too, which can be averted by not approaching the Holy and maintaining an attitude of awe and respect.

This feeling of fear and respect towards the Man of God, which in these stories is demanded of the secular characters, hints at the inner tendency of these stories, that is, their unconscious message. These tales express the attitude of fear and admiration of the simple believer towards the Holy Man, his wonder at the supernatural acts of the Man of God and his excitement at the involvement of the Divine in daily affairs. These emotions were readily transmitted by the narrator of the story. Even if the audience at first listened only out of curiosity or for entertainment, by the end of the tale it would certainly be deeply moved and inspired by the perception of the presence of the Divine. This religious emotion was evidently capable of inspiring unusual acts of piety or charity as in the incident of Gehazi and the king in 2Kgs 8:1–6.[5]

The attitude of fear and admiration towards the Man of God is also evident in the way in which he is addressed. Instead of a direct request for his assistance, his petitioners merely state their troubles. This indirect appeal expresses the intense faith of the common people in the ability of the Man of God to render aid and succor, but at the same time allows him the possibility of not intervening and still preserving

---

4   On the primitive notion of holiness, see R. Otto, *The Idea of the Holy*[2] (Pelican Books, 1959).

5   Regarding this story, see below, chap. 2, sect.1.

his self-respect. It can be said that the miracles performed by Elisha, his small acts of deliverance, are carried out by request, though the request is a silent one.

How are the miracles performed? Usually by magical action: throwing salt out of a *new* dish (2Kgs 2:20), *looking* at the youths while cursing them in the name of God (2:24), *closing the door* of the widow's house while the oil is poured (4:4), *throwing the flour* into the bitter stew (4:41), and *throwing a stick* at the spot where the axehead had sunk (6:6). All these are magical acts well known from other cultures and periods.[6] It is therefore understandable that nowhere, not even when Elisha is for the moment totally perplexed (4:2a), does he pray to God. He acts not through the power of prayer, nor through the power of God's word which he hears and transmits, but through the use of powers residing within himself, or through his knowledge and rule over the hidden forces of nature.

In two of these stories, however, the miracle also involves the word of God. In purifying the waters of Jericho's spring, Elisha says, as he casts in the salt: "Thus said the Lord: 'I heal this water; no longer shall death and bereavement come from it!'" (2:21). And when he multiplies the "first fruits"[7] he answers the doubting servant: "Give it to the people and let them eat. For thus said the Lord: They shall eat and have some left over" (4:43). In both cases the prophetic utterance "Thus said the Lord" is not the sole cause of the miracle. In the story of the spring, the salt is spilled from the new dish, and in the multiplication of the loaves, it is Elisha's repetition of the command: "Give it to the people and let them eat" which overcomes the servant's words of doubt. It is thus difficult to determine whether the narrator was originally undecided as to the cause of the miracle, and attributed it therefore to both Elisha's magical powers and God's Word of

---

6 Studies by anthropologists of the old school are still valid in characterizing and classifying the various types of magic acts; see J. G. Frazer, *The Golden Bough: Part I – The Magic Art and the Evolution of Kings*[3] (London, 1911), pp. 52–219; Hut. Webster, *Magic: A Sociological Study* (Stanford, CA-London, 1948). For magical traces in prophecy, see G. Fohrer, "Prophetie und Magie," *Studien zur alttestamentlichen Prophetie (1949-1965)* [BZAW 99] (Berlin, 1967), pp. 242-264.

7 The word לחם here means "food" as in 1Kgs 5:2.

creation,[8] or whether the Word of God was a later addition.[9] It seems that both these references to the Word of God were added together with the concluding statements "in accordance with the word spoken by Elisha" (2:22), and "as the Lord had said" (4:44), by the editor of the Book of Kings, who missed no opportunity to stress the fulfillment if the Word of God by His servants, the prophets.[10]

The absence of any literary shaping which is evident in the lack of narrative development and of three-dimensional characters, as well as the somewhat primitive religious conceptions, can point to the source of these stories. These are popular tales, which were transmitted orally by the people of the Northern Kingdom. That these stories were handed down by word of mouth is also attested by the king's request of Gehazi to relate to him "all the wonderful things that Elisha has done" (2Kgs 8:4–6). Evidently, even among the sophisticated court circles, stories about Elisha circulated orally. It may be assumed that at least one generation passed after the death of Elisha before these stories were committed to writing.

What was the relationship between the original folk tales and the stories in their present written form? It seems unlikely that these stories, as they are presented in the Book of Kings, are a faithful and exact transcription of the popular legends. The longest of these stories takes about seventy-five seconds to read. It is inconceivable that the ancient Israelite storyteller could not hold his audience's attention for longer than this. If these stories had any *Sitz im Leben* – and, as we shall see, they most certainly did – unless they were passed on informally in conversations on the street, their relating could take hours.[11] We must thus conclude that the original oral versions were much longer than the present stories, and what we have before us is a condensation. The writer who recorded the stories preserved only their kernel – the miracle and its circumstances – and left out most

---

8   In this case, as well, the Word of God is not described as being transmitted to the prophet, but as spontaneously issuing from him at the moment of need. The prophet is a "Man of God" in the sense that he incorporates Divinity, a kind of Godly emanation, by whose power he acts.

9   See B.O. Long, "2 Kings III and Genres of Prophetic Narrative," *VT* 23 (1973), pp. 337–348, ad p. 346.

10 See below, chap. 5, sect.5.

11 Compare the description of the creation of folk epic by A.B. Lord, *The Singer of Tales* (New York, 1968).

of the other details. In this way he created a concise and simple type of wonder tale: a wonder tale about the Man of God.[12]

Such wonder tales are not unique in the history of literature. They are well known from various cultures. In medieval Europe, legends abounded about miracles performed by the Christian saints, or about their torture and martyrdom. These stories were collected from time to time and arranged according to a calendar of saints, and read on their days in monasteries and feudal courts. This also indicates the origin of the word *legenda,* whose meaning is "those things which should be read, things worthy of being read."[13] This term, which originally applied to the entire corpus of saints' tales, came in the course of time to refer also to individual stories, and was so used to designate the same class of stories in other cultures. It is in this sense that the term is used throughout this book.[14]

Legends of this type are also found in the Jewish tradition. Well-known stories from rabbinic literature, for example, are the tales of Honi Ha-Meʻaggel and R. Hanina b. Dosa.[15] It is in the hassidic age, however, that this genre comes into its own. Here the *legenda* achieves almost canonical status as the official literature of the hassidic sects, which served to instruct their members. The dictum: "It is enjoined to speak the praises of the saints" clearly expresses this intention,[16] as does the Latin term *legenda.* The Hebrew term *šebah* (praise) which was applied to R. Isaac Luria, R. Israel Baʻal Shem Tov and other

---

12 It seems that not much time passed between the oral composition of these stories and their written summaries. Cf. G. Widengren, "Oral Tradition and Written Literature ... with Special Regard to Prose Narrative," *AcOr* 23 (1959), pp. 201–262.

13 Of great importance for the understanding of the *legenda* is the comprehensive discussion of A. Jolles, *Einfache Formen*[3] (Tübingen, 1965), pp. 23–61. An extensive study with rich bibliography on the subject can be found in H. Rosenfeld, *Legende*[2] (Stuttgart, 1964).

14 Conversely, its secondary meaning – that of a fantastic tale in general (as in the English "legend" and Spanish "leyenda") – will not be employed here. The problems of the use of the modern English term "legend," if used with the connotations of the medieval Christian *legenda*, are evident in the study of R. Hals, "Legend: A Case Study in OT Formcritical Terminology," *CBQ* 34 (1972), pp. 166–176.

15 This material has been studied by G.B. Sarfatti, "Pious Men, Men of Deeds, and the Early Prophets" (Heb.), *Tarbiz* 26 (1957), pp. 126–153.

16 Cf. S.A. Horodetsky, ספר שבחי הבעש״ט[2] "Introduction,"(Tel Aviv, 1947), p. יב.

kabalistic and hassidic personalities, is the Jewish equivalent of the medieval Christian *legenda.*

In some ways the Hassidic *šebah* is more akin to the prophetic *legenda* than are the above-noted Christian parallels. Whereas the Christian *legenda* is partially composed of stories of the martyrdom on behalf of the faith, the prophetic *legenda* at this stage of their evolution include no such tales, and this, for the simple reason that no such situation occurred in Israel before the end of the seventh century BCE.[17] True martyrologies, i.e. tales describing heroes whose lives and deaths testified to God's glory, appear only during the Second Temple period (cf. Dan 3; 6). In the same manner, the hassidic tale does not describe martyrdom, or as it was then known, the Sanctification of God's Name, but was rather an account of wonders performed by the hassidic rabbi. Similar historical situations in different and widely separated eras gave rise to the same literary genre. The prophetic *legenda,* like the hassidic wonder tale, is the creation of a band of believers who had gathered around a Holy Man, and to express their admiration for him, recounted his miraculous acts.

André Jolles has maintained that *legenda* are still being composed in modern, secular society. The heroes of these, however, are the heroes of our time – sports stars, for example, whose performances in the arena are followed anxiously by millions of fans in hope of witnessing a "miracle": a world record broken, or some other feat of skill or endurance.[18] This analogy, while tempting, is nevertheless somewhat misleading. The prophetic, Christian, and hassidic *legenda* all sprang up around a local figure whose miracles benefited a small group of admirers, and who therefore was known to only a restricted group. The sports star, on the other hand, in the era of modern media, gains widespread, even international fame. In this respect he represents a type of popular hero which never existed before the twentieth century. Moreover, the sports star's "miracles" have no effect on the personal lives of his admirers. He does not save them from famine, poverty, or oppression, nor does he protect them from

---

17　On the reports of the slaughter of prophets by Jezebel and the people in 1 Kgs 18:4, 13, 22; 19:10, 14, see below, chaps. 9 and 10.

18　See Jolles (above, n. 13), pp. 23–61.

illness or death. A modern analogy to the Man of God may be found by asking which of the functions performed by him still have a place in contemporary society. These functions would seem to be mainly "minor miracles," performed in matters of sickness and health: healing the terminally ill, "reviving the dead," and curing barren women. In modern society these tasks are performed by doctors, and just as the Man of God replaced the primitive medicine man, he himself was eventually replaced by the modern medical doctor.

Indeed, there are a number of interesting parallels between the status of the Man of God and that of the modern doctor. It is enough to note the high expectations which the average person has for his doctor's ability to cure him. I think the following comment, offered by a patient at a New York hospital,[19] is typical:

> Because especially now, we don't have Gods anymore really and truly. Hardly anybody believes in that. So the doctor's job is one that never existed – far beyond any of the others. There were some Gods that were all of these things, and there was Jesus. Because you had another world. But since we don't believe in it anymore, the doctor is now God.

These remarks are of interest to our study of the *legenda,* since the doctor appears to inherit the role of the Holy Man. This is demonstrated by the personal stories of patients, especially elderly people who are more intensely concerned with their personal health. They tell tales, with great vividness and emotion, of undetected illnesses, improper treatment, patients who stood at death's door, until . . . until the modern Holy Man, the doctor (often a "specialist") appeared, examined, diagnosed, prescribed swiftly and accurately, and saved the patient from certain death. The patient, who went on to live a long and happy life, now relates the story with a distinct feeling of self-importance – "It happened to me!" – adding another incident to the legend of the "Wonder Rabbi" . . . .

Who began relating the stories of Elisha's miracles? In 2Kgs 8:1–6 the King requests Gehazi to tell him of the great deeds performed by his master. In other words, Gehazi is a "reliable source" for these

---

19 Quoted from E.J. Cassel, "In Sickness and in Health," *Commentary* 49/6 (June 1970), p. 64.

stories. Nevertheless, it is unlikely that Gehazi was the primary person responsible for transmitting the Elisha tradition, as the two main stories in which he appears (2Kgs 4:8–37; 5) paint a negative picture of him. Moreover, Gehazi is not mentioned at all in the short *legenda*.[20] |Rather, the Sons of the Prophets בני הנביאים are mentioned there several times as companions of Elisha and recipients of his miraculous acts. In these stories the Sons of the Prophets have no prophetic power.[21] Nothing is known of them, save that they "were sitting before" Elisha (2Kgs 4:38; 6:1). That they were not an organized communal sect is certain from the fact that they did not share communal property (4:1–7; 6:5). It seems that these groups were bands of the prophet's admirers, who, drawn by his fame and charismatic personality, gathered around him. They ministered to him when necessary, listened to his preaching and discussed his words. These circles of disciples, similar to the coteries surrounding the hassidic masters in Eastern Europe, were the originators of the traditions of the prophetic *legenda*.

2. *Legenda and Reliquiae*

The Man of God heals, resurrects, and brings good fortune through his supernatural power. This is a unique kind of hidden energy which

---

20 Orally, by Dr. Yair Zakovitch of the Hebrew University. See also the distinctions drawn by O. Eissfeldt, *The Old Testament, An Introduction* (Oxford, 1965), p. 294.

21 Indeed, in 1Kgs 20:35 a true prophet is referred to as "one of the Sons of the Prophets"; in 2Kgs 2:1–15 the Sons of the Prophets are described as knowing the future and inheriting part of Elijah's spirit (Elisha receiving the firstborn's double portion); and in 2Kgs 9:1 one of the Sons of the Prophets is sent by Elisha to anoint Jehu; yet all these cases can be proved to be of a late date and consequently not to reflect the original meaning of the term "Sons of the Prophets." On 2Kgs 2:1–18, see below, chap. 3, sect. 1; and on 2Kgs 9:1, see chap. 5, sect. 2. I therefore cannot accept the view of M.A. Vanden Oudenrijn, "L'Expression 'fils des prophètes' et ses analogies," *Biblica* 6 (1925), pp. 167–171, and (more recently) A. Bartal, "The Rise and Fall of the Prophetic Movement in the Days of Elijah and Elisha" (Heb.), ספר יעקב גיל (Jerusalem, 1979), pp. 41–63, and J.R. Porter, "Běnê-hanněbî'îm," *Proceedings of the Eighth World Congress of Jewish Studies 1981* (Jerusalem, 1982), pp. 41–46. See P. Joüon's important comment in *Grammaire de l'Hébreu Biblique* (Rome, 1923), p. 390. The analogy from the history of Hassidism is instructive; just as the members of hassidic circles did not necessarily display excessive personal piety, neither did the Sons of the Prophets possess special prophetic gifts.

never dissipates. Even after his death, the body of the Man of God is capable of effecting miracles. His supernatural energy is transmitted by contact; it is "contagious." It can therefore also be transferred to his personal effects – his staff, mantle, and utensils, which preserve his power even after his death.

Such notions are well known from medieval Christianity. Relics of the saints – their bones, hair, fingers, and skin – were objects of veneration in the Catholic church. They were preserved as charms in cathedrals. They were stolen, looted, bartered and moved from one place to another in an effort to enjoy the power of blessing they could bestow. This power was also attributed to the personal possessions of the saints, to their clothes and utensils. All these *reliquiae* had a double role: they served as charms of good fortune for their owners, either an individual or community, as well as material proof for later generations of the existence of the saint and of his wonders and miracles.[22]

In Judaism, the *reliquiae* lost much of their significance, mainly because of the struggle against the cult of the dead (Deut 26:14),[23] and the laws of defilement by corpses (Num 19). Still, under the influence of Islam, many burial sites of saints and scholars were maintained as places of prayer and pilgrimage. The custom of visiting and praying at the tombs of saints was, and still is, practiced at the graves of several hassidic masters in Eastern Europe. Another hassidic custom which recalls the veneration of *reliquiae* is the partaking of "leavings" שיירים i.e., food served on formal festive occasions at the hassidic rabbi's table, which is tasted by the rabbi and then divided among the Hassidim. The sons and relatives of the Holy Man constitute a further class of *reliquiae*. The principle of hereditary succession among hassidic leaders originated in the notion that the descendants of the Holy Man inherit or preserve his supernatural abilities.

There are also modern *reliquiae*. The mausoleums of state and class leaders, museums which display not only the personal papers but also the effects of public figures, attest to the modern survival of the idea. The Zionist movement, for example, transferred to Jerusalem

22 See again Jolles (n. 13), pp. 23–61.
23 See A. Rofé, *Introduction to Deuteronomy* (Heb.) (Jerusalem, 1974), pp. 35–39. In my opinion, the evidence of Deut. 26:14 qualifies the claims made by Y. Kaufmann, תולדות האמונה הישראלית[2], Vol. 2 (Tel Aviv, 1952), pp. 544–556.

Theodor Herzl's study from Vienna, and the desk at which he wrote *Der Judenstaat* from a Paris hotel. These relics are considered to have taken part in the miracle of the rebirth of the Jewish people. Descendants in modern movements are also seen as a kind of *reliquiae*. But the secular attitude towards inherited charisma is more complex; often the emotional appeal of the descendant of the great leader is rejected on the rational level. The sons of the great and famous are, on the one hand, expected to have inherited their fathers' talents and abilities, but on the other, an automatic assumption of their positions is challenged. And worse, the descendants' own talents and abilities are rarely appreciated.[24] The difficulty of being the son of a great man was already recognized in classical literature, as the figure of Telemachus in the Odyssey so poignantly demonstrates.[25]

Though the concept of *reliquiae* has scarcely survived in the Bible, it is nevertheless present. According to Josh 24:32, Joseph's remains were buried in Shechem, in the plot purchased by Jacob. There is evidence that this plot was considered a sacred precinct; in Gen 33:19–20 Jacob is said to have erected an altar on the same spot.[26] Such stories, which describe the Patriarchs as building altars, erecting stelae, and planting sacred groves and trees in open fields, do not imply that these sacred objects were still in empty fields at the time of the stories' composition. The authors refer to altars and other monuments that did indeed exist in their own times but were now in the courtyards of sanctuaries. This is indicated by the story about Jacob at Beth-el (Gen 28:10–22), for in the early Monarchy period, and possibly even at the end of the period of the Judges, Beth-el was one of the main temples for the worship of YHWH. Coming back to Shechem, in its sanctuary both an altar built by Jacob and the tomb

---

24 A contemporary Israeli example is provided by the controversial remarks made at the burial of Prof. Eri Jabotinsky, Zeev Jabotinsky's son, cf. הארץ, June 9, 1969, p. 4.

25 Homer, *Odyssey,* especially Books 1–3. Can we call the syndrome of a son overshadowed by and constantly judged by himself and others in comparison with a deceased father a "Telemachus complex?" A tragic modern example is that of the son of Theodor Herzl; see J. Weinschall, *Hans Herzl* (Heb.) (Tel Aviv, 1945).

26 The phrase ויצב שם מזבח "He set up an altar there" (Gen 33:20), is puzzling. It probably read originally ויצב שם מצבה "He set up a pillar" and was emended by copyists because of the law of Deut. 16:22 forbidding *maṣṣebot*. See J. Wellhausen, *Die Composition des Hexateuchs etc.*[4] (Berlin, 1963), p. 48.

of Joseph were shown. Joseph's remains were preserved in the *temenos* of Shechem, just as the remains of Greek heroes were buried in the local shrines,[27] and the *reliquiae* of the saints were kept in cathedrals. In full agreement with such ideas is the biblical statement that Joseph's bones became a heritage of the Josephites (Josh 24:32).[28] The remains of the eponymous hero of the tribe were preserved as a talisman of good fortune for his descendants.

The Bible also attests to the opposition to the veneration of the nation's leaders. Of Moses, who died on Mt. Nebo, it is written: "And no one knows his burial place to this day" (Deut 34:6). On the Mesha Stone, however, we read that the utensils of the sanctuary at Nebo, the only Israelite city mentioned there to have a sanctuary, were plundered by the King of Moab.[29] It seems likely that the sanctity of the site was based on the belief that Moses was buried there,[30] and Deuteronomy opposes this claim in accordance with its doctrine of centralization of the cult in the place chosen by God. Of Joshua it is said that: "They placed in the tomb with him . . . the flint knives with which he circumcized the Israelites when he took them out of Egypt" (LXX Josh 24:31).[31] This verse, however, was omitted from the Masoretic text. What was later done to the text had earlier been done to the objects. Hezekiah smashed the bronze serpent made by Moses

---

27 See L.R. Farnell, *Greek Hero Cults and Ideas of Immortality* (Oxford, 1921); A.C. Pearson, "Heroes and Hero-Gods (Greek and Roman)," *Encyclopaedia of Religion and Ethics* VI:652–656. The memory of a Phoenician cult of city-founding heroes has been preserved in the remarks of Philo of Byblos regarding Shamaim-Ramim and Ushu, who dwelt at Tyre; after their death a cult was dedicated to them: Eusebius, *Praeparatio Evangelica* I:10:9–11. Cf. O. Eissfeldt, "Schamem-rumim 'Hoher Himmel,' ein Stadtteil von Gross-Sidon," *Kleine Schriften* II (Tübingen, 1963), pp. 123–126.

28 The *NJPS* translation: " . . . The piece of ground which Jacob had bought for a hundred *kesitahs* from the children of Hamor, Shechem's father, and which had become a heritage of the Josephites" ignores the reliquarian implications of the verse.

29 See J.C.L. Gibson, *Textbook of Syrian Semitic Inscriptions,* Vol. I (Oxford, 1971), pp. 71–83.

30 See A. Rofé, "Moses' Blessing, the Sanctuary of Nebo, and the Origin of the Levites" (Heb.), *Studies in Bible and the Ancient Near East Presented to Samuel E. Loewenstamm . . .,* ed. Y. Avishur and J. Blau (Jerusalem, 1978), Hebrew Volume, pp. 409–422, ad pp. 413ff.

31 See A. Rofé, "The End of the Book of Joshua According to the Septuagint," *Henoch* 4 (1982), pp. 17–36.

to cure the people (2Kgs 18:4), and so destroyed an ancient relic which had been used by Moses to perform his miracles, and which later became an object of naive veneration by the nation.

The idea of *reliquiae* survived with greater vitality in the prophetic *legenda.* The story in 2Kgs 13:20–21 of the man who was resurrected by contact with Elisha's bones is the only such case, but an indisputable one.[32] The location of Elisha's grave is not specified, but the reference to a Moabite raid in this incident hints that it was situated in Abel-Meholah, in the Jordan Valley, his native town. The author appears to have assumed that his listeners or readers would be aware of this fact, whereas the editor of the book, being of the Deuteronomistic school, was not particularly interested in informing his audience of the location of the holy grave where such miracles took place.

An example of a human *reliquiae* is found in 2Kgs 8:1–6. This story seems to have taken place after Elisha's death.[33] The king wishes to hear stories of Elisha's miracles from Gehazi, who had been his servant. An atmosphere of piety, awe, and veneration of the Man of God, of true belief in God and in Elisha, His representative on Earth, permeates the story and grips the audience: "While he was telling the king how (Elisha) had revived a dead person, in came the woman whose son he had revived." The miracle, while being told, suddenly comes to life: the woman and her son stand before the king and court, not only as witnesses, but as living *reliquiae,* objects which were touched by the prophet's supernatural powers. The circumstance of their arrival at the court at the precise moment their story was being told is no mere coincidence. Gehazi is immediately affected by this marvel. His words take on a breathless, staccato, pace: "My lord king! This is the woman, and this is her son, whom Elisha revived!" The king is also seized with emotion. He asks to hear the story again, this time from the woman; not because of any doubts regarding Gehazi's story, but rather to "speak the praises of the saints." In this spirit, and out of respect for the deceased Man of God and the living *reliquiae* standing before him, he grants the widow her request.

---

32 Cf. R. Hallevy, "The Origins of Prophecy in Israel" (Heb.), *HUCA* 31 (1960), pp. 1–14, ad p. 3, n. 5.

33 The evidence will be presented below, chap. 2, end of sect. 1.

Chapter Two

ELABORATIONS OF THE *LEGENDA*

1. *The Literary Elaboration.*[1]

In 2Kgs 4:8–37 two miracles performed by Elisha are described: the granting of a son to the Shunammite woman (vv 8–17), and the resurrection of the child after his death (vv 18–37). These are not, however, two separate *legenda,* but two miracles recounted in a single *legenda.* The unity of plot is evident not only in the fact that all the characters in the two incidents are identical, but also in the inner connection between the episodes. The Shunammite woman's plea to Elisha after the boy's death, her chastisement of him and his positive response (vv 25–29), can be understood only against the backdrop of the first miracle, whose details are given in full (vv 12–16). This story is thus one long *legenda* comprising thirty verses, a single framework which incorporates two separate miraculous acts.

The ability to construct so long and complex a story attests to greater literary talent than was displayed in the short *legenda.* Obviously it is not the length of the story alone which attests to this skill, but the complexity of the story. A full explanation is presented here of the *circumstances* of Elisha's initial acquaintance with the Shunammite, and reasons for his granting her a son and for being eager to attempt the boy's resurrection. All these aspects of the story, here fully developed, are lacking in the short *legenda.*

The detailed descriptions are carefully structured. The phrase ויהי היום "one day," which occurs here three times (vv 8, 11, 18), divides

---

1 This section is an expanded and revised version of a section of my article: "The Classification of Prophetical Stories," *JBL* 89 (1970), pp. 427–440, pp. 433–435; see there a discussion of the earlier literature.

the story into three parts: Elisha's introduction to the Shunammite (vv 8–10), his curing of her barrenness (vv 11–17), and his resurrection of her child (vv 18–37).[2] In the Bible the phrase ויהי היום is employed primarily for the purpose of focusing on a particular incident, especially if preceded by the description of a long-standing situation or a recurring action.[3] In this story the term concentrates the action into three days: the day the characters meet (v 8a), the day of Elisha's promise (vv 11–16), and the day of the child's death and resurrection (vv 18b–37). The events which take place between these days – Elisha's repeated visits and the construction of the upper chamber for him (vv 8b–10), the woman's pregnancy, the birth and growth of the child (vv 17–18a) – are a direct result of the preceding events and preparation for those to follow. There is thus a lengthy description of the intermediate episodes after the first day, a somewhat shorter one after the second day, and none after the third. As the intermediate narrative becomes condensed, the description of the "days" themselves expands from a short, casual description of the day of meeting (v 8a) to a longer, detailed account of the day of Elisha's promise (vv 11–16) and a very thorough account of the day of death and resurrection (vv 18b–37). Thus, the structure parallels the development of the story: as the plot becomes more complex, in terms of the relationships between the heroes, the seriousness of the crisis and the difficulty of finding a solution, the tale becomes longer and more complex.[4]

In the course of the narrative, the characters of the protagonists are described. First, the woman who benefits from these miracles. She is no longer anonymous; though her name is not disclosed, she has a title: the Shunammite. Many details of her biography are disclosed to the reader: she is the wife of an old farmer (v 14), she is of a respected

2   See T. Rudin-O'Brasky, *The Patriarchs in Hebron and Sodom* (Heb.) (Jerusalem, 1982), pp. 66–74. A. Schmitt, "Die Totenerweckung in 2 Kön 4, 8–37 etc.," *BZ* (N.F.) 19 (1975), pp. 1–25, ad pp. 1–8, suggests a division into five episodes.

3   This formula is similarly employed in the story of Elkanah's family at Shilo (1 Sam 1:4, in contrast to vv 1–3); in the story of Jonathan and his attendant (1 Sam 14:1, in contrast to 13:15–23); and in the story of Job's afflictions (1:6, in contrast to vv 1–5; 2:1, in contrast to 1:22). Only in 2 Kgs 4:8 and in Job 1:13 does the formula appear without a prior continuous or recurring action.

4   "... telling time is expanded very noticeably precisely at the moment of the decisive deed" – J. Licht, *Storytelling in the Bible* (Jerusalem, 1978), p. 102.

family (v 3), she possesses fields and servants (v 18), domestic animals (v 22), and is therefore able to build an attic chamber on to her house and to furnish it comfortably (v 10). In short, she is an אשה גדולה "wealthy woman" (v 8).[5] Of greater significance are the spiritual aspects of her life. She had no children and no longer hoped for any. She therefore did not ask for a son when Elisha inquired what could be done for her (v 13). The Man of God's promise filled her with trepidation; she feared bitter disappointment (v 16b). Then came the end of her barrenness, but after that – tragedy. The woman's worst fears were realized, though in an unforeseen fashion. But now a change occurs in the Shunammite's character. No longer is she the childless woman resigned to her fate in abject despair. She is now a mother and so, in the manner of mothers eternal, she acts swiftly and forcefully to save the life of her child. She suppresses her grief, hides her child (v 21), conceals the true situation from her husband (vv 22–23), hastens to the Carmel (v 24), bursts into Elisha's presence (vv 26–27), upbraids him (v 28), and implores him to help her (v 30). All these uncharacteristic actions of the Shunammite attest to the nobility of her maternal spirit. The Shunammite is clearly the dominant character of this story. She also overshadows Elisha when she castigates him for his deceptive, disappointing miracles (v 28), and forces him to follow her to Shunem (v 30).[6]

Despite the honor and veneration Elisha receives from the other characters, here he is reduced to human proportions. He readily admits his inability to understand what has happened (v 27). Immediately thereafter he fails in his first attempt to revive the boy through magic (vv 29,31). Even more significant is that in having performed a wondrous act which ordinary men might consider a great feat, Elisha has in fact really failed. In bringing about a miracle that was not sought, he caused a major transformation in the Shunammite's life – motherhood – and so set into motion deep and lasting emotions which he had never anticipated. As he openly admits, the Lord had hidden from him the bitter distress of the bereaved

---

5 Cf. Gen 26:13; 1Sam 25:2; 2Sam 19:33; Job 1:3. In all these cases the root גד"ל indicates wealth.

6 Cf. H. Gressmann, *Die älteste Geschichtsschreibung und Prophetie Israels*[2] (SATA) (Göttingen, 1921), p. 294.

mother (v 27).[7] Without any understanding or regard for the Shunammite's feelings, Elisha burst into her life and performed his miracle. Like the sorcerer's apprentice, however, he could not foresee the consequences of his act. It is no wonder that the woman thereafter reproved him and reminded him of his moral obligation towards her!

Indeed, in this story the Man of God also has moral obligations. The story is not confined to the relating of a miraculous deed wrought by the Man of God but represents an attempt to understand the soul of man. Thus the author has, consciously or unconsciously, crossed the narrow boundaries of the prophetic *legenda* entering the realm of literature, since the nature of man's soul is the proper study of all true literary compositions.

As is expected in a work of literature, the description of the characters presented here is a dynamic one, and throws light on the changes in their nature and behavior.[8] Just as the Shunammite is shown transformed from a resigned childless woman into a mother fighting for her son, so too is Elisha portrayed dynamically. In the second episode of the story, it is mentioned incidentally how Elisha, the guest of the Shunammite and her family, insists on proper respect for his person; when he wants to speak to the woman, she is called and approaches him, standing near his bed (v 12). Elisha, however, does not address her directly, but speaks to her through the intermediacy of Gehazi: "Tell her" (v 13). The next time, the Shunammite has learnt her place and stands at the door (v 15).[9] But these formal gestures of

---

7   Though the general thrust of Elisha's statement is that God did not tell him that the child had died, what he actually says is that God did not reveal to him that the Shunammite was bitter.

8   See the perceptive remarks of Sh. Bar-Efrat, *The Art of the Biblical Story* (Heb.) (Tel Aviv, 1980), pp. 110–112. We must add, however, that sometimes, as in the stories of Samuel and David, variations in characterization stem from the diversity of the material, and not from the artistic shaping of complex characters.

9   Cf. D. Altschuler's commentary מצודת דוד (in מקראות גדולות) *ad loc.* Some modern critics explain vv 13–15 as an addition intended to stress Gehazi's role and the greatness of the miracle, the woman's husband being old. According to this view, the end of v 15 is merely a resumptive repetition of the end of v 12. Therefore, neither the different places she stood in nor the manner in which Elisha addresses her are relevant. But the information that the woman's husband was "old" (= impotent, cf. Gen 18:12) is the main point of the story; without it there would be no miracle! This kind of old age would not prevent the "old man" from going out to supervise the reapers. In other words, there is no contradiction between vv 4 and 18. Such hypercriticism, which detects additions while misinterpreting the

etiquette are totally disregarded when it becomes apparent that his miraculous favors are fleeting and meaningless (vv 36–37). She, with one stroke, breaks down all barriers between them.

At the end of the story, however, Elisha is restored to his lofty position as a Holy Man of God (vv 26–27). After reviving her son, he turns to the woman with a short, two-word command: שאי בנך "Pick up your son," saying no more, as if he found it difficult to converse with her. The next sentence is all movement, five of its eight words being verbs: ותבא ותפל על רגליו ותשתחו ארצה ותשא את בנה ותצא "She came, fell at his feet, bowed low to the ground, picked up her son and left"– a gesture of silent respect and awe in the presence of the holy. Not a word is spoken.

The Shunammite picks up her son as commanded – "and left," an appropriate conclusion to the story, and the Man of God remains alone, far removed and alienated from human society, alone with his God. That this interpretation is not merely read into this story can be illustrated by comparison with a similar scene in 1Kgs 17:23–24. There it is Elijah who *descends* from the *attic* into the house, approaches the mother and calls out in ringing tones of victory: "See, your son is alive!" He speaks in the natural enthusiastic joy of a healer who has triumphed over death and shares in the exhilaration of the patient's family. There is no atmosphere of holiness here despite the widow's *declaration* of her faith in Elijah as a Man of God. The Shunammite woman, in contrast, makes no declarations, but her respect for and admiration of the Man of God is more effectively expressed in her mute obeisance and silent departure from Elisha's presence.

The literary craftsmanship of this story is also evident in the presentation of the subordinate character of Gehazi. What is his role in this story? Firstly, he provides Elisha with information on the Shunammite's family. Secondly, he drives her away in her moment of despair. Thirdly, he takes Elisha's staff to the boy in a vain attempt to revive him. With a few strokes of the brush, the author draws a vivid portrait of his figure: gossipy, crude, violent, and in the end –

story, will not concern us here, *pace* H.C. Schmitt, *Elisa – Traditionsgeschichtliche Untersuchungen zur vorklassischen nordisraelitischen Prophetie* (Gütersloh, 1972), pp. 93–99; A. Schmitt (above, n. 2), pp. 1–25.

a miserable failure. Gehazi is a vapid, worthless person who nevertheless has succeeded in achieving a position of respect as a result of his close relationship with Elisha. The Man of God's staff is entrusted to him – it is his position that makes him important. Gehazi's role is familiar from the hassidic world: he is the rabbi's attendant, who keeps him informed on current happenings in the outside world and prevents troublesome persons from disturbing the Holy Man. Yet, we know about Gehazi from circumstances other than *legenda*; he is the eternal bureaucrat, lacking in sensitivity and consideration for others, a gossip and intrigant, possessor of an insatiable appetite for power, narrow minded and covetous – and above all, ineffectual. This is the type of person who often manages to seize the staff of the Great Man.[10]

These three elements of the story – the ability to combine different miracles, then to relate them in one unified, carefully woven account, the ability to examine and recount the circumstances and causes of events, last not least, the ability to describe the characters as real, living figures with all their strengths and weaknesses, and the transformations which they undergo in their positions and personalities – all these factors mark the story of the Shunammite as a special type of *legenda,* one which has undergone literary elaboration.

This evaluation, which is based on an internal examination of the Shunammite's story, is borne out by a comparison with 2Kgs 8:1–6. As we have noted, this pericope attests to the initial stage of the story's development – its oral transmission. It presupposes that Elisha has already died; hence Gehazi's presence in the king's court and not in Elisha's service.[11] The king nostalgically asks Gehazi to retell Elisha's miracles, knowing that he will never again personally witness either Elisha or his acts. This is also why the Shunammite goes directly to

---

10   Gehazi, no doubt, serves in the development of the plot as the antithesis of Elisha to emphasize the latter's holiness and generosity. See U. Simon, "Secondary Characters in the Biblical Narrative" (Heb.), *Proceedings of the Fifth World Congress of Jewish Studies* (Jerusalem, n.d.), Vol. I, pp. 31–36.

11   This story, incidentally, does not seem to be aware of the tradition preserved in 2Kgs 5, according to which Gehazi was stricken with leprosy, along with all his descendants, for taking Naaman's gifts. A leper would not have been allowed into the king's presence.

the king to appeal for her lands;[12] Elisha, her protector, is gone. This is exactly what the story wishes to convey: even after Elisha's death, his memory and fame alone are capable of carrying out acts of kindness on behalf of his believers. We can therefore conclude that this *legenda* contains an allusion to another orally-transmitted *legenda*. But not to 2Kgs 4:18–37. The woman of 2Kgs 8:1–6 is nameless; she is called "the woman whose son he revived," not the Shunammite. She is a widow (like the mother of the child in Zarephath in 1Kgs 17:17–24), she is not married to an old man (2Kgs 4:14). She is destitute and escaped starving during a time of famine only by fleeing to Philistia and living there as a sojourner, in a lowly position of humiliation and insecurity.[13] In these details as well she more closely resembles the widow of Zarephath than the wealthy woman of Shunem. Even the "people" of the Shunammite (2Kgs 4:13), her important clan, are not mentioned; when oppressed she must appeal to the king for justice. It is possible to explain most of these differences as changes which occurred during the course of time (except for her not being identified as the Shunammite of 2Kgs 4). It is possible, but probably not correct. In my opinion, there is no reason to attempt to harmonize these differences. What we have here is simply two different crystallizations of the same *legenda*. 2Kgs 8:1–6 represents the earlier, oral phase, and the story of the Shunammite the later, literary version. The time between these two tales elapsed not for the woman and her family, but for the story and its narrators.

2. *Epigonic Devolution*[14]

An epigone is one who arrives, comes into being, or is created in later times: an heir or replacement. In the sphere of politics the Diadochi, the heirs of Alexander the Great, are called epigoni. In literature the term is used to describe authors writing in a post-classical period, who tend to be less creative, more conformist, imitative, and artificial than

---

12 Hebrew צע"ק, meaning to appeal for correction of a legal injustice.
13 This is the meaning of לכי וגורי באשר תגורי in biblical Hebrew: Be a soujourner in some other land.
14 This section is a revised version of my article "Baal, The Prophet, and the Angel (II Kings 1)" (Heb.) *Beer-Sheva* 1 (1973), pp. 222–230; earlier literature is discussed there.

their more inventive predecessors. Such an epigonic *legenda* may be found, in my opinion in 2Kgs 1:2–17a, which tells of Ahaziah, King of Israel's inquiry of Baal Zebub, and of Elijah's prediction of the King's death and of the immolation of the officers and companies sent to capture him.

It is generally agreed that this story contains two strata: one which tells of Elijah's prediction of Ahaziah's death, a second about Elijah, the officers and the fire from heaven. There is a difference of opinion, however, as to the boundaries of these two strata. In one view the first stratum includes vv 2–4 and 17a , the second vv 5–16. Another view regards vv 2–8 and 17a as the first stratum, and limits the second to vv 9–16.[15] This differentiation between the strata is based on the assumption that it allows us to reconstruct the original nucleus of the story. In the present case, the nucleus was a purely factual account of Elijah's encounter with Ahaziah's messengers. Here Elijah, as was his custom, appeared suddenly in accordance with God's command, fulfilled his charge, and disappeared. Where he came from and where he went no one knows. Elijah's character, as presented here, is that of a fearless prophet, who challenged kings and their emissaries and fought a total war of destruction against Baal and his manifestations. He is deeply imbued with a sense of mission and devotion to his task: war of the monotheistic faith against foreign gods and pagan practices. This characterization of Elijah is familiar from 1Kgs 17–19 and 21. The second, interpolated story (vv 5–16 or 9–16), tells of Elijah and the officers. It is concerned solely with Elijah's test of strength, with the intention of demonstrating his divine power. This being the second author's purpose, he is not disturbed by the immoral punishment meted out to the officers and their men. This factor, as well as the similarity between this story and 1Sam 19:18ff, and the fact that v 16 repeats v 3 without adding any new information, point to a late date for its stratum.

The division of the narrative into strata is characteristic of the Documentary Hypothesis, with one difference. The Documentary Hypothesis usually maintains the existence of separate and inde-

---

15 The first view is that of I. Benzinger, *Die Bücher der Könige* [KHAT] (Freiburg i.B. etc., 1899); the second is that of R. Kittel, *Die Bücher der Könige* [GHAT] (Göttingen, 1900). Most modern commentators have followed Kittel, as have most biblical introductions and monographs on Elijah.

pendent source documents which were combined by later editors, while this analysis assumes only a single source document which was later expanded by a redactor. Yet, one may question whether this analysis in fact adheres to the principles of biblical criticism. The division of a story into discrete documents should be based on three considerations: firstly, the detection of unnecessary repetitions or contradictions in the contents of the story; secondly, the presence of obvious stylistic differences (vocabulary, personal names, syntax) between the repetitive or contradictory sections; and thirdly, that each of the units distinguished by the above criteria should display ideational or conceptual differences. A close study of the critical analysis of this chapter reveals that it relies almost exclusively on the third consideration, and completely disregards the first two. This is not coincidental: a careful examination will discover no signs of disunity in the contents of the story, while the language, though unusual, is uniformly so.

Prominent among the linguistic irregularities are the Yahwistic theophoric names, most of which end in יה instead of יהו. Thus we find not אחזיהו (1Kings 22:40, 50, 52; 2Kgs 1:18) but אחזיה (2Kgs 1:2); not אליהו (appearing about fifty-five times in the Book of Kings) but אליה (2Kgs 1:3, 4, 8, 12; also Mal 3:23).[16] This is the common form in the Second Temple period (in names such as נחמיה, חנניה and זכריה, whereas in the First Temple period we find ירמיהו and חלקיהו[17]. The fact that Second Temple period scribes generally transcribed theophoric names in their ancient forms indicates that they endeavored to preserve the language of the original biblical Hebrew despite the influence of the vernacular. This tendency occasionally led to *hypercorrection*, in which later forms were changed into archaic ones. This explains why the form אליהו does appear four times in our chapter (vv 10, 13, 15, 17). However, the predominance of יה – suffixes, which occur only here out of all the prophetical stories, attests to the late date of this story.

Several other features also indicate a late date for this story. One

16 This was already noted by E. König, "Elijah, Critical View," *The Jewish Encyclopaedia*, Vol. 5 (1907), p. 128.

17 Harry Torczyner, et al., *Lachish I: The Lachish Letters* (Oxford, 1938), pp. 24–25; E.Y. Kutscher, *The Language and Linguistic Background of the Isaiah Scroll* (Leiden, 1974), pp. 4–5, 96–125.

is the unusual interrogative forms. In general, biblical Hebrew employs the interrogative ה, and only if the question is repeated does it add אם e.g. המלך תמלך עלינו אם משול תמשל בנו (Gen 37:8) or היפלו ולא יקומו אם ישוב ולא ישוב (Jer 8:4). In our chapter, however, the simple interrogative sentence is introduced by אם: אם אחיה מחלי זה: (2Kgs 1:2), which is the common form in rabbinic Hebrew.[18]

The phrase חלי זה is typical of rabbinic Hebrew, as in מה נאה ניר זה מה נאה אילן זה (Abot 3:7). In biblical Hebrew we would expect חליי זה or החלי הזה,[19] as in 10:19 and Zeph 2:9.

The expression לדרוש ב־ appears in our chapter four times (vv 2,3, 6, 16). Biblical Hebrew generally prefers לדרוש את or לדרוש אל except for two occurrences in the Book of Chronicles, and in one of them לדרוש ב־ replaces לדרוש את in the parallel passage in the Book of Kings.[20] The combination לדרוש ב־ is also found in Qumran literature.[21] It seems that this form was current during the Second Temple period alongside the other, earlier forms.

Ahaziah's title, "King of Samaria," is probably also a late idiom. The rulers of the Northern Kingdom were called "Kings of Israel," not "Kings of Samaria," just as the rulers of the Southern Kingdom were "Kings of Judah," not "Kings of Jerusalem." The title "King of Samaria" is anachronistic and reflects the period which began with the establishment of the Assyrian province of Samaria in the south-central part of the former Kingdom of Israel. 1Kgs 21:1 is no proof of the antiquity of this title, as this entire chapter shows signs of late composition.[22] On the other hand, we read in Hos 10:7: "Samaria's monarchy is vanishing, like foam upon the waters." It is therefore possible that when the Northern Kingdom was greatly reduced in size after 731 BCE, its king was called the "King of Samaria."

18 M. H. Segal, *A Grammar of Mishnaic Hebrew* (Oxford, 1970), p. 220, section 461.
19 Cf. C.F. Burney, *Notes on the Hebrew Text of the Book of Kings* (Oxford, 1903), ad. loc.: "The const. חלי זה (for the normal החלי הזה) is regular in Rabbinic Heb. but extremely uncommon in Bib. Heb."
20 See 1Chr 10:14 and 2Chr 34:26, as opposed to 2Kgs 22:18. This was pointed out to me by Dr. Y. Avishur.
21 CD 1:18; 1QS 6:6.
22 1Kgs 21 contains other examples of late language: חרים 'nobles' in vv 8, 11; cf. Jer 27:20; 39:6; Neh 2:16; 4:8, 13; 5:5 [LXX]; 7:6, 17; 7:5; 13:17; Isa 34:12; Eccl 10:17; Sir 10:25. Cf. further: A. Rofé, "The Vineyard of Naboth – The Origin and Message of the Story," *VT* 38 (1988), in press.

The use of the verb דבר in this chapter is extremely unusual. It appears many times in place of the verb אמר as if they were exactly synonymous as, for example, in v 3:‏ ומלאך ה' דבר אל אליה התשבי קום: עלה לקראת מלאכי מלך שמרון ודבר אלהם וגו'. "An angel of the Lord said to Elijah the Tishbite: 'Go and confront the messengers of the king of Samaria and say to them'." דבר (אל) is also found in vv 6, 7, 9 (twice) 10, 11, 12, 13, 15 and 16. We find it elsewhere in the Bible,[23] but nowhere in so great a concentration. This usage is not attested in rabbinic or Qumran Hebrew. Lacking any other explanation we can only surmise that an author for whom Hebrew was no longer a living language interchanged two closely related verbs.

We may conclude from the above survey that the language of this story is also uniform in its irregularities. This evidence refutes the view that the story should be divided into separate strata[24] but, on the other hand, supports its attribution to a late date,[25] as does the study of its contents.

Elijah's portrayal in this story agrees fully with what is related about him elsewhere in the Bible, and our story can thus represent a kind of synthesis of all the Elijah narratives: (a) His distinctive garment is the mantle (1Kgs 19:19, 2Kgs 2:13–14), which may have been made of hair cloth, which was the usual prophetic attire (Zech 13:14). This is alluded to in its description of Elijah as "a hairy man" (בעל שער) in v 8. (b) His sudden and frightening appearances are described in 1Kgs 18:7, 12. (c) His vehemence, effrontery and brutal

---

23 Gen 41:17; Exod 32:7, 13; 33:1; Lev 10:12, 19; Num 18:8; Josh 22:21; 1Sam 4:20; 1Kgs 13:7, 12, 17(?), 22; 21:5–6; Ezek 40:4, 45; 41:22; Ps 116: 10; Dan 2:4; and in Aramaic Dan 6:22. Of these examples the following may be identified as late occurrences on the basis of other considerations: Exod 32:7–14; Josh 22; 1Kgs 13 (see below, chap. 8, sect.4); 1Kgs 21 (see previous note); and passages in Ezek, Ps, and Dan. On the other hand, it seems that דבר was used as an imperative before a direct speech in Standard Biblical Hebrew as well: Num 5:6; Judg 9:2; 20:3; Jer 9:21; 1Kgs 20:11; Ezek 37:19, 21.

24 This raises serious doubts as to the attempt made by J.R. Lundbom, "Elijah's Chariot Ride," *JJS* 24 (1973), pp. 39–50, to explain 2Kgs 1–2 as a single consecutive unit as a result of which he had to resort to several unacceptable interpretations.

25 As was already noted by A.B. Ehrlich מקרא כפשוטו, Vol. II (Berlin, 1900), p. 330: "This seems to me a very late story . . . because the verb דב״ר is used without the accompanying לאמר in vv 7, 10, 12, 13, 15, 16 which was not done in early writings." See also O. Thenius, *Die Bücher der Könige²* [KEHAT] (Leipzig, 1873), *ad loc.*

words before kings are told of in 1Kings 18:8; 21:17–24 (cf. 2Kgs 9:26). (d) The unsuccessful attempts at Elijah's capture by the royal authorities are recounted in 1Kgs 17:3; 18:1–16; 19:1–3. (e) Elijah is characterized by zealousness on behalf of God in fighting the Baal worship in 1Kgs 18; 19:10–18. (f) His cruel treatment of his opponents is demonstrated by his massacre of the prophets of Baal in 1Kgs 18:40. (g) His ability to bring down fire from heaven is revealed in 1Kgs 18:24–39.

This last point demands some consideration. In the confrontation on the Carmel fire descended from on high to resolve the deadlock in Israel's dilemma of faith. This was a spectacular miracle designed to decide the contest between God and Baal. Its echoes will reverberate for generations; all those present tremble in awe of the revealed Holiness. They fall upon their faces and proclaim: "The Lord alone is God! The Lord alone is God!" Moments of tension preceded the miracle; in his prayer before the altar, Elijah beseeches God: "Answer me, O Lord, Answer me, that this people may know that You, O Lord, are God. . . " The suspense surrounding God's response begins in verse 24 and continues through most of the story. In 2Kings 1:2–17, on the other hand, the point is developed ad absurdum: fire descends from the skies with no delay, and not once, but twice! Elijah speaks and fire appears at his command; no prayer is required to accomplish the deed. And, in final analysis, the miracle is superfluous. There is no need for Elijah to destroy the companies to save his own life. In the end he goes to Ahaziah of his own volition. The fire serves only to glorify and exalt Elijah.

To glorify and exalt – in the manner of later believers and admirers. Elijah here is characterized not by the emphasis on his uniqueness as a prophet – his devotion to God, his struggle against evil and idolatry, and his fearless defiance of kings, his very person is exalted. He is depicted as an other-wordly being, almost a god, perhaps – almost a demon. First and foremost is his *honor* and his *sanctity*. Elijah must be addressed as one would address God; he is certainly no less dangerous than He.[26]

But, what essential difference is there between this story and a short

26　Cf. Z. Adar, *The Biblical Narrative,* trans. M. Louvish (Jerusalem, 1959), pp. 95–97.

legenda, such as the tale of youths and the bears discussed above (2Kgs 2:23–24). That story as well was based on the honor and sanctity of the Man of God! Are these too not the fundamental elements of the *legenda*? There are, nevertheless, subtle but important differences between our story and the short *legenda*. In the story of the youths and the bears, for example, the youths taunted Elisha, while here the soldiers merely commanded Elijah in the name of the king. In Elisha's story the violent miracle put an end to the derision and abuse of the Man of God; in Elijah's the miracle accomplishes nothing substantive. And most important, in the *legenda* about the youths the attitude of holy awe and veneration toward the Man of God is a natural one, unconsciously expressed. The story of the captains and their companies, on the other hand, by contrasting the two cases in which the prophet is first addressed insultingly and then approached respectfully, is intended as a lesson on the proper attitude toward the Man of God: kneeling before him and imploring his mercy!

Such a portrayal is closer to the outlook of later generations. Ben Sira, who attempts to summarize the deeds of the Tishbite (48:1–11) in a few verses, stresses his awe of him[27]: מה נורא אתה אליהו ואשר כמוך יתפאר "How awesome are you, Elijah; one such as you is to be praised." Our story is mentioned twice in his description – in v 3: גם שלוש [הוריד] אשות "He brought down fire thrice," and in v 6: המוריד מלכים אל שחת ונכבדים [מ]מטותם "He brings kings down to destruction and nobles from their bed." In these verses Ben Sira emphasizes the catastrophic, numinous aspects of Elijah's nature. The Midrash, as well (Tanhuma, Bereshit 7), in a disputation with Hiram King of Tyre (which probably reflects a late polemic against the deification of kings), stresses those actions of Elijah which would allow him to be compared with God:

> The Holy One, blessed be He, said: 'I revive the dead and Elijah revived the dead, and he never said: "I am a God." I cause rain to fall and Elijah caused rain to fall, I hold back the rains and so Elijah, as it is said: "As the Lord lives, there will be no dew or rain except at my bidding" (1Kgs 17:1). I brought down fire and brimstone upon Sodom and so Elijah brought them down, as it is said: "If I am a Man of God, let fire come down from

---

27   M.Z. Segal, ספר בן־סירא השלם² (Jerusalem, 1959), p. 330.

heaven" (2Kgs 1:10,12), and he never said: "I am a God." And
you say: "I am a god; I sit enthroned like a god . . .'" (Ezek 28:2).

Another characteristic of the later attitude towards the prophets and
holy men is Elijah's portrayal in this story as a potential martyr. When
he sits alone atop the mountain, and the king's officers are sent one after
another to fetch him, he is viewed as a victim of and a witness to God's
war against idolatry. His excessive and uncompromising reaction to the
king's summons can be understood in the light of a basic presupposition which is left unstated: a prophet's summons by the authorities
means the prophet's death. In this sense the story contains a martyrological quality which is the final stage in the formation of the prophetical stories.[28]

In summary, this *legenda,* in which a miracle is performed not as
a result of the force of circumstances for the benefit of the faithful,
but rather for the greater glory of the Holy Man, belongs to one of the
final stages of composition of the legend of Elijah. It represents the
epigonic stage; instead of stressing Elijah's greatness in the context of
his historical mission, it exalts Elijah beyond human proportions,
transforming him into a supernatural figure. The powerful impression
that this prophetic figure left on his generation, fully convincing in its
innocence, is replaced here by a portrayal which attributes to Elijah
divine powers of which he has no need, and which go far beyond the
internal logic of the situation he faced.

---

28   The martyrological tendency of this story was pointed out to me several years ago
     by Dr. Y. Zakovitch of Jerusalem, see below, chap. 10.

Chapter Three

THE *VITA*

1. *The Genre and Elisha's Appointment*

The *legenda* were told, retold, and disseminated throughout the country. Some preserved their original oral character, eventually being written down in summary form. Others underwent literary elaboration. Still others underwent other kinds of transformation which will be described below. But as the *legenda* spread, questions arose among their audiences which soon added a new dimension to the development of this literature.

One question concerned the origins of the Holy Man. This was not merely a matter of idle curiosity but involved a more fundamental question: what were the factors, innate or arising from the Man of God's early life, by means of which he received the supernatural powers that were later revealed in his performance of miracles and wonders? This type of straightforward inquiry into causes naïvely accepted the truth of the miracle stories. Yet, not content with a spontaneous emotional response to the reconstruction of the miracles offered by the storyteller, it seeks out the inner causes. The response to such a question is given in the same spirit – a mixture of innocence and inquisitiveness; it takes the form of a tale of the Holy Man's birth or of an incident which occurred shortly before his appearance.[1]

Another related question is that of the Man of God's end. Did he merely die like everyone else? Could he really have escaped the fate

---

1   See the opening sections of שבחי הבעש״ט, שבחי האריז״י, שבחי האריז״י and שבחי מהר״ם, (cited below). Cf. J. Dan, הסיפור החסידי (Jerusalem, 1975), p. 85: "So this story (about R. Adam) strengthened the claim that the Besht had superhuman powers, which are attributed to him in most of the stories about him."

of mortal man? The account of the Holy Man's death must take this question into consideration. This can be done in a number of ways, depending on his position and the beliefs of his disciples. One possible answer is that the Man of God does not die, but ascends to a hidden world of goodness and light.[2] Another could present a description of the Man of God's supernatural powers struggling with the forces of Sheol, and continuing to perform new,[3] and even greater miracles. A third possibility, especially fitting for a spiritual leader, is the portrayal of his hour of death as the moment of the realization of his life's teachings, illuminating his greatness in all its splendor.[4]

These tales of birth and death presuppose a large existing body of *legenda,* and they provide an explanation or fitting climactic ending for them. Written with a broad perspective on their subject's life, they display a genuine attempt at biography. But such attempts may also occur for a different reason, namely the wish to immortalize the Man of God, to transmit to coming generations every detail of his wondrous existence. Here again the specific miracles are not so important as the acquaintance with the great man's person. To commemorate his personality and preserve it, the stories are written down, collated, edited and sometimes arranged chronologically. The finished product is a biography of the Man of God consisting entirely of a consecutive recitation of miracles: a biography of *legenda.*

Such legendary biographies flourished in Christian literature of the Middle Ages. They were called by the Latin name of *vita,* meaning "life" (in the sense of "the history of a life"), identical to the Greek *biographia.* The latter term, however, referred to personal histories which aspired to historical accuracy, in the manner of the ancient Greek and Roman biographies, while the Latin *vita* preserved its

---

2 This is hinted at in ספר שבחי מהר"ם (R. Mordechai Labaton of Aleppo), (Jerusalem; Pinhas Anav, 1932), p. 43: He died as a result of being struck by a bolt of lightning," and "his pure soul rose heavenwards to the celestial vaults."

3 ספר שבחי האר"י (Jerusalem; Hamesorah, 1955), p. 32: "And the Master told him, that if the generation had merited it, that year would have seen the Redemption and the true End, since none had arisen like him since the days of R. Simon b. Yohai . . . and after his death his students came to perform the ritual immersion before burial, and brought him to the ritual bathhouse, and he stood up in the water. They said to him: 'Let the Master excuse us and we will immerse him'; he immediately dipped his head and immersed himself."

4 On the death of R. Akiva, see the legend preserved in b Ber 61b; Socrates's death is described in the *Crito* and the *Phaedo.*

medieval connotation: histories of religious personalities which were embellished with accounts of their miraculous acts and signs of their faith.[5]

The process of transformation of *legenda* into *vita* is a very slow one. The שבחי הבעש"ט which can be considered the *vita* of R. Israel Baal Shem Tov, the founder of Hassidism, was first published in 1815, some fifty-five years after his death.[6] It is indeed amazing that among the "People of the Book" (even the Hassidim, although many were simple and untutored, were on the whole literate), more than two generations should be required to produce a popular account of so famous a figure! The שבחי הבעש"ט even displays some trace of reluctance at recording the words and deeds of the Holy Master. Alongside the popular adage: "It is proper to speak in praise of the righteous," is quoted the Besht's saying: "Anyone who speaks in praise of the saints (צדיקים) is as if he dabbled in the account of the Chariot (i.e., mysticism)." This indicates the exceptional holiness with which the praises of the zaddikim were regarded and the care to be taken in telling about them. So much for telling the tales. As for writing them down a more explicit warning was given. R. Gedaliah of Luncz said of the publication of the שבחי הבעש"ט "When hell is harrowed its author will remain, as he has made the Besht into a subject of idle conversation."[7] This statement attests to the general attitude towards committing the acts of the Holy Man to writing. He was a charismatic figure, possessed of incredible powers of mind and will, who had the power to arouse religious emotion, inspire devotion and lead men. Set down on paper, however, forced to convince rather than awe, he loses this charisma and becomes banal. Hence the opposition to writing.[8] Only after several generations, when the danger of oblivion outweighed these considerations, could the task be accomplished without remorse. Sometimes external events hastened the process: the שבחי הבעש"ט was published in 1815 by the Habad-Lubavitch Hassidim, after its members suffered persecutions at the hands of the anti-Hassidic movement and the authorities.

---

5 I use the term *vita* in a slightly different sense from that defined by A. Jolles in his classic *Einfache Formen*[2] (Tübingen, 1965), pp. 25–61.
6 See S.A. Horodetsky, ספר שבחי הבעש"ט[2] (Tel Aviv, 1947), Introduction.
7 שבחי הבעש"ט Introduction, p. טו, n. 13.
8 שבחי הבעש"ט, p. קמד, which opposes committing the Besht's teachings to writing.

Do *vita* appear in the Bible? The first candidate for this genre would seem to be the entire account of Elisha, from 2Kgs 2 (more exactly 1Kg 19:19–21)[9] to 2Kgs 13:14–19. In their present sequence there is no continuity between these stories. Especially long is the gap between 2Kgs 8:15 and 2Kgs 13:14. But the present disposition of these stories is the responsibility of the author of the Book of Kings, who arranged the available material to the order of kings, and who erred in any case in assigning most of the Elisha stories to the period of the Omrides.[10] It is difficult, from the present version of the Book of Kings, to ascertain the original order of the stories.[11]Neverthess, it seems possible to distinguish in the Elisha cycle the attempt to construct a consecutive *vita.* Comments such as: "He went on from there to Mount Carmel, and from there he returned to Samaria" (2Kgs 2:25), or: "Elisha, returned to Gilgal" (4:38a) are attempts to present a unified history of acts explaining why his miracles are connected with various, distant places. Such comments, however, are relatively scarce. More important is the fact that the history of Elisha opens with a story which certainly cannot be considered a *legenda,* but must be regarded as a component of the larger *vita.*

The story recorded in 2Kgs 2:1–18, which is usually called "The Ascension of Elijah," actually belongs to the Elisha cycle.[12] Though Elijah is the main character, and his ascension is the outstanding incident in the story, it is not Elijah's fate which is the issue here but Elisha's. The account therefore does not conclude with Elijah's ascension but continues until it ascertains that Elisha's request for a double portion of his master's spirit (v 9) is granted (vv 13-15). Similarly, the author makes no effort to keep us in suspense regarding Elijah's extraordinary fate, but in his introductionary sentence reveals exactly what will happen (v 1a, a relative temporal clause).[13] The

---

9   As was demonstrated by A. Alt, "Die literarische Herkunft von 1 Reg 19, 19–21," *ZAW* 32 (1912), pp. 123–125. See below, beginning of chap. 9.

10 See below, chap. 4, sect. 5.

11 On the present arrangement of the Elisha cycle, see sect. 2 of this chapter.

12 On this story, see H. Gunkel, *Geschichten von Elisa* (Berlin, 1922), in English: "Elisha – The Successor of Elijah (2Kings II, 1–18)," *ExT* 41 (1929–30), pp. 182–186; G. del Olmo Lete, *La vocación del líder en el antiguo Israel* (Salamanca, 1973), pp. 165–178 .

13 I obviously cannot accept the suggestion that v 1a was interpolated by a later editor who thereby undermined the story's dramatic suspense. Cf. K. Galling, "Der Ehrenname Elisas und die Entrückung Elias," *ZThK* 53 (1956), pp. 129–148.

author assumes that the reader knows of Elijah's ascension and proceeds directly to his real subject – Elisha's role in that crisis.

Other details in the story also indicate that it originated in the Elisha cycle. The Sons of the Prophets who appear here (vv 3, 5, 7, 15–18) never played a role in the Elijah stories, but are often mentioned in conjunction with Elisha. The title "O father, father, Israel's chariots and horsemen," by which Elijah is denoted here (v 12), was transferred to him from Elisha (2Kgs 13:14). Elisha was originally granted this title by the people because of his salvation of Israel during the Aramean oppression (2Kgs 5; 6:8 –23; 6:24–7:20).[14] Elijah, on the other hand, never aided Israel in war. He was even known as the "Troubler of Israel" (1Kgs 18:17) because of the three-year drought which he brought upon the people. But the author of the story, a disciple of Elisha, assumed that his master's teacher had borne the same title as his master.

These arguments point to a late date for the story. The transference of Elisha's characteristics to Elijah could easily have happened when actual memories about both men had become dim. The blurring of once-accepted distinctions may lead to anachronisms; here the Sons of the Prophets know the future (vv 3, 5) and inherit part of Elija's spirit (the firstborn's share going to Elisha, v 9),[15] but nowhere else in the Elisha cycle are they portrayed as enjoying supernatural powers. Just the opposite; in general they are portrayed as impoverished, defenseless, simple people, in need of the Man of God to provide protection and their basic necessities (2Kgs 4:1, 38–41; 5:22, which attests to the same effect, may be of later origin). The idealization of the Sons of the Prophets in this story is probably due to their being considered actual prophets, an idea which corresponds to later conceptions. Thus the internal evidence contained in 2Kgs 2:1–18

---

14   Attempts to fit this title into the context of 2Kgs 2, whether as a cry of despair (Bork, Sadan), or as a general title of the prophets based on the ancient Israelite Passover liturgy (Beek), are not convincing. See F. Bork, *OLZ* 35 (1932), pp. 153–165; M.A. Beek, "The Meaning of the Expression 'The Chariots and the Horsemen of Israel", *OuTS* 17 (1972), pp. 1–10; D. Sadan, " 'Father, Father, the Chariots of Israel and its Horsemen' – the Biblical Sense" (Heb.), in י"ב מחקרים (Jerusalem-Tel Aviv, 1977), pp. 52–68.

15   The portion of the first born is double that of each of the other sons. When there is only one other son, it is two-thirds, which is the meaning of פי שנים in Deut 21:15–17; Zech 13:8. It seems that by the time of Ben Sira (Sir 48:12) this meaning had already been forgotten.

fully agrees with its *gattunggeschichte:* this section of Elisha's *vita* is one of its latest elements.[16]

That this is part of a *vita* is also shown by examination of the miracles appearing in the story. Two miracles are performed here: the two partings of the Jordan, once by Elijah and once by Elisha. These miracles are not warranted by the situation: the prophets could easily have crossed without dividing the waters. Therefore the miracles are not the small acts of salvation typical of the *legenda*. The purpose of the miracles is to prove by a comparison of the two prophets that Elisha is the true heir of Elijah, inheriting not only his mantle but also his spirit. The group of fifty Sons of the Prophets witness the miracles and like a Greek tragic chorus proclaim among themselves and to the reader: "The spirit of Elijah has descended upon Elisha" (v 15). All the previously circulating *legenda* about Elisha to be written down subsequently are thus placed into perspective.[17]

At the same time, it is still possible to sense to what degree this story has evolved beyond its original role of introducing the *vita*. An ordinary storyteller might be content recounting the transfer of Elijah's spirit to Elisha, but not our narrator. He provides a master portrait of psychological changes which Elisha undergoes. At the beginning of the story he is depicted as a student in the presence of his teacher, refusing to be parted from him – "As the Lord lives and as you live, I will not leave you" (vv 2, 4, 6) – he silences, through fear

16   The relative lateness of stories about a hero's beginnings is a known phenomenon. See, e.g., B.S. Childs, "The Birth of Moses," *JBL* 84 (1965), pp. 109–122; on David's anointment (1Sam 16:1–13), see A. Weiser, "Die Legitimation des Königs David," *VT* 16 (1966), pp. 325–354, ad pp. 325–328. The story of David's anointment is never again referred to in the Book of Samuel, though he surely needed this legitimation in his encounters with Saul and his struggle with Ish-bosheth. The story is not referred to by the author of the Book of Chronicles either! His mention of "the Word of the Lord through Samuel" (1Chr 11:3) may refer to 1Sam 13:14; 15:28; 28:17. 1Sam 16:1–13 is first mentioned in the late, apocryphal Ps 151, also found in Qumran Cave 11. See also T. Veijola, *Die ewige Dynastie* [AASF 193] (Helsinki, 1975), p. 102, n. 156; T.N.D. Mettinger, *King and Messiah* [CoBOTS 6] (Lund, 1976), pp. 174–179.

17   Besides this basic connection between the story of Elisha's appointment as prophet and the other stories about him, there is also an external connection: both this story and the colligative verses of the *vita,* which we have noted, stress Elisha's itinerary. Our story lists Gilgal, Bethel, Jericho, the Jordan, and Jericho again; the linking verses mention Bethel, Mt. Carmel, Samaria (2Kgs 2:23a, 25), and again Gilgal (4:38a).

of the future, all rumors of his teacher's impending tragedy: "I know it, too; be silent" (vv 3, 5).[18] But by the end of the story, Elisha, who calls upon the Lord (no longer upon Elijah) and is answered by Him (v 14; cf. v 12), dwells in Jericho, having reconciled himself to reality: he is no longer despondent as an orphaned disciple (v 12). He understands clearly that Elijah will never return. There is no point in searching for him – not even his body will be discovered (vv 16–18). The disciple becomes transformed into a leader who demands for himself the obedience and loyalty of the other followers.[19]

In the same manner, the narrator presents Elijah's departure not as a mere physical phenomenon, but primarily as the completion of a process taking place in the depths of his soul. Elijah is ever the wonder man, lacking permanent ties with any social group, moving with suddenness from place to place: Gilgal, Bethel, Jericho, the Jordan. But here a new feature is added. He wishes to leave, to rid himself of his permanent travelling companion, he seems to be trying to isolate himself completely from even the slightest contact he had with human society. Something is happening between God and Elijah ("For the Lord has sent me") to which no one else is to be witness. And yet, Elijah submits to Elisha's insistent presence, in a kind of weak apathy. These two themes – withdrawal from the present world and apathy – are expressed in Elijah's parting words: "If you see me as I am being taken from you, this will be granted to you; if not, you will not" (v 10). This from the decisive personality, Elijah, whose very

18 Cf. the story about the death of R. Judah the Prince, b Ketub 104 a: "The Rabbis decreed a fast and implored God's mercy, and proclaimed: 'Anyone who says that Rabbi (R. Judah) died will be stabbed'."

19 The position taken by the Sons of the Prophets in this story is somewhat contradictory. At the beginning of the story, they know of Elijah's impending departure, but at the end they want to search for him! Gunkel (above, n. 12), therefore concluded (as did others following him) that vv 16–18 were not part of the original story. In my opinion, these verses are a necessary part of the tale: as we have noted, the renewed meeting of Elisha with the Sons of the Prophets, adds a dynamic dimension to the prophet's characterization. As for the contradiction, the Sons of the Prophets knew of Elijah's departure, but did not necessarily understand the nature of his ascension; therefore they wanted to search for his body. It is, however, possible that various originally contrasting oral traditions are embedded in this story. Moreover, vv 16–18 close the circle of the story: it begins with a dialogue between Elisha and the Sons of the Prophets and ends in the same way. See G. del Olmo Lete, "La vocación de Eliseo," *Es Bib* 26 (1967), pp. 287–293.

word was law! Always at the forefront of the struggle, against his people, king and God, never had he appeared neutral or vacillating. But here, there are no promises, prayers, or entreaties. The matter is out of his hands – greater powers alone will decide it. The cares and troubles of this world no longer concern him. His reality will soon be revealed: a fiery chariot with fiery horses, ascending to heaven.

The last dialogue between Elijah and Elisha is a moment of truth, in which the conspiracy of silence surrounding Elijah's departure is broken. Up to that time both Elijah and Elisha had refrained from speaking about the subject. Any whisperings and hints by the Sons of the Prophets had been silenced by Elisha. But when the mental anguish is finally lifted and the two men talk freely of Elijah's departure, the event occurs taking them by surprise and cutting short their communion: "As they kept on walking and talking." Even though Elisha had for a whole day dreaded the imminent departure of his master the shock of its materializing was no less real or painful.

Elijah's ascension is portrayed as the death of a beloved teacher. A storm in which chariot and horses of fire lift him to heaven[20] could have provided the author with an opportunity to explore the celestial spheres, to describe God's mansions in the sky and His hosts of angels. But the author chooses to turn his gaze earthwards, to focus on Elisha, the lonely, orphaned disciple, who weeps and rends his clothes in the fury of his despair. The realities of man and his emotions are the author's concern. Of these emotions, the pain of separation is the primary one, even greater than Elisha's soon to be realized hope of emulating his teacher. 2Kgs 2:1–18 goes far beyond its purpose as the initial component of Elisha's *vita*. Not only does it provide an explanation of Elisha's future miracles, but like other great literary compositions, it offers a new insight into reality – and above all, into the inner depths of man's soul.

20 Despite the explicit statements of 2Kgs 2:1, 11, there have been attempts – some contemporary – to explain Elijah's ascension rationally, as if he had died in a tornado: S. Grill, "Die Himmelfahrt des Elias," *BZ* 24 (1938–9), pp. 242–48. No less farfetched is J.R. Lundbom's contention ("Elijah's Chariot Ride," *JJS* 24 [1973], pp. 48–49) that Elijah was snatched by Israel's chariots and horsemen, i.e. – by the chariots of King Jehoram!

2. The Arrangement of the Elisha Narratives

The Elisha cycle, as has been shown above, represents an attempt to construct a *vita* of the Holy Man out of the individual *legenda*. This attempt is evident both in the verses linking the stories (such as 2Kgs 2:25) and in the story of Elisha's inauguration (2:1–18), which forms the opening section of the *vita*. The *legenda* about Elisha and Joash (2Kgs 13:14–19) also belongs to the account of Elisha's life and serves as a fitting conclusion to the Man of God's supernatural career. It thus remains for us to determine the order of the *legenda* within the main body of the *vita* to detect the principle according to which the stories were arranged and what can be learned from their order about the history of Elisha and the history of the stories. It is evident that the original order of the stories has been disturbed, since continuity between the stories is lacking. The story of Elisha's appointment as Elijah's servant (1Kgs 19:19–21) has been severed from its continuation, his prophetic inauguration; the stories of Elisha's death and burial (2Kgs 13:14–21) similarly are removed from the main body of *legenda* concerning him in 2Kgs 2–8. Such editorial revision, however, resulted from the desire to integrate these stories with other sources about contemporaneous events. Therefore, the lapse in continuity does not mean that the original sequence of these stories has in any way been disturbed. What then is the nature of this sequence?

In my opinion the stories were not arranged in the *vita* chronologically[21] but mainly according to the typical biblical manner of associative order, i.e., arrangement by external associations, such as similarity of words or phrases.[22] This arrangement, however, is not

---

21   This was the approach taken by A. Šanda, *Die Bücher der Könige*, 2 Halbband [EHAT] (Münster, i. Westf., 1912), pp. 86–88.
22   For this ancient method of arrangement, see U. Cassuto, "The Sequence and Arrangement of the Biblical Sections," in *Biblical and Oriental Studies*, Vol. 1, trans. 1. Abrahams (Jerusalem, 1973), pp. 1–6. Cf. also: N.M. Sarna, "Psalm 89: A Study in Inner Biblical Exegesis," in *Biblical and Other Studies* [ed. A. Altmann] (Cambridge, Mass., 1963), p. 30 and n. 7; Y. Zakovitch, "The Associative Principle in the Arrangement of the Book of Judges, etc.," in *I.L. Seeligmann Volume*, Vol. 1 (Heb.) (Jerusalem, 1983), pp. 161–183; A. Rofé, "The Arrangement of the Deuteronomic Laws" (Heb.), in *Cassuto Memorial Volume* (Jerusalem, 1987), 217–235. Earlier bibliography can be found in these works.

the sole principle followed here, some examples of chronological-logical considerations are found.[23]

Chronology and logical succession determine the position of the stories of the inauguration and illness-death-burial (2Kgs 2:1–18; 2Kgs 13:14–19, 20–21) at the beginning and end of the *vita*, respectively. All the other *legenda* seem to be arranged associatively. The inauguration (2Kgs 2:1–18) is followed by two stories related to its location – Jericho (2:19–22) and Elisha's ascent from there to Bethel (2:23–24).[24] The campaign against Moab (ch. 3) has no connection with these stories, and there is some doubt whether it originally belonged to the Elisha cycle.[25] The miracle of the oil (4:1–7) may originally have been contiguous with the incident of the bears (2:23–24), as both of them concern children. A child also plays a role in 4:8–37, but its main link with 4:1–7 is that in both stories the main characters are women, who refer to themselves as "your maidservant" (4:2, 16). The miracle of the stew (4:38–41) may succeed the resurrection of the child, because of the association of "death in the pot" (v 40) with the death of the child. The multiplication of the loaves is, like the purification of the stew, a miracle concerning food and there are similar commands in both stories: "Serve it/give it to the people and let them eat" (4:41, 43, 44).

The position of the story of Naaman (ch. 5) remains problematic. Was it placed in its present position because Naaman brought a gift (ברכה) (5:15) for the Man of God, as in the previous tale Elisha received bread of the first reaping (בכורים) (4:42)?[26] The miracle of the axe (6:1–7), like the healing of Naaman was performed in the Jordan. The story of the Dothan incident immediately follows, because of the similarity between the cry of despair: "Alas, master, it was a borrowed one!" (6:5) in the axe story and that uttered by the servant at Dothan:

---

23 Cassuto (above, n. 22), p.2.

24 R. Joseph (cited in b Sota 46b) suggested that the incident happened at Naʿaran.

25 This is also confirmed by the consideration of the date of Elisha's activity; see below, chap. 4, sect. 5.

26 Cf. Cassuto (above, n. 22), p. 5: "The parable of the adulterous woman (chapter xvi) comes after the allegory of the vine due to the fact that the latter contains the words (xv.4) היצלח למלאכה ['Is it useful for any work'], and in the former we find the expression (xvi 13) ותצלחי למלוכה ['and come to regal estate']. We find another such case in the arrangement of Deuteronomy: Deut 23:17 לא תוננו. "You must not ill treat him" is followed by 23:19 לא תביא אתנן זונה "You shall not bring the fee of a whore."

"Alas, master, what shall we do?" (6:15). The siege of Dothan leads into the siege of Samaria (6:24–7:20). This is clearly an associative, not a logical, connection, because the end of the Dothan story (6:23) directly contradicts the beginning of the story following it (6:24).

In the story of the siege of Samaria (6:24–7:20), a woman cries out to the king (6:26); in the next story another woman does the same (8:3). In both cases there is an appeal for justice against a background of famine. In 8:1–6, it is stated four times that Elisha revived the dead (החיה), and in the following story, concerning Hazael's appointment (8:7–15), Ben Hadad's question is repeated twice: "Will I recover (האחיה) from this illness?" (vv 8, 9) Elisha's answer is also repeated twice: "You will recover and live (חיה תחיה) (vv 10, 14). The verb חי"ה is the central concept in both stories, albeit in two different senses: the first in the sense of to revive, to resurrect; the second in the sense of to recover, to get well. This is a common phenomenon in the arrangement of biblical passages.[27] Hazael' s appointment leads to the story of Jehu's anointment, as both deal with officers who plot against their kings, assassinate them, and rule in their stead.

Returning to the question whether anything can be learned about the history of Elisha or the stories from their arrangement, the answer must be essentially negative. An associative arrangement cannot possibly shed light on the phases in the history of Elisha's prophetic career. As for the history of the stories, whether the editor had different collections of stories before him cannot be ascertained from the present arrangement of the *vita*. Moreover, since the associative arrangement is common in biblical literature, it is impossible to determine whether the original sources were oral or written. This arrangement of the stories most likely began in the oral stage, later becoming the accepted system even after they were committed to writing.

It therefore seems that whatever may be learned about the history of Elisha or about the stories of his life must be derived from their contents, and not from their order in the Bible.

27　Cf. Deut. 23:14, והיה בשבתך חוץ "And when you have squatted," with 23:17, עמך ישב בקרבך "He shall live with you . . . in your midst" – two different meanings of the verb יש"ב.

PART TWO

LEGENDA, HISTORIOGRAPHY, BIOGRAPHY

Chapter Four

THE *LEGENDA* IN POLITICAL LIFE

1. *Elisha and Joash*

The series of *legenda* recording the acts of Elisha concludes with a brief account of the prophet's meeting with Joash, King of Israel (2 Kgs 13:14–17; on vv 18–19, see below). As Elisha lies mortally ill, the king bemoans the fact that upon the prophet's death "Israel's chariots and horsemen" would be lost – referring to Elisha's repeated assistance in the struggle against the Arameans. The king's plaint inspires Elisha to one final effort on behalf of his people. He conducts a short ceremony: through an eastward-facing window, he orders the king to shoot an arrow in the direction of the Arameans, while he lays his hands on the king's arms and cries out: "An arrow of victory of the Lord! An arrow of victory over Aram! You shall rout Aram completely at Aphek!"

This ceremony is a magical act, very typical of the *legenda*. Elisha's exclamation is not merely a promise, but a kind of spell which he casts upon the arrow. This is not an arrow of a human being, but an arrow of God and because of Elisha's incantation, uttered at the correct moment, the arrow will succeed in striking Aram, its intended target. The magical character of these statements is attested to by Elisha's actions. He places his hands in the king's in order to transfer his – the Man of God's – supernatural power to Joash before he shoots the arrow. In addition, the overall structure of the story – a short description of the circumstances, the king's cry of despair, the Man of God's magic solution – bears a close resemblance to that of the other short *legenda* of the Elisha cycle.[1]

---

1 The detailed descripition of Elisha's instructions to the king and their execution conforms with magical ritualism, especially as such detail is not common in

At the same time, this story displays several unique features. It records Elisha's last miracle, performed shortly before his death, the effect of which would be evident in later times, and would be greater than all his other miracles combined. The prophet from Samaria had saved the King of Israel more than once from Aramean ambushes (2Kgs 6:10), had taken an Aramean band captive at Dothan without the use of sword or bow (6:18–20), and had liberated a besieged Samaria on the verge of collapse (6:24–7:20). This time, however, Elisha promises nothing short of complete victory over Aram. What Elisha had failed to accomplish during his lifetime he will achieve posthumously. This demonstrates a characteristic of the *vita* which was noted above: their concluding sections often describe the supernatural powers of the Man of God struggling with the forces of Sheol often achieving greater miracles than at any time throughout his career.[2] The closing *legenda* about Elisha, which contains allusions to many of his earlier miracles, juxtaposed by one which equals them all, is firmly stamped with the impress of the *vita*.

The scope of this *legenda* has also been expanded to embrace new features. Its milieu is no longer the circle of the בני הנביאים the prophet's provincial followers-admirers from the outlands and border towns. Here the prophet's audience is none other than the King of Israel himself, and the object of his miracle is the deliverance of the nation. The miracle is not a "minor act of salvation," but Israel's victory over Aram, which will produce far-reaching changes in the future balance of power between the two nations. This *legenda* thus takes on a new perspective: the political arena. And, accordingly, the story includes the type of details unusual in *legenda* but common in historiography: Joash is mentioned as king, and Aphek as the scene of battle.[3]

---

biblical narrative. See W. Baumgartner, "Ein Kapitel von hebräischen Erzählungsstil," *Eucharisterion ... H. Gunkel* (Göttingen, 1923), pp. 145–157. At the same time Elisha's ceremonious actions befit this dramatic turning point in his people's history.

2 See above, chap. 3, sect. 2.

3 See the identification suggested by M. Dothan, "Aphek on the Israel-Aram Border and Aphek on the Amorite Border" (Heb.), *Eretz Yisrael* 12 (*Nelson Glueck Volume*), (Jerusalem, 1975), pp. 63–65. The fact that the Omride wars against the Arameans took place in Ramoth-gilead, far south-east of Aphek (see below, n. 28) is additional evidence that the battle at Aphek described in 1Kgs 20 was also

This striving for historical accuracy is therefore probably responsible for the expansion of the *legenda* by the addition of vv 18–19. In vv 14–17 Elisha assures Joash that he will rout Aram once and for all, while in vv 18–19 the totality of Israel's victory is made dependent upon the number of times Joash strikes the ground – a dependence typical of the practice of magic! Since Joash struck the ground three times only, Elisha's promise would not be fulfilled.[4] It therefore seems that vv 18–19 are an addition which seeks to explain why Joash's *reconquista,* which began so auspiciously, was limited to three victories, or, in terms of the *legenda's* conceptions – why Elisha's magic did not achieve its goal.

The fact that later authors attempted to harmonize the *details* of the *legenda* with the events of history (cf. 2Kgs 13:22–25) confirms the general reliability of the *legenda.* It seems that though most of the *legenda* concerning Elisha have provincial backdrops (Shunem, Mt. Carmel, Gilgal, Jericho), the authenticity of this account, which portrays the prophet as the king's associate involved in national political life, should not be doubted. The authenticity of this aspect of Elisha's career is similarly attested to by the fact that it recurs several times in other *legenda* as well (2Kgs 5, 6:8–23, 6:24–7:20), and is presupposed in some of the "provincial" *legenda* (2Kgs 4:13, 8:1–6). These stories should not be viewed as later legendary embellishments. In fact, charismatic personalities, such as prophets, sorcerers, and other holy men, often appear at the royal court, especially in times of crisis. One example which immediately comes to mind is Joan of Arc's appearance at the court of Charles VII when he claimed the crown of France (1429–31) against the English and the Burgundians. Another is the monk Rasputin and his activities during the later years of the House of Romanoff. In Israel, there was an established tradition of the prophet's participation in national political affairs, whether as court adviser (Gad, Nathan) or as leader of the opposition (Ahijah the Shilonite, Jehu the son of Hanani). Elisha's magical acts on behalf of the King of Israel and his army are therefore only a variant of accepted prophetic activity.

fought by Joash son of Jehoahaz; see A. Jepsen, "Israel und Damaskus," *AOF* 14 (1942), pp. 153–173.

4   Pointed out to me by my student Yair Zakovitch at Haifa College (1968).

As will be seen in the following, there is a group of stories of this type describing Elisha's political activities. These stories, which belong to a very early layer of *legenda* about the prophet, have been designated here as "political *legenda.*"

2. The Character of the Political Legenda

The political *legenda* contains most of the distinctive features of the *legenda*. Its structure is familiar; a description of the problem: despair, an appeal to the prophet for intervention, the prophet's action and the miraculous deliverance which follows in its wake. However, since political crises are by nature infinitely more complicated than personal and group problems, the account of the circumstances of the crisis and its resolution is more detailed than in the ordinary *legenda*. For this reason too, the political *legenda* is generally longer than the simple *legenda*.

Detailed descriptions of political life are also typical of another literary genre – historiography. As will be seen below, biblical historiography possesses a special sub-group whose purpose is to highlight the prophet's role in national events. This raises the question of how political *legenda* can be distinguished from prophetic historiography. This can be done in several ways. An essential feature of the political *legenda* is the miracle, which is performed at a moment of crisis after all human efforts seem to have failed and only the supernatural intervention of the Man of God can deliver the people from calamity. Aside from this, the *legenda,* and the political *legenda* as well, displays a basic lack of concern with politics *per se,* even when describing the prophet's political activities. These political *legenda* rarely mention the names of kings, generals, locations, dates, or the strength of military forces.[5] This indifference towards political details is similar to that displayed in the simple *legenda* towards details of any kind. In the political *legenda,* however, this attitude is even more striking because political life is usually described with more accuracy.

Just as the composition of *legenda* differs from that of historiography, so too the hero of the legend – the prophet, the holy

---

5   Note, however, that the *legenda* in 2Kgs 13:14–19 is an exception to this rule in a number of details.

Man of God – differs from the usual heroes of political histories – kings and ministers, who rule the state according to practical considerations. The determining factors are the political realities, such as stories of provisions, the construction of fortifications, the size of their forces and equipment, the battle array of chariots, allies, alliances, taxes and tributes. The Man of God, on the other hand, acts by means of supernatural powers which are concentrated in him or granted him because of his nearness to God. The "invasion" of the Man of God into the political realm accentuates the fundamental difference between him and the political leaders. This gives rise to the appearance of another character in the political *legenda,* the prophet's antagonist: the scoffer, who belittles the Man of God's ability.[6] In the name of practical realism he ridicules the Man of God, or attempts to fight him with whatever means available. The political *legenda* makes a great effort to describe how the Man of God overcomes his opponent, defeats him, sometimes actually destroying him, and at other times merely convincing the doubter of his own superiority.

Thus, the political *legenda* is concerned not only with the Man of God's activity in the political arena, but also with the tensions and conflicts generated by his presence. This latter point is at first surprising for both in Israel and in the neighboring countries, the prophet in the biblical period was a well-established social institution. His counsel was sought by commoners and kings alike, and especially by the nation's leaders before they reached major decisions. Such a situation, in which the Man of God was fully accepted by the Establishment – even *within* the Establishment – did not lend itself to the creation of ideological polarizations between the prophet and the national leaders. And yet there are political *legenda* which represent a "modern" account of the struggle between the Man of God and men of action. They recount a situation which is similar to that of battles fought in the name of faith – Christianity versus Paganism, Hassidism versus Mitnagdism. We must therefore infer that such *legenda* were the product of periods of social disintegration, and evolved among circles of disciples who nurtured ideas and traditions differing from, even hostile to, the current ideas predominant in the royal court.

6 Cf. A. Jolles, *Einfache Formen*[3] (Tübingen, 1965), pp. 51–55.

Conflict also requires self-appraisal and self-correction. The assumed conflict between the disciples of the prophets and the court circles is no exception. Attempts at improvement and expurgation can therefore be found in the political *legenda*. In some of these *legenda*, the miracle is no longer accomplished by a magical act, but rather through actual religious means – a prayer directed to God by the Holy Man or a prophetic utterance delivered in the name of God. The transition from faith in the supernatural powers of the Holy Man to an emphasis on the active intervention of God may perhaps be explained by the need felt by the narrators to improve and strengthen the religious character of the stories in order to make them more effective in combatting the doubting or derisive attitudes of the political realists. In this sense, the political *legenda* bears a closer resemblence to another form which will be examined below, the ethical *legenda*.

3. Elisha in Dothan

Among the political *legenda* is the story of Elisha in Dothan (2Kgs 6:8–23). Here too we find the characteristic elements of the short *legenda*: the threat (v 14), the moment of fear or despair (v 15), the deliverance through a miraculous act (vv 18–20). However, unlike the typical short *legenda*, this story contains a more detailed account of the circumstances leading to the main event: the assistance given the King of Israel by Elisha and the decision of the King of Aram to capture him (vv 8–13). This diffuseness is necessitated by the nature of the subject: political events require a more lengthy explanation than private events. This is true even if the story is not intended for a politically sophisticated audience. Even so, the details provided are completely neutral: kings and officers are anonymous, incidents are not dated, and places are nameless. The identification of Samaria, the capital city and residence of the "King of Israel," is taken for granted; otherwise, Dothan is the only location named. This lack of detail attests to the origin of the story: not in the court or military circles but among the common people, the prophet's followers and admirers. They expressed their conviction that after the great military defeats which Israel suffered at the hands of the Arameans, only Elisha was capable of withstanding the enemy's might. Not only did he frustrate their plans through his supernatural omniscience, but he also proved his might in vanquishing "horses and chariots and a strong force" (v 14). "Fear not," says Elisha, "There are more on our side than on theirs " (v 16).

Elisha as portrayed in this account has undergone a process of refinement; indeed, here he is the very paradigm of religious morality. He no longer performs miracles through magical acts, but through prayer (v 18). Towards his mortal enemies he displays not vengeful cruelty (cf. the story of the children and the bears in 2Kgs 2:23–24),[7] but mercy, sending them home in peace, and making his actions a lesson to the King of Israel (vv 21–22). The result of Elisha's noble gesture is that "the Aramean bands stopped invading the Land of Israel."[8] Elisha appears here not only as a savior, but as one who puts an end to war. We have here a lofty folk expression of the idea of universal peace.[9] The attacking enemy must be fought with no quarter and forced into submission, but after its defeat it is to be shown mercy and sent back home. Only thus will its violence be deflected.

Opposite Elisha, the magnanimous Man of God, who calmly holds to his conviction that "there are more on our side than on theirs," stands his antagonist, the King of Aram. As one after another of his war plans are frustrated, he becomes increasingly agitated and angry,[10] suspecting treachery among his officials. Even when his servants explain the reason for their failures, he still cannot grasp the nature of Elisha's superiority. He fails to understand that one who warns the King of Israel of potential danger can very well look after himself. Thus he sends men to take Elisha captive. But this "blindness," the inability to understand which factors are decisive in war, results in

7 See A.B. Ehrlich, מקרא כפשוטו, Vol. II (Berlin, 1900), p. 347.
8 But the following *legenda* 2Kgs 6:24–7:20, opens with an even greater Aramean campaign. The contradiction may be explained by harmonization (see, for example, Kimhi's comment on v. 23), but it is more likely that the two *legenda* were originally independent and unrelated. This agrees with what we know about the formation of this genre of stories.
9 I doubt whether the origins of these ideas can be identified. Along with the well-known Isa 2:4 = Mic 4:3, Ps 46 and 76 should be taken into account. Ideas later developed by classical prophets, e.g., "Assyria, the rod of my wrath," already began to take shape among Elisha's disciples who edited the stories of their master's career. Cf. E. Ruprecht, "Entstehung und Zeitgeschichtlicher Bezug der Erzählung von der Designation Hasaels durch Elisa (2 Kon viii 7–15)," *VT* 28 (1978), pp. 73–82.
10 So I interpret the phrase ויסער לב מלך ארם a unique biblical expression.

physical blindness, when God, at Elisha's request, strikes the Aramean force with blinding light, and the captors become captives. In a polemic against the political "realists" (represented here by the King of Aram), their defeat, or even worse – their frustration, is presented as the consequence of their total lack of understanding of the supernatural forces forming the world of the prophet. And, as if to dispel the misconception that this constitutes solely an anti-Aramean polemic, the King of Israel gets his share of admonishment as well. "Father, shall I strike them down?" he asks. And Elisha answers. "No, do not. Did you take them captive with your sword and bow that you would strike them down?" In other words, Elisha refuses to allow the king to treat God's captives as if they were his own.[11] How petty and pitiful is this ruler, for whom the great miracle which occurred before his very eyes does not inspire a renewal of faith, but only greed for temporary gain, a reaction characteristic of a "hard-headed realist." He intends to exploit this great moment to settle his private accounts and does not pause to consider that by slaying his prisoners he will remove the most trustworthy witnesses to God's act of salvation!

One aspect of the story – the appearance of the horses and chariots of fire around Elisha – does not seem to belong to the original text. The horses and chariots are beheld by Elisha's servant after he is reassured by the prophet. They are meant to explain and illustrate Elisha's statement: "Have no fear, there are more on our side than on theirs" (v 16). But after the horses and chariots make their appearance and come down to Elisha, they play no further role in the tale,[12] even though the main task at hand, victory over the Arameans, still awaits

11   Cf. Radak's comment on v 22: "What right have you to slay them? Did you capture them with your bow and sword?" For the use of the participle מכה in the future sense, see: S.R. Driver, *A Treatise on the Use of the Tenses in Hebrew*[3] (Oxford, 1892), pp. 168ff, and note that "with your sword and bow" serves to contrast human and divine victory (Gen 48:22; Josh 24:12; Ps 44:4); thus here, too, the prophet probably maintains that these captives should not be treated as the king usually treated his prisoners.

12   Traditional exegetes therefore attempt to attribute them a role. See, e.g., Gersonides's comment on v 18 (in מקראות גדולות): "Even though Elisha was not helped by them, it was useful for him to show them to his servant, to calm his fears, that he should not cry out in fear, which would cause the whole city to be afraid; this would have aided (the Arameans) to achieve their aims, for then they would know that Elisha was there."

accomplishment. Who would be more suited to achieve this than Elisha's celestial cavalry? Yet the victory over the Arameans is brought about directly by God, while Elisha's great auxiliary force is left without any task to perform. Therefore it seems that v 17 and the words "and they came down about him" in v 18 were added by a later writer[13] who wished to stress Elisha's supernatural character. He does this through a mythological interpretation of the title given to Elisha in 2Kgs 13:14 : "Israel's chariots and horsemen." The epigonic character of this interpretation is revealed by a comparison with 2Kgs 2:1–18. Fiery horses and chariots descended from the sky once only – to transport *Elijah* to heaven. In contrast to this is the assumption, implied by the addition in 2Kgs 6:17–18a, that fiery horses and chariots would surround Elisha whenever he was in trouble. This is the same epigonic tendency as that appearing in the story about Elijah and Ahaziah's messengers (2Kgs 1:2–17a), in which fire descending from heaven was made into one of Elijah's distinctive features.

4. *Elisha and the Siege of Samaria*

The story of Elisha and the siege of Samaria (2Kgs 6:24–7:20) also displays the characteristics of a political *legenda*.[14] The familiar

13 The subordinate nature of this passage is also attested by the *resumptive repetition (Wiederaufnahme)*:
     v 17: Then Elisha prayed and said: Lord . . .
     v.18: And Elisha prayed to the Lord and said . . .
It is a well-known phenomenon in the Hebrew Bible that scribes who inserted additions into the text smoothed their interpolations by beginning or ending them with wording similar to the existing text. This was noted by H.M. Wiener, who coined the term *resumptive repetition* for the phenomenon, and pointed out many examples. See H.M. Wiener, *The Composition of Judges II 11 to I Kings II 46* (Leipzig, 1929), pp. 2–3, etc. sub indice, cf. below, chap. 8, sect. 2.
    A. Momigliano, "Eliseo e il Re di Siria in II Re VI–VII," *SMSR* 7 (1931), pp. 223–226 (= *Quinto contributo alla storia degli studi classici e del mondo antico* [Rome, 1975], pp. 751–755), believes this passage is a later addition, but in his opinion it was transferred from the following story which relates: "The Lord had caused the Aramean camp to hear a sound of chariots, a sound of horses – the din of a huge army . . ." (7:6). However, Momigliano did not realize that the main point here is that the horses and chariots of fire surround Elisha (see text below). Momigliano's theory that the stories of Dothan and of the siege of Samaria are two versions of the same account seems to me farfetched.
14 The literary qualities of this story, as well as its religious nature were first recognized by H. Gunkel, "Die Belagerung Samariens," reprinted in *Geschichten*

structure is followed: it opens with the detailed description of the suffering in the city of Samaria due to the Aramean siege (6:24–29), proceeds to the crisis in the king's despair when confronted with the atrocities resulting from the famine in the city and in his decision to kill Elisha (6:32–7:2), and concludes with a description of its fulfillment, with particular stress on the manner in which the city became aware of its deliverance (1:3–20).

In the manner of political *legenda,* the story lacks concrete details about persons and events. Only Elisha is mentioned by name. The king, his aide, the messenger, the women who cook their children, the lepers, the gatekeeper(s), the king's servants – all are anonymous. Similarly, there are no chronological, political, or geographical details. However, the story is quite rich in details of another sort. It has absorbed several subordinate narratives, such as the women who argue over the live and the dead child and the lepers bearing tidings of salvation, both of which seem to have been drawn from the store of ancient Israelite folklore. In this exceptionally long tale (thirty verses in its present form and originally perhaps even longer, see below) some five distinct themes are interwoven: the main story about the siege of Samaria and its deliverance, and the secondary episodes of the two women, the king's attempt on Elisha and the doubting aide, and the story of the lepers.

Elisha plays a relatively small role in this large narrative – he is mentioned in only five verses (6:31-7:2). There the narrator (or the editor?) attempted to magnify his importance by means of a brief synopsis (7:17b–20) in which the incidents leading to Samaria's deliverance are presented as merely the fulfillment of Elisha's prior predictions. Some contemporary critics, however, infer from Elisha's limited role that his presence in this story was a late interpolation, the original tale having portrayed the salvation of the city as God's intervention on behalf of the desperate king and people (6:30; 7:6).[15]

Indeed, there are a number of "rough edges" in the story. The King of Israel appears both as a righteous king who physically afflicts

---

von Elisa (Berlin, n.d. [1922]), pp. 46–66, and H. Gressmann, *Die älteste Geschichtsschreibung und Prophetie Israels* [SATA²] (Göttingen, 1921), pp. 300–304.

15 H.Ch. Schmitt, *Elisa: Traditionsgeschichtliche Untersuchungen zur vorklassischen nordisraelitischen Prophetie* (Gütersloh, 1972), p. 38.

himself in secret over the people's suffering (6:30), a cautious and temperate ruler (7:12), and, in contrast, the "son of a murderer" who swears in the fury of despair to relieve Elisha of his head (6:31–32). Yet, it is doubtful whether the discrepancies can support the contention that the story is composed of distinct phases and layers. The portrayal of the king changes in accordance with the context: he is an ideal figure in comparison with the people, but when contrasting him with the prophet he is found wanting and his faults and weaknesses are revealed.[16] As for Elisha's role in the story, it is a recognized feature of biblical narrative that the hero appears not at the beginning of a story but only in the middle after the stage has been set with other characters and the action is underway. This is true both in short legendary-folkloristic stories (1Sam 11:5; 17:12; 2Kgs 5:8, [but note the allusion in v 3]), and in longer, more elaborately constructed *novellas* (Gen 41:12–14, 42:6–7, 1Kgs 1:10–11). In later narratives it is an almost constant device in the structure of the stories (Dan 2:13, 3:1–30 [v 12], 3:31–4:34 [4:5], 5:11; Esth 2:5; Jdt 8:1). At times an appearance of the hero at the very end of the story is necessitated by the course of events, as in the two coronation stories in 1Sam (10:17–27, 16:1–13). A class by themselves are historical narratives incorporating prophetic speeches. In such cases, the story flows until it reaches a crisis point when the prophetic prediction or command is delivered. The story then continues, describing how this prophecy is fulfilled, but the prophet himself is not mentioned again. Examples of this type are the story of the plague during David's reign (2Sam 24) and the first story of Sennacherib's campaign (2Kgs 18:17–19:9a 36–37).[17] The present account of the siege of Samaria is different in this respect from the other *legenda* about Elisha and in structure displays a similarity to historiography, with the exception here that folkloristic elements replace historical ones.

At the same time Elisha is portrayed as involved in events in his special, characteristic way: by hidden rather than overt actions.

16 We may say that the king is portrayed as a complex multifaceted character. His initial response to the suppliant woman is a curse: "Let the Lord not help you!" אל יושעך ה' (6:27); but later his piety is disclosed (6:30), after which we witness a display of fury in his hour of despair (6:31). From the point of view of the *legenda,* his military caution borders on lack of faith (7:12).

17 See below, chap. 5, sect. 3, for the differentiation between two accounts of Sennacherib's campaign.

Samaria's prosperity and the death of the king's aide are exact fulfillments of Elisha's predictions. Furthermore, even the drama that occurred on the wall of the city during the king's walk and his subsequent despair (6:26–31), is fully known to the prophet through his powers of second sight (6:31), even though he was not present during these events. This can in a way, provide an explanation for the contemporary critics' question as to why Elisha is scarcely mentioned in this tale; even when physically absent from certain events, Elisha nevertheless participated in them.

The story's unity is also demonstrated by its uniform literary character. While displaying a broad epic perspective, it integrates its folkloristic elements into a single unit, in which humor, though macabre, is the dominant vein. The introduction to the story in 6:24–25 sets the scene: the siege of Samaria and the famine in the city. The author chooses to illustrate this fact through the market prices of various comestibles,[18] just as the promise of the city's deliverance (7:1) and its fulfillment (7:16) are designated by food prices. Thus attention is drawn away from the siege outside the city and focused on the events within. The choice of the "donkey's head" as an illustration of prices, and the aide's ridicule of God who is to "make windows in the sky" display an ironic-humoristic point of view.

The first main scene [19] (6:26–31) depicts how the king, walking atop the walls is approached by a woman who seeks justice from him, which is apparently a folkloristic motif, by analogy with a similar Solomon story (1 Kings 3:16–28). Her tale is a horrifying one – "With their own hands merciful women cooked their own children, they sated themselves with them. . . " (Lam 4:10; cf. Lam 2:20; Jer 19:9; Deut 28:53–57; this seems to be a recurrent motif in accounts of siege) – and the king rends his garments. It is impossible not to sense that the motif of the besieged eating their own children is employed here in a strange, sarcastic fashion. "Help me, Your Majesty" cries the woman (6:26), imitating the plea of the oppressed calling out for

---

18 On ראש חמור and חריונים see Har. Schweizer, *Elischa in den Kriegen* [StANT 37] (München, 1974), pp. 311–313; M. Held, "Studies in Comparative Semitic Lexicography," *Studies. . . B. Landsberger* [AsSt 16] (Chicago, 1965), pp. 395–406, ad pp. 395-398.

19 For a similar division into scenes, see B. Uffenheimer, *Ancient Prophecy in Israel* (Heb.), (Jerusalem, 1973), pp. 264–268.

justice (2Sam 14:4), but this time the woman complains that she had been cheated out of a cannibal feast she had been promised!

The king, in his rage, swears to behead Elisha, and this introduces the second scene (6:32–7:2), which depicts Elisha at ease in his house. This scene underlines the sharp contrast between the desperate, anguished king and the confident prophet that is characteristic of the political *legenda*. Elisha is fully aware that the king has sent a messenger to slay him, and knows that the king himself will arrive shortly after his messenger, probably to ascertain that his order had indeed been carried out.[20] At this point Elisha plays a practical joke, ordering those present to "press" the assassin in the "door" that is, to squeeze him between the door and the doorpost. This episode as well contains an element of humor: the city is dying of famine, the king walks about in sackcloth, there is a price on Elisha's head, but the prophet ignores everything and finds time for farcical pranks. Several verses which told how Elisha's order was carried out, are apparently missing here.[21] The king, arriving at the prophet's house and finding his crushed messenger bent over in pain, alters his tone and speaks imploringly to Elisha. But his aide still dares to taunt the prophet of deliverance. Now the farce becomes serious: since the fate of the messenger crushed in the doorway did not teach the aide to fear the prophet, his end will be even worse, he will be trampled to death by the crowds rioting in the city marketplace. What happened at Elisha's doorway is a prototypical warning of what will happen on the morrow at the gate of Samaria. The practical, sceptical aide, who refuses to believe in supernatural deliverance and mocks its herald, is branded a heretic, the anti-hero of the political *legenda*. The salvation which he rejects will prove his undoing.

In the third scene (7:3–5), the peak of epic breadth and humoristic style is attained. While the fate of the city, Elisha's head, and the

---

20 Or perhaps to annul his order?

21 There seems to have been a homoeoteleuton in 2Kgs 6:33. The words והנה המלאך indicate the arrival of the messenger sent by the king to kill Elisha followed by a description of his being crushed in the door by the elders, and possibly of his screams of pain. Next appear the words והנה המלך which herald the arrival of the king, already foreseen by Elisha (v 32: "No doubt the sound of his master's footsteps will follow"). The copyist's eye skipped from והנה המלאך to the similar והנה המלך. Traces of this error can be found in v 33b, where the subject is the king (המלך) and not the aforementioned messenger (המלאך).

fulfillment of the Word of God are hanging in the balance, the narrator leisurely proceeds to introduce four new characters – the lepers. These lepers dwell outside the city, cut off from all human contact; their status is almost subhuman. They lack all national consciousness, like the fatally ill, the retarded, the insane, and – on quite another plane – the genius.[22] They are apathetic, almost neutral, completely uninvolved in the war which rages about them.[23] With the light-hearted nonchalance of those who have nothing left to lose, they prepare to desert to the Aramean camp.

These "happy-go-lucky" lepers, wandering from camp to camp, represent the outlook of those who are inured to tragedy and continue joking despite all – like the Shakespearean figures of the gatekeeper in *Macbeth,* opening the castle doors after the king's murder, and the grave diggers in *Hamlet* preparing Ophelia's grave.[24] It is through their eyes that we witness the turning point in the story: "When they came to the edge of the Aramean camp, there was no one there" (7:5). Not the king who craves deliverance (6:33), nor Elisha who predicted it, nor the aide who casts doubt on it, discover this miracle; the four pitiful lepers do, they who neither hoped nor cared are made the heralds of salvation, thus heightening our surprise and expanding the circle of those who benefit from the miracle.

In the intermezzo (7:6–7), the author reveals to his audience (but not to his characters) what the Lord had done. God did not have to open windows in the sky and cause bounty to descend miraculously (Mal 3:10) upon the besieged in order to deliver Samaria, as the doubting aide had mockingly suggested. The *qôl* He produced was not the expected thunder and storms, but "a sound of chariots, a sound of horses – the din of a huge army." This unusual ploy indicates that

---

22 Cf. the anecdote about Archimedes's behavior during the fall of his city Syracuse: Plutarch, *The Lives of Noble Grecians and Romans* [John Dryden translation, revised by A.H. Clough] (Chicago, 1952), pp. 254–255.

23 Indeed, they bring the news to the city only because of their fear of punishment: "We shall incur guilt" (7:9).

24 Cf. A.P. Rossiter, *Angel with Horns and Other Shakespeare Lectures* (London, 1961), pp. 274–292. Rossiter stresses that such scenes do more than provide comic relief. While advancing the plot they offer a different perspective which presents the heroes of the tragedy in a burlesque, non-heroic light and provides an antithesis to the self-centered pride of the tragic hero. I am grateful to Dr. Zvi Jagendorf, who referred me to Rossiter's work.

salvation may be achieved through finesse as well as through force. The lepers, however, know nothing of all this. At first approaching the edge of the camp, they take no notice of what has happened; finding no one to molest them, they fall upon one of the tents and gorge themselves, after which they loot its valuables. Only after looting a second tent (and carefully hiding their new found treasures) do they begin to notice the mysterious silence which surrounds them – "There is not a soul there, nor any human sound"; gradually their self-absorption lessens and they begin to identify with the fate of their people: "Come, let us go and inform the king's palace." The denouement of the story – the flight of the Arameans discovered by the lepers – which appears in the third scene (7:3–5, 8–10), constitutes the center of the tale, and its core is the announcement of God's act of salvation (7:6–7).

The fourth scene (7:11–15) takes us to the palace, paralleling the second scene which occurred in Elisha's house. The king gathers his advisers for a midnight conference. As a sober military leader and diplomat, he tries to ascertain the reason for the Arameans' sudden and unexpected withdrawal, suspecting it to be a tactical ploy of his wily opponent. Though the king is righteous, afflicts himself and prays to God on behalf of his beleaguered city, he is totally concerned with material causes and effects and cannot conceive that such a miracle has indeed taken place. One of his courtiers suggests that a reconnaissance team be dispatched; his reasoning, however, is not military but fatalistic: even if they are destroyed, their fate will be no different from those staying in the city, who are doomed to die of hunger, or from their brethren, "the whole multitude of Israel that have perished," who have already fallen in battle. This reasoning is similar to the fatalistic argument advanced by the miserable, forsaken lepers. Such are human hopes and plans. Samaria's deliverance comes only after all have learned that "the help of man is worthless" (Ps 60:13; 108:13). Slowly the extent of God's salvation is revealed: though it happened suddenly, it takes some time for the people to assimilate it. In the end, however, they understand what has happened. The fourth scene ends as it began, with the messengers returning to tell the king that the Arameans had indeed fled across the Jordan. The surprise of the characters, and their gradual acceptance of the reality of their deliverance, lends credibility to the miracle.

The fifth scene (7:15–20) returns us to the market place of Samaria and its prices. Elisha's prediction has been fulfilled, and immediately thereafter, his curse. Whoever doubts the Lord's power to save will not live to benefit from His salvation.

As was pointed out above the political *legenda,* in polemicizing against the political realism of the temporal leaders, refines and develops the character of the Holy Man. The process is especially evident in this *legenda,* because of its ambivalent presentation of the character of Elisha. This ambivalence, in my opinion, attests that the refining process had not been completed by the time this *legenda* took literary shape. Elisha, on the one hand, is presented as a sorcerer possessing supernatural powers, who sees and hears from afar (6:32), and who by himself brings down curses upon his enemies without God's intervention (7:2, 19–20). But, on the other hand, he also appears as a prophet of God who speaks in His name in formulae familiar from the classical prophets (7:1: "Hear the word of the Lord. Thus said the Lord," but cf. 7:18), he speaks with the king, who awaits God's salvation (6:27) and who recognizes God as being the source of the calamity which had fallen (6:33). The city's deliverance is similarly accomplished directly by God without the intermediacy of the Holy Man. This ambivalence therefore, rather than providing a basis for the recognition of different strata in the development of the story, displays a fluidity in the perception of Elisha's character. The more primitive perception of Elisha as a Holy Man possessing magical powers, typical of the simple *legenda,* is united here with the more sophisticated conception of Elisha as the herald of God's acts in times of crisis.

5. *The Date of Elisha's Activity*

The inevitable questions which arise from the existence of these political *legenda* concern the historical background of Elisha's activity, the identity of the king with whom Elisha had so close a relationship and on whose behalf he intervened on numerous occasions. These points are important for the appreciation of Elisha's character and actions as well as for the understanding of the history of Israelite prophecy.

Most of the *legenda* concerning Elisha appear in 2Kgs 4–8, that is, within the context of the account of the reign of Joram the son of Ahab (2Kgs 3:1–3; 8:29). This arrangement was apparently based on the two considerations of chronology and continuity. Since Elijah's last recorded act was related with the death of Ahaziah the son of Ahab (2Kgs 1), the editor concluded that Elisha's prophetic mission began at the time of Ahaziah's successor, his brother Joram. Indeed, Elisha's first political appearance took place, according to 2Kgs 3, during Joram's campaign against Moab. As for the second consideration, the editor endeavored to preserve a continuity between the various stories about Elisha, and he therefore linked together all the tales in which Elisha was the main character. Their arrangement, however, from several standpoints, is problematic, and must be reconsidered.[25]

First of all, according to the present arrangement it is difficult to understand Elisha's attitude towards Joram. In the *legenda* Elisha is portrayed as having close relations with the king. He aids him repeatedly in his wars (2Kgs 6:8–23; 6:24–7:20), and in the resolution of delicate political problems (2Kgs 5). The king respects him (2Kgs 8:1–6) and Elisha is able to influence his judgment in favor of various citizens (2Kgs 4:13). After all this would Elisha send a messenger to anoint Jehu king over Israel, inciting him to rebel against his master and murder him (2Kgs 9:1–13)! In light of this totally inconsistent behavior, it seems evident that the anonymous king of 2Kgs 4–8 was not Joram, but a king of the Jehu dynasty. Indeed, Elisha's close connections with Jehu's house are demonstrated in 2Kgs 9, where the dynasty's claim to legitimacy is predicated upon an act of Elisha.

This assumption is further supported by the political realities reflected in the Elisha *legenda*,[26] in which the Kingdom of Israel is

---

25 This is one more instance of Abraham Kuenen's pioneering work in modern biblical criticism. See his *Historisch-Kritische Einleitung in die Bücher des Alten Testaments,* 1er Theil, Zweites Stück: *Die Prophetischen Bücher* (Leipzig, 1890), pp. 80–82. More recently this point has been made by J.M. Miller, "The Elisha Cycle and the Account of the Omride Wars," *JBL* 85 (1966), pp. 441–454; it can also be found in Moshe Wilensky's apologetic work איחודו של התנ"ך (London, 1964), pp. 116–127.

26 The political background and regnal years given here generally follow H. Tadmor, "Chronology" (Heb.), *Encyclopaedia Biblica* 4 (Jerusalem, 1963), pp. 245–310, and idem, "The Period of the First Temple, the Babylonian Exile and the Restoration," in H.H. Ben-Sasson, ed., *A History of the Jewish People* (Cambridge, Mass., 1976), pp. 91ff. See below, n. 29.

described as being in a severe state of decline. Aramean bands raid the Land of Israel and take captives (2Kings 5:2). Aramean ambushes regularly set up roadblocks in Israelite territory (2Kgs 6:9–10). Without encountering resistance, the Arameans besiege Dothan (6:13–14), as well as Samaria, which cannot withstand them as it possessed only two chariots and few horses (2Kgs 7:13–14). These circumstances are fully consistent with the conditions prevailing during the reigns of Jehu and Jehoahaz. In Jehu's time (842–814 BCE) the King of Aram conquered all Israelite Transjordan (2Kgs 10:33); during his son Jehoahaz's rule (814–800 BCE) the situation worsened and Israel was "trampled to dust under the feet" (2Kgs 13:3–4, 22, 25). The size of the fighting force mentioned here also clearly indicates the extreme weakness of the Israelite army (2Kgs 13:7). Israel had ceased to be a power of consequence to such an extent that at the end of Jehoash's reign in Judah (836–798 BCE), which was roughly contemporaneous with Jehoahaz's reign in Israel, Hazael attacked Gath of the Philistines, just beyond Israel's south-western border in preparation for embarking on an expedition to Jerusalem (2Kgs 12:18–19). The rise of Aramean power at this time was made possible by the relative weakness of Assyria. In 839 BCE Shalmaneser III's final attempt at subduing Damascus was repulsed. That marked the end of Assyrian expeditions in the west until 806 BCE, when Adad-Nirari III conducted a campaign against Syria. This long period of tranquility was exploited by Hazael, King of Damascus, to attempt an expansion into the southern country. Under the Omrides, on the other hand, stability had reigned on the border between Aram and Israel. The Bashan had been ruled by Aram and the Gilead by Israel.[27] Towards the end of Ahab's rule the Arameans succeeded in establishing control over Ramoth-gilead, on the northern approaches of Israelite Transjordan.[28] Ahab set out to expel the Arameans from Ramoth-gilead and was killed in battle (1Kgs 22:35) but his army

---

27 This situation seems to have developed at the end of Solomon's reign: 1Chr 2:23 relates that Geshur and Aram took Havvoth-Jair from the Gileadites. The kingdom of Geshur, however, is mentioned only in documents dating to the tenth century BCE. It appears that it was subsequently incorporated into Aram; cf. 2Sam 15:8.

28 Identified with Tel Ramith, south of the Yarmuk; see Y. Aharoni, *The Land of the Bible*[2], trans. A.F. Rainey (London, 1979), pp. 314, 441.

apparently succeeded in capturing the city, as it was in Israelite possession during the reign of his son Joram (2Kgs 9:14–15), and it was there that Jehu's revolt began. We may therefore conclude, on the basis of the historical events, that the background of Elisha's *legenda* is not to be sought in the Omride period, but in that of the House of Jehu.

The chronological examination also supports this conclusion. Joram's assassination and Jehu's coronation took place in the year 841 BCE, or shortly before, as in that year Jehu sent tribute to Shalmaneser III of Assyria. Elisha died after 800 BCE, since Joash, who visited him during his last illness, ascended to the throne at or around that date.[29] The *legenda* which describes Joash's visit to Elisha assumes (as was noted above) that in the eyes of Joash, Elisha was a constant source of assistance during war, from which we must conclude that Elisha's acts of deliverance were a recent occurrence, and not something which had happened forty years earlier. This is further proof that the Elisha *legenda* in 2Kgs 4–8 were told about the times of the House of Jehu. Furthermore, a comparison of 2Kgs 7:13–14 with 13:7 shows that most of them should be assigned to the days of Jehoahaz.

These chronological considerations are also significant for the assessment of the reliability of other historical relationships appearing in the Elisha cycle. It is difficult to conceive – though not altogether impossible – that Elisha's prophetic career could have lasted more than forty years. If he died during Joash's reign, i.e., after 800 BCE, then there can have been no connection between him and Jehu's rebellion (2Kgs 9:1–13) or with Joram son of Ahab (2Kgs 3:11–18), as the stories of these two kings must be dated before 841 BCE, the year in which Jehu paid tribute to Shalmaneser.

---

29 But the stela of Adad-Nirari III from Tell al-Rimah indicates that Joash had already paid tribute to Assyria in 802 BCE. See S. Page, "A Stela of Adad-Nirari III and Nergal-Eres from Tell-al-Rimah," *Iraq* 30 (1968), pp. 139–153; A. Jepsen, "Ein neuer Fixpunkt für die Chronologie der israelitischen Könige?" *VT* 20 (1970), pp. 359–361; J.A. Soggin, "Ein ausserbiblisches Zeugnis für die Chronologie des Jehoas/Joas König von Israel," *ibid.*, pp. 366–368; H. Donner, "Adadnirari III. und die Vasallen des Westens," *Fs K. Galling* (Tübingen, 1970), pp. 45–59. It is possible, however, that Joash was then co-regent with his father Jehoahaz. See A. Cody, "A New Inscription from Tell al Rimah and King Jehoash of Israel," *CBQ* 32 (1976), pp. 324–340.

Even more suspect is the connection between Elisha and Elijah, because all of the Tishbite's prophetic activities occurred during the reign
of Ahab and his son Ahaziah, i.e., before 850 BCE. Thus the tales linking the two are all unreliable: 1Kgs 19:16, in which God commands
Elijah to anoint Elisha as prophet in his stead, and 1Kgs 19:19–21;
2Kgs 2:1–18; 3:11–14, which depict the relationship between Elijah
and Elisha as those of master and disciple-servant. As for the story of
Elisha's appointment in 2Kgs 2:1–18 we have already demonstrated
above that it was the latest of the Elisha stories, pointing out besides,
several anachronistic features in its composition.[30] It should also be
noted that the study of historical consciousness is familiar with the tendency of later generations to link famous figures who were originally
widely separated in time or place. In Classical Greece, for example, the
sophist Alcidemus (c. 400 BCE) composed a work called *Agon,* which
describes a lyric competition between Homer and Hesiod, which is
won, of course, by . . Hesiod![31] It is therefore not surprising that later
narrators connected Elisha and Elijah. If they belonged to Elisha's circle, they described Elijah in their master's image – as a fighter against
Aram ("Israel's chariots and horsemen," 2Kgs 2:12) and as the center
of the Sons of the Prophets בני הנביאים (2Kgs 2:1–18); if they were part
of the Elijah tradition, they depicted Elisha as waging a war of annihila-
tion against the Tyrian Baal and its cult – "And whoever escapes the
sword of Jehu shall be slain by Elisha. I will leave in Israel only seven
thousand – every knee that has not knelt to Baal and every mouth that
has not kissed him" (1Kgs 19:17–18). Originally there was absolutely
no connection between the two prophets, Elijah and Elisha, and each
represented a different trend and stage in the history of Israelite prophecy.

30 See above, chap. 3, sect. 1.
31 Cf. A. Momigliano, *The Development of Greek Biography* (Cambridge, Mass.,
    1971), pp. 26–27, and literature cited there. This trend was nurtured by the rabbis,
    who naturally assigned great importance to the chain of tradition; cf. b Bava Batra
    121b: "There were seven whose lives spanned the history of the world between
    them . . ., " and each was his follower's master as is told in *Seder Olam Rabbah.*

Chapter Five

PROPHETIC HISTORIOGRAPHY

1. *Historiography and Prophetic Historiography*

We employ the term historiography here to denote a sequential account of events of general interest.[1] Historiography therefore deals with peoples, states, and their leaders. The treatment of smaller groups – the recounting of the history of cities, communities, institutions, parties, or societies – is an invention of modern historiography. Ancient historiography was characterized by broader horizons. In Greece, it transcended political and ethnic limitations in an attempt to encompass all the known civilized lands within its scope. In ancient Israel, it traversed the boundaries of national realities – back to the beginning of mankind and creation.[2]

Historiographical concern with public affairs, i.e., with politics, sets the tone for its basic approach to the description of events, since the natural writers and readers of such accounts were usually the same politically active public. The origins of historiography are thus associated with the existence of a political class, which was trained to appreciate and realistically appraise events.[3] Historiography,

1 I employ the term "historiography" here to designate the recounting of events. Originally, this was the meaning of "history," but in the course of time this term came to refer to the events themselves, and "historiography" took on its earlier meaning. The following section has been strongly influenced by B. Croce, *Teoria e storia della storiografia* (Bari, 1948).

2 See G. de Sanctis, *Studi di storia della storiografia greca* (Florence, 1951), pp. 3–19, 21–45; Ch. G. Starr, *The Awakening of Greek Historical Spirit* (New York, 1968), pp. 37–56; A. Momigliano, "Time in Ancient Historiography," *History and Theory, Beiheft* 6 (1966), pp. 1–23 [= *Quarto contributo alla storia degli studi classici etc.* (Rome, 1969), pp. 13–41].

3 Ed. Schwartz, "Ueber das Verhältnis der Hellenen zur Geschichte," *Gesammelte Schriften,* I. Band (Berlin, 1938), pp. 47–66, ad p. 56.

therefore, reflects this type of proficiency, in which miracle and the supernatural play only an infinitesimal part. In this respect historiography is the direct opposite of the *legenda,* which is full of awe in the presence of miracle while historiography does not entirely avoid metaphysical explanations of events, but merely minimizes them.[4]

Historiography links the events it describes with an ideational concept in order to explain them and their relationship.[5] The word is derived from the Greek *historia,* which means investigation – originally of the events of the past "as they really occurred" and later the investigation of their causes. Thus, historiography is a creation of human intellectual endeavor, which takes the past as its subject of inquiry,[6] and as such is distinguished from the chronicle, which merely notes events in the sequence of their occurrence, with no attempt to explain them or their interrelationship. Of course the selection of events worthy of record and the very fact that they have been recorded also reflect a historical outlook. Therefore, the difference between chronicle and history should not be considered an essential but rather a qualitative one. The historiographer is fully aware of his role as interpreter and explainer of events while the chronicler merely records them.

A more sophisticated level of historical thinking is displayed by the historian in his criticism of the sources, his inquiry into the reliability of the available historical sources; which sources are reliable and how reliable are they? What caused them to give a biased picture of events? Source criticism is the basic requirement of modern historiography. Its origin is attributed to the Greek historians Thucydides and Polybius,[7] who, however, limited its use to information submitted

4   H. Gunkel, "Geschichtsschreibung: I – im AT," *RGG*[2] II (1928), pp. 1112–1115; A. Momigliano, "Pagan and Christian Historiography in the Fourth Century A.D.," in (idem. ed.) *The Conflict Between Paganism and Christianity in the Fourth Century* (Oxford, 1963), pp. 78–99.

5   Cf. F. Jacoby, *Abhandlungen zur griechische Geschichtsschreibung* (Leiden, 1956), pp. 73–99; and especially his discussion of Herodotus and Thuycidides, pp. 80–95.

6   See Croce (n. 1, above), and I. Kopelowitz, "Ibn Khaldun's Thought" (Heb.), in (idem, ed.) Ibn Khaldun, *The Muqaddemah, Prolegomena to History* (Heb.), (Jerusalem, 1966), introduction, pp. 28–29.

7   See J.B. Bury, *The Ancient Greek Historians* (London, 1909), pp. 83–87, 197–198.

orally by eyewitnesses.[8] There is no evidence of source criticism by Israelite historians of the biblical period. Just the opposite: the fusion of parallel and conflicting sources attests to uncritical historical writing. It has already been noted, however, that this was not the result of an underdeveloped sense of historical thinking, but of the fact that the biblical historians treated their sources as sacred materials whose authenticity was not to be doubted.[9] If the ancient Israelite historiographers exercised any critical control over their sources, it was probably limited to the supression of documents which they judged to be unreliable.[10]

The first Israelite historiography appears some two generations after the establishment of the monarchy, during the flourishing years of Solomon's reign. This was probably the period of the composition of the comprehensive history of David's reign, including most of the material in 1Sam 27–1Kgs 2.[11] The more succinct account, known by

8   Cf. R.G. Collingwood, *The Idea of History* (Oxford, 1963), pp. 25–36. One should bear in mind, however, that these authors, and Herodotus before them, in any case used only oral sources. And see A.D. Momigliano, *Studies in Historiography* (London, 1966), pp. 127–142, 211–220. Probably the boldest historical source critic was the first historian, Hecataeus of Miletus, who even dared to criticize the Greek mythical and genealogical traditions. See Jacoby (above, n. 5), pp. 73–80.

9   Momigliano (above, n. 2), pp. 35–37.

10   One would expect the Chronicler to be the most conservative and uncritical in consideration of his historical context and his attitude towards ancient tradition. Yet examination reveals that he was a foremost practitioner of just this kind of historical expunging. Since Wellhausen, the Chronicler's omission of the reign of Eshbaal, son of Saul, the court scandals during David's reign, the conflict over David's succession, and Solomon's sins of dotage have been repeatedly pointed out. See the recent treatment by I.L. Seeligmann, "The Beginnings of *Midrash* in the Books of Chronicles" (Heb.), *Tarbiz* 49 (1980), pp. 14–32, especially pp. 17–19, and n. 10. It should be stressed that in 1Chr 17:1 the author deleted the words: "and the Lord had granted him safety from all the enemies around him" from the original source (2Sam 7:1). On the Book of Chronicles as historiography, see S. Japhet, *The Ideology of the Book of Chronicles and its Place in Biblical Thought* (Heb.), (Jerusalem, 1977), pp. 423–432.

11   1Sam 27 represents a shift from legendary and anecdotal accounts (David feigning madness in Gath, Saul in David's power) to a realistic, reasoned and continuous presentation. It is also possible that several sections preceding this chapter, such as those which tell of David and Abiathar, and of David in Keilah (22:6–23:14), belong to this historical work. The existence of a continuous history of David's ascension which began with his flight from Saul has already been suggested in the past. See M.H. Segal, ספרי שמואל (Jerusalem, 1956), pp. 20–28; S. Mowinckel, "Israelite Historiography," *ASTI* 2 (1963), pp. 4–26.

scholars as the Succession Narrative (*Thronnachfolge Geschichte*), which has been identified in 2Sam 7–20 and 1Kgs 1–2,[12] is in my opinion not an independent work but part of the aforementioned composition. In any event, this work, in either form, displays most of the characteristics associated with historiography: an account of political matters, a realistic, non-metaphysical description of the events and a continuous narrative linking the incidents in terms of cause and effect – with explanations being offered in terms of the personal motivations of the various leaders, or of the will of God (as in 1Kgs 2:15), not in terms of group interests (national, tribal, class, or economic) as in modern historiography. A certain degree of historical criticism can also be detected in this work, in the absence of the common biblical practice of presenting the same story in two or three different versions, as if they reflected different incidents. The author of this work chose one version only and presented it in a convincing fashion. Modern scholarship considers this monarchial history of David as marking the beginning of ancient historiography, almost five hundred years before Herodotus.[13] According to this view, this composition, the first of Israelite historiography, gave impetus to the later effort to compose a complete ancient history, from God's promise to Abraham to its fulfillment through Joshua.[14]

If Israelite historiography began as early as the tenth century BCE, it is not surprising that in the course of time, as the prophets acquired influential positions in political affairs, writers of history fell under

12 See L. Rost, *Die Ueberlieferung von der Thronnachfolge Davids* [BWANT III 6] (Stuttgart, 1926). It has recently been questioned whether this story should be considered history; see R.N. Whybray, *The Succession Narrative* [SBT 2:9] (London, 1968).

13 Cf. Ed. Meyer, *Geschichte des Altertums*[2], 2er Band, 2te Abteilung (Stuttgart and Berlin, 1931), pp. 284–286; G. von Rad, "The Beginnings of Historical Writing in Ancient Israel" (1944), in *The Problem of the Hexateuch and Other Essays* (Edingburgh, 1966), pp. 166–204, ad pp. 176 ff.

14 This progression, though logical, is by no means obligatory. Historiography in ancient Greece started with Hecataeus, during the Persian domination of Miletus, with his reworking of ancient myths; see de Sanctis (above, n. 2), pp. 3–19. On the same lines, U. Cassuto describes "the Beginnings of Historiography among the Israelites" as being the didactic reworking of the ancient epic poems, followed later by the narratives about David, which attempted to present a factual description of events and to explain them causally. See his article of the above name in his *Biblical and Oriental Studies*, trans. I. Abrahams (Jerusalem, 1973), Vol. 1, pp. 7–16.

their influence and created a new literary genre, which until the advent of Christianity was uniquely Israelite – prophetic historiography. The distinctive features of this genre can be easily recognized. In contrast to the political *legenda,* prophetic historiography has all the characteristics of general historiography: the treatment of a series of continuous political developments rather than individual episodes; a realistic approach to events with a minimum of supernatural explanations and miracles; historical accuracy, and the suggestion of causal relationships between events. Prophetic and general historiography differ from each other in as far as in the first the cause of events is often purported to be the prophetic word, whether as oracle, doctrine or admonition. The predictive oracle serves as sufficient cause for an event, in the sense that developments may be interpreted as the fulfillment of the oracle; doctrines propounded by the prophet may explain why events follow a certain necessary course; while the refusal to obey a prophetic admonition may result in retaliation.[15] In the following sections of this chapter we shall examine several stories which may be considered products of prophetic historiography.

2. Jehu's Coup and the Suppression of Baal Worship

In 2Kgs 9:1–10:28 appears a lengthy account (some sixty-five verses) describing Jehu's anointment, his rebellion against Joram, his murder of the royal family and its supporters, and the elimination of Baal worship from Israel. The story contains several features which prove its authenticity. These are especially evident in the account of Jehu's actions: Jehu acts decisively, swiftly, cruelly and deviously, and this seems to be the secret of his success. Those passages in which these qualities are portrayed may be expected to contain an authentic portrait of Jehu as seen by his contemporaries. This is especially true of the descriptions which display his cunning, his use of others and his casting some of the blame on them to achieve his aims.[16] Jehu

---

15 Cf. P.R. Ackroyd, "Historians and Prophets," *SEÅ* 33 (1968), pp. 18–54.

16 This was aptly described by B. Uffenheimer in "The Significance of the Story of Jehu" (Heb.), in עז לדוד: *The David Ben Gurion Jubilee Volume* (Jerusalem, 1964), pp. 291–311, and in his book, *Ancient Prophecy in Israel* (Heb.), (Jerusalem, 1973), pp. 248–264. I do not agree, however, with his conclusions on the meaning of the story; see the end of this section.

maneuvers the other officers at Ramoth-gilead to voluntarily acclaim him king, in response to a prophetic mandate which Jehu himself ostensibly rejects; he manages to draw the wounded Joram from the city of Jezreel out to the Beth-Shean road, and to slay him there; Bidkar, his aide, mutilates the dead king's corpse, throwing it out of his chariot into Naboth's field; the eunuchs cast Jezebel out the window at his bidding, and following his ambiguous command – "Take the heads ... of your master's sons and come to me" (10:6) – the elders of Samaria behead the seventy sons of the king. In all these cases, Jehu acts as if supported by God's word, considering himself a messenger of Divine Providence, carrying out its will. This repetition of the same *modus operandi* bears the stamp of personality, without doubt that of a genuine historical personality: Jehu son of Nimshi, general and king.

And yet, though we sense that a single personality is acting in all these stories, it is doubtful that they are the work of a single author. On the contrary, there are clear signs that the stories were assembled by a number of writers drawing on varied traditions.

Firstly, a stylistic difference between the first part of the story (chapter 9) and most of the second part (10:1–28) is readily discernible. The first section is factual and detailed; it strives for accuracy in presenting details and gives the impression of authenticity. Not so the second part. The story about Ahab's sons (10:1–10) more closely resembles an anecdote. The elders and officers of Samaria and the guardians of Ahab's children are all anonymous. Ahab's seventy sons are described as children who were reared by the town elders. Yet we know that at least some of Ahab's children, such as Ahaziah, Joram, and Athaliah, were already adults! They numbered seventy, a conventional numeral representing perfection, like the number of sons of Asherah in Ugaritic myth,[17] the sons of Jacob (Gen 46:27; Exod 1:5) and the sons of Abdon son of Hillel the Pirathonite (Judg 12:14). Their fate is to be slain together, in one place and at one time by a new tyrant. This is a typical folkloristic motif which also occurs in the story of Abimelech (Judg 8:30; 9:1–5, 18) and

---

17 "*šh šb'm bn aṯrt*": C.H. Gordon, *Ugaritic Textbook* [AnOr 38] (Rome, 1965), 51:VI:45 –46. See S.E. Loewenstamm, "Inheritance of the Lord," *S. Dim Memorial Volume* (Heb.), (Jerusalem, 1958), pp. 120–125, ad p. 121.

in the inscription of BRRKB king of Y'DY.[18] Moreover, it is evident that this incident is not in harmony with the main story. In 10:11, the narrator describes Jehu's purge in Jezreel: "And Jehu struck down all that were left of the house of Ahab in Jezreel – and all his notables, intimates, and priests – till he left him no survivor." This seems to be the continuation of the story of the seizure of the palace and city of Jezreel (9:30–37). From there Jehu proceeds next to Samaria. On his way, at Beit-eked of the shepherds, he meets the kinsmen of King Ahaziah of Judah, who have not heard of the rebellion, and kills them. If these nobles whom he met on the road from Samaria to Jezreel had not heard of the slaughter of the sons of Ahab which took place in Samaria, it becomes evident that the account of this slaughter in 10:1–10 did not belong to the present story.

The story of the eradication of the Baal worship (10:18–28) also has an anecdotal flavor. The categorical distinction between servants of God and servants of Baal (v 23) is naively non-historical. In reality, the people worshipped both the Lord and Baal, or united the two in a syncretistic cult, i.e., they assigned to the Lord some of Baal's attributes.[19] The impression of non-historicity is strengthened by the description of Jehu masquerading as an adherent of Baal. Surely his origins and ideological allegiance were public knowledge. In any event, it is difficult to imagine that an author who thrice portrayed Jehu as relying on the Lord's word to Elijah (9:25–26, 36–37; 10:10) would at the same time portray him as attempting to disguise himself as a worshipper of Baal. But on the other hand the historical reality underlying this anecdote and the one describing the slaying of the sons of Ahab is not to be doubted: Jehu did indeed destroy the temple of Baal (10:27) and purge Israel of the Baal worship (10:28).

---

18   והרג אבה ברצר והרג שבעי . . . איחי אבה H. Donner & W. Röllig, *Kanaanäische und aramäische Inschriften* (Wiesbaden, 1962–64), No. 215; J. Gray, *I & II Kings – A Commentary*[2] [OTL] (London, 1970), p. 533; F.C. Fensham, "The Numeral Seventy, etc." *PEQ* 102 (1977), pp. 113–115.

19   The following verses express this unequivocally: 2Sam 5:19–20: "And the Lord answered David: 'Go up . . .' Thereupon David marched to Baalperazim (בעל פרצים) and David defeated them there. And he said: 'The Lord has broken through (פרץ ה') my enemies before me as the waters break through (כפרץ מים). That is why the place was named Baal-perazim"; Hos 2:18, 21–22: "And in that day – declares the Lord – You will call [Me] אישי (my man), and no more will you call Me בעלי (my husband). And I will betroth you forever: I will betroth you with righteousness

Moreover, some revision can be distinguished in the roles of the prophets and their utterances. Firstly, it is doubtful whether Elisha really played the part in Jehu's rebellion which is assigned to him in 2Kgs 9:1. We have already noted above that if Elisha died during the reign of Joash, after 800 BCE, it is difficult to believe that he was active as a prophet as early as 841 BCE, which is the latest possible date for Jehu's revolt.[20] An additional problem is the lack of clarity regarding the prophetic status of Elisha's messenger. Was he merely one of the בני הנביאים "Sons of the prophets" (9:1), i.e., one of the prophet's admirers ready to serve at his command,[21] or was he "the young prophet," הנער הנביא – a prophet in his own right? In other words, did he merely transmit a message sent by Elisha, or did he utter the word of God which he himself heard? From the question asked by the officers – What did that madman come to you for? – it seems that the lad was indeed a prophet, relating a message which he himself had received. His transformation into Elisha's prophetic messenger, a phenomenon unparalleled in the history of prophecy, is possibly a secondary development. Finally, it is strange that Elisha is named at the beginning of the story (9:1a) not to be mentioned ever again.

Time and again, Jehu justifies his actions by invoking the Word of God, but never once does he refer to his anointment at the behest of Elisha.[22] It therefore seems likely that Jehu's anointment was originally attributed to an anonymous true prophet, and not to a mere messenger; only later, possibly in order to legitimatize Jehu's dynasty, was this usurper's anointment related to Elisha, who in any event was considered the patron of the later kings of this dynasty. This tradition did not take root quickly enough to prevent later writers from assigning Jehu's anointment to a higher authority: Elijah himself (1Kgs 19:16).

and justice, and with goodness and mercy, and I will betroth you with faithfulness; then you shalt be devoted to the Lord." I have no doubt that vv 19–20, which break the flow, were interpolated by a later scribe.

20 Above, chap. 4, sect. 5.
21 See above, chap. 1, sect. 1, and chap. 3, sect. 1. *NJPS,* "The servant of the prophet" reflects such an understanding.
22 This was already noted by scholars in the past; see I. Benzinger, *Die Bücher der Könige erklärt* [KHAT] (Freiburg, etc., 1899), p. 149; and H. Ch. Schmitt, *Elisa. Traditionsgeschichtliche Untersuchungen zur vorklassischen nordisraelitischen Prophetie* (Gütersloh, 1972), pp. 27– 28, but strangely enough, no one drew the appropriate historical conclusions.

The prophecies show signs of having undergone revision. The message to Jehu is repeated twice (vv 3, 12): "Thus said the Lord: I anoint you king over Israel." But later, in the actual story of the anointment, an additional long speech is appended: "You shall strike down the House of Ahab your master; this will avenge on Jezebel the blood of my servants the prophets and the blood of the other servants of the Lord. The whole House of Ahab shall perish, and I shall cut off every male belonging to Ahab, bond and free in Israel. I will make the House of Ahab like the House of Jeroboam son of Nebat, and like the house of Baasha son of Ahijah. The dogs shall devour Jezebel in the field of Jezreel, with none to bury her" (9:7–10a). This speech includes details about the murder of the prophets of the Lord and other servants of God by Jezebel, which are apparently anachronisms relating to episodes dating from the end of the monarchy in Judah.[23] Moreover, it contains historical reflections on the fate of the Northern Israelite dynasties rather than marching orders delivered by a prophet to a king (who is himself about to found a new dynasty); besides, the speech employs the standard prophetic terminology used widely by the author of the Book of Kings whenever he presented prophecies regarding political matters.[24] We may conclude that these verses (vv 7–10a) were not part of the original story, but were added by the editor of an early version of the Book of Kings which included most of the information on the Northern Kingdom.[25]

---

23 See below, chaps. 9 and 10.
24 Compare the following statements in 1Kgs:
   14:10 "Therefore I . . . will cut off from Jeroboam every male, bond and free in Israel."
   14:11 "Anyone who belongs to Jeroboam who dies in the town shall be devoured by dogs . . ."
   16:3 "I am going to sweep away Baasha and his house. I will make your house like the House of Jeroboam son of Nebat."
   16:4 "Anyone belonging to Baasah who dies in the town shall be devoured by dogs . . ."
   21:21 " . . . I will cut off from Israel every male belonging to Ahab, bond and free."
   21:22 "And I will make your house like the House of Jeroboam son of Nebat and like the House of Baasha son of Ahijah . . . "
   21:23 "The dogs shall devour Jezebel in the fields of Jezreel."
25 *Aliter* P.R. Ackroyd, "The Vitality of the Word of God in the OT," *ASTI* 1 (1962), pp. 7–23, who believes that there are no editorial additions here, but rather successive reinterpretations of the Word of God at different points in history, all

A much more complex problem is raised by two additional prophecies quoted by Jehu in 9:26, and 36–37. The familiar prediction in v 36b: "The dogs shall devour the flesh of Jezebel in the field of Jezreel," appears again in 1Kgs 21:23 and 2Kgs 9:10. This triple repetition leads one to suspect the interpolative hand of an editor.[26] This does not seem to be the case, however, with v 37: "And the carcass of Jezebel shall be like dung on the ground, in the field of Jezreel, so that none will be able to say: 'This was Jezebel'." This verse differs from the other prophetic statements known as the "editorial prophecies" of the Book of Kings.[27] On the other hand it corresponds with the earlier statement that Jezebel was trampled by the horses. These animals crushed Jezebel's corpse until it became unidentifiable, thus fulfilling the prophecy. It therefore seems that the prophecy quoted by Jehu included v 37 only, and the editor supplemented it with v 36b in order to harmonize the statement with Elijah's prediction in 1 Kgs 21:23.

The prophecy quoted in 9:26 seems to be original as well. In form and substance it differs both from the story of Naboth and from the prophecy addressed to Ahab in 1Kgs 21.[28] Here the object of Ahab's craving is a plot – a field – not a vineyard, and it is located not adjacent to his palace, but at some distance, a chariot's ride, from it. Naboth was not slain alone, but with his sons; he was not killed during the day, nor even in the early morning, after the conclusion of a trial,[29] but at

based on the belief in the vitality of the Word of God, which transcends historical boundaries. In my opinion, however, the fact that this phenomenon is limited to the Book of Kings indicates that this was not a general belief prevalent during the period of the classical prophets; rather the inclusion of inappropriate cliches, as in our chapter, demonstrates that these belong indeed to an editorial revision.

26 See below, sect. 5 in this chapter.
27 At most it bears a similarity to several examples in Jeremiah. In the Deuteronomistic sections of that book, the curse: "They shall not be gathered for reburial; they shall become dung upon the face of the *earth*" (or some similar form) appears several times (8:2; 16:4; 25:33). On the other hand, the original prophecy spoken by Jeremiah (9:21) reads: "The carcasses of men shall lie like dung upon the *fields*, like sheaves behind the reaper, with none to pick them up."
28 For the following see O.H. Steck, *Ueberlieferung und Zeitgeschichte in den Elia-Erzählungen* [WMANT 26] (Neukirchen-Vluyn 1968), pp. 32–35; I.L. Seeligmann, "Die Auffassung der Prophetie in der deuteronomistischen und chronistischen Geschichtsschreibung," *SVT* 29 [*Congress Volume-Göttingen, 1977*] (Leiden, 1978), pp. 254–284, ad pp. 260–262.
29 This is the background of statements such as "Render just verdicts morning by

night, by murderers who came upon him stealthily. This is the point made in God's statement: "I swear: it was the blood of Naboth and the blood of his sons which I saw last night[29a] – declares the Lord" – even though the murder was carried out secretly, at night, God did see it. The many differences between the Naboth incident as described in our chapter and in 1 Kgs 21 indicate that the former does not represent an editorial addition, for a later author or editor would have only copied the information contained in 1 Kgs 21. The dissimilarities in the accounts are therefore evidence of the authenticity and the relatively early date of these verses.[30]

This distinction between original prophecies and those which are products of editorial revision provides us with the means of distinguishing other editorial intrusions. As we have noted, the editor's goal was to harmonize the prophecies quoted here with Elijah's statements in 1 Kgs 21. On the other hand, Jehu twice quotes the Word of God but not once does he mention that it was proclaimed by Elijah. This may lead us to conclude that any marginal annotations to Jehu's statements or deeds which explicitly identify them as the fulfillment of Elijah's prophecies are suspect of being editorial additions. This applies to the comment in 10:10b: "For the Lord has done what he announced through his servant Elijah," and in 10:17: "Fulfilling the word that the Lord had spoken to Elijah." Similarly, part of 9:36a may also fall into this category: "It is just as the Lord spoke through His servant Elijah." These statements, as we shall see below in our discussion of the redaction of the Book of Kings, also fully agree with both the outlook and terminology of one of the recensions of the book.

To recapitulate, the account of Jehu's rebellion is composed of a historical document which originally included most of chap. 9

---

morning" (Jer 21:12); "He issues judgment every morning, never missing at first light" [cf. *NJPS*] (Zeph 3:5), and of the situation described in 2 Sam 15:1–6.

29a *NJPS* "yesterday" misses the nuance of אמש "last night."

30 On the other hand, there is also evidence (see above, n. 28, and chap. 2, n. 22) that the Naboth story in 1 Kgs 21 was composed at a very late date, probably in the Post-exilic age. In any event, the date of composition of this story should be clarified before correcting it on the basis of assumed analogies from the Bronze Age! – as does F.I. Andersen, "The Socio-Juridical Background of the Naboth Incident," *JBL* 85 (1966), pp. 46–57.

(excluding, of course, the verses derived from the Royal Annals of Judah: vv 28–29) and 10:11–17. This document was expanded by the addition of two anecdotes, which preserved historical reminiscences colored by folklore – the slaughter of the House of Ahab (10:1–10) and the eradication of the Baal worship (10:18–28). Using these three sources, the author composed a continuous account of the rebellion, which was at one and the same time a political and a religious revolt. The complete story was later supplemented by various editorial additions. The attribution of the initiative for the revolt to Elisha (9:1a) was appended at a later date, though still probably during the period of Jehu's dynasty. Still later additions were made in order to correlate some of the prophecies in the story with others, characteristic of the editorial strata of the Book of Kings, especially with the oracle against Ahab in 1Kgs 21. Another aim was to identify the prophet in question as Elijah. These additions account for 9:7–10a, 36; 10:10b, 17b. Finally, definitely belonging to the editorial layer are the remarks accusing Jehu of following in the sins of Jeroboam, namely, in setting up the golden calves at Bethel and at Dan (10:29, 31).

The main point made in the story of Jehu, before its expansion by recensional and editorial alterations, was the recognition of the power and the authority of the Word of God. By means of this Word, announced by the young prophet, God anointed Jehu king over Israel. This Word caused the officers to recognize his kingship; it caused Jehu to rebel against his master, slay him, massacre his family and supporters, and reign in his stead in Jezreel and Samaria. God's Word against Ahab is repeated by Jehu at each of the three stages of the rebellion: first at the murder of Joram, then at the "casting out" of Jezebel, finally at the slaughter of the seventy sons of Ahab (9:25–26, 37; 10:10a). At each opportunity he emphasizes the wondrous fulfillment of the Word. The last time, he stresses this conclusion to all those present. Wily Jehu, of course, knows how to exploit the inexorable Word in order to absolve himself from responsibility for the bloodbath which he carries out, representing himself as the chosen instrument of destiny. He exploits the Word to advance his interests and to crush his enemies. Jehu plays a perfect Machiavellian politician – cynically using religion as a political tool in order to galvanize public support and justify the use of brutal force.[31] But such a sanguine evaluation represents only the critical reaction of the modern historian to our story. The ancient historian, who commenced the account with Jehu's anointment by a prophet of God and concluded it with the eradication of the Baal worship from Israel, considered the rebellious officer an instrument in God's hand, by which He carried out His will and fulfilled His Word, despite his realization that Jehu used God's Word to advance his own aims. The fact that in the original story it is Jehu, and not the author, who declares that God's Word has come to pass, does not signify that the author rejected the idea that Jehu's actions against the House of Ahab were a fulfillment of the Word of God; in other biblical stories, such as the Succession Narrative and the story of Joseph, the moral drawn by the authors is expressed by one of the characters: Adonijah (1 Kgs 2:15) and Joseph (Gen 50:20).[32]

The idea that the Word of God is fulfilled through the course of historical events was not new in Israel. It was deeply rooted in the mantic character of early prophecy. An ancient legend about Saul's ascension said of Samuel: "Everything that he says comes true" (1 Sam 9:6). But in the course of Jehu's rebellion something noteworthy happened: several different oracles of doom against Ahab's house were fulfilled simultaneously. This did not go unnoticed. The ancient popular conception of prophecy was confirmed in the political sphere. It became a standard for historical appraisal – in other words, a historiographical criterion. In this way a new historiography was created: prophetic historiography. Based on the conviction that God's Word never goes unfulfilled, this form of historiography attempted to portray all Israelite history as a sequence of prophetic realizations. This school of thought emerged by the end of Jehu's dynasty, or at the very latest with the fall of the Northern Kingdom (see below). It was most likely responsible for the statements that through Jehu God carried out "that which He announced through His servant Elijah" (10:10b; cf. 9:36; 10:17b). If we are correct in our analysis, Jehu's rebellion, besides marking a political turning point (the end of the pact with Tyre and the collapse of the Aramean entente) and a religious one

---

31   Cf. H. Gunkel, *Geschichten von Elisa* (Berlin, 1922), p. 75.
32   See G. Von Rad, "The Joseph Narrative and Ancient Wisdom," *The Problem of the Hexateuch and Other Essays* (Edinburgh, 1966), pp. 292–300.

(the eradication of the Baal worship), also constitutes a turning point in historical thinking and writing – the beginning of prophetic historiography.

3. *Sennacherib's Campaign*

Once born out of a particular perception of the course of national events, prophetic historiography endeavored to encompass additional events and periods within its purview, in order to adduce further proof for its thesis. Appropriate material, such as the prophecies against Ahab fulfilled in Jehu's rebellion, was not always available. Therefore, the "editing" of available historical material was frequently practiced. This presented no great difficulty if the historical information at the author's disposal was fragmentary and not sufficiently clear; under such circumstances the, historian in any event would have had to supplement his sources and this would assuredly be done according to his own perspective. Such was the case with the story of Sennacherib's campaign in 2Kgs 18:13–19:37.[33]

This story does not appear to be a unified composition.[34] Firstly, the description in 18:14–15 of Hezekiah's capitulation and his paying tribute to Sennacherib somewhat contradicts the continuation of the story, which depicts Hezekiah as persisting in his rebelliousness, Jerusalem refusing to surrender, and Sennacherib returning to Nineveh in shame. Of course, it is possible that two different stages of the campaign are portrayed here, that at first Sennacherib acted as if he were satisfied with the tribute paid to him, but afterwards attempted to capture the city and exile its inhabitants.[35] In the

---

33 A partially revised parallel version occurs in Isa 36–39. We shall deal here only with the version found in the Book of Kings; despite reservations expressed by H.M. Orlinsky, "The Kings-Isaiah Recensions of the Hezekiah Story," *JQR* 30 (1939/40), pp. 33–49, the version of Kings is closer to the original. See also below, chap. 7, sect. 5.

34 I include here a brief discussion of the subject found in my book, *Israelite Belief in Angels* (Heb.), (Jerusalem, 1979), pp. 203–218, where full bibliographical references are given. Additional references only are included here.

35 So even recently H.M.I. Gevaryahu, "Sennacherib's War Against Hezekiah and the Deliverance of Jerusalem" (Heb.), עז לדוד: *The David Ben Gurion Jubilee Volume* (Jerusalem, 1964), pp. 351–375. It will become clear below why Gevaryahu's alternative suggestion, that we have here *one story* about two missions, is not acceptable to me.

continuation of the story (18:17 ff.), however, there is no mention of any such Assyrian duplicity. Verses 14–15, moreover, differ from the rest of the story in that they employ the name Hezekiah (and not Hezekiahu). They are annalistic in character (v 16 may come from a Temple Chronicle) and their style is not that of prophetical stories. They apparently originated in a different source.[36]

The remainder of the story, 18:17–19:37, also seems a composite work. The following repetitions can be noted: twice a mission is sent by Sennacherib to demand Hezekiah's surrender (18:17; 19:9b); twice Hezekiah responds by appealing to God in the Temple (19:1, 14–15); twice God answers him through Isaiah (19:6–7, 20–34). Such repetitions, frequently found in biblical literature, usually do not indicate that events happened twice, but point to the existence of two versions of the same incident which later editors tried to weave into a single story.[37]

In addition to the repetitions, there are contradictions and inconsistencies. In 18:22, 25, Rab-shakeh claims that Hezekiah had sinned against the Lord who therefore sent Sennacherib to inflict punishment on the country. But in 18:32b–35; 19:10–12 the Assyrians mockingly claim that, like the gods of the other nations, the Lord is powerless, unable to save Jerusalem from the Assyrians; it is this contention which Hezekiah refers to in his prayer (19:4; 15–19). There is also an inconsistency in Isaiah's prophecy: in 19:7 he promises Hezekiah that the King of Assyria will hear a rumor and return to his land, while in 19:34 he prophesies that God will defend Jerusalem (cf. Isa 31:5), which gives the impression that Sennacherib will ascend from Lachish to besiege the capital. These examples are quite sufficient reason to doubt the unity of the story.

A separate problem is the matter of the fulfillment of Isaiah's prophecies. Prophets' predictions do not always come to pass, as we

---

36   See J. Meinhold, *Die Jesajaerzählungen-Jesaja 36–39* (Göttingen, 1898), who convincingly rejects the possibility that 2Kgs 18:13–16 concerns an earlier incident of Hezekiah's rebellion and submission in the days of Sargon.

37   Some of the most famous examples are the three stories concerning danger to a matriarch (Gen 12:10–20; 20; 26:6–11); three stories of how Saul became king (1Sam 9:1–10:16; 10:17–27; 11); two stories of how David spared Saul (1Sam 24; 26); and in the prophetic literature, two stories about Zedekiah's mission to Jeremiah (Jer 21:1–7; 37:3–10).

know from many examples in the Hebrew Bible.[38] Yet the present case is somewhat different. Here pride of place is given to Isaiah's oracles because the author wished to stress that they were true prophecies. It is therefore surprising that his first prediction: "I will delude him; he will hear a rumor and return to his land, and I will make him fall by the sword in his land" (19:7), is not fulfilled. To be more precise, it seems at first that it will materialize, in the light of the statement that "(The King of Assyria) heard that King Tirhakah of Nubia had come out to fight him, and he returned . . . " (10:9a).[39] But if the beginning of this verse appears as the fulfillment of the prophecy contained in v 7, its end, "So he again sent messengers to Hezekiah, saying: . . . " (19:9b), begins the series of repetitions which we mentioned: another Assyrian mission to Hezekiah! From this biblical scholars[40] have deduced that 19:9b is the seam between two accounts of the Sennacherib episode, and that the first story, interrupted after 19:9a, originally continued with 19:36–37: "So King Sennacherib of Assyria broke camp and retreated, and stayed in Nineveh. When he was worshiping in the temple of his god Nisroch, his sons Adrammelech and Sharezer struck him down with the sword . . . " Thus Isaiah's detailed prophecy (19:7) is fulfilled exactly, and the two stories about Sennacherib's campaign are clearly differentiated; the first is preserved in 18:17–19:9a, 36, 37, the second in 19:9b–35.

This is the solution to the problem of the composition of these stories proposed by the Documentary Hypothesis. It is primarily based on the various repetitions and contradictions in the verses. Though there does not seem to be any major stylistic difference between the two stories, they can be differentiated by the nature of the facts contained in them. The first story is rich in historical details. It provides the titles of Sennacherib's officers, the names of the Judean officials who met with them, and the location of their meeting (18:17–18). The arguments presented by the Assyrian officers are

38 This point was often stressed by Y. Kaufmann, e.g., in תולדות האמונה הישראליתVol. 3 (Tel Aviv, 1948), pp. 37–32 (= *The Religion of Israel*, trans. M. Greenberg [Chicago, 1960], pp. 353–355).

39 See H. Haag, "La campagne de Sennacherib contre Jerusalem en 701," *RB* 58 (1951), pp. 348–359, ad p. 356. On וישב cf. *NJPS*; in my view וישב here refers not to his second dispatch of messengers but to his turning to meet the threat posed by Tirhakah.

40 The first was probably B. Stade, "Miscellen," *ZAW* 6 (1886), p. 122–189.

authentic and relevant in their historical context.[41] They mock Hezekiah's impetuosity in rebelling (18:20) and dismiss his expectation of aid from Egypt, (18:21, 24); they observe the weakness of the Judean army (18:23), and the famine and thirst in Jerusalem which will result from the siege (18:27); they attempt to convince the people to desert their king and surrender by promising them a life of peace and prosperity in exile (18:29, 31, 32a). In their speech the Assyrians even present details of Hezekiah's religious reforms – the centralization of worship in Jerusalem – and depict them as blasphemous acts and as the defilement of holy places (18:22), which caused God in His wrath to send Sennacherib to punish Judah (18:25). The second story, on the other hand, contains almost none of this. Sennacherib's emissaries are anonymous "messengers"; they bring certain "letters", containing blasphemous words against the Lord. Hezekiah sets the letters before the Lord, prays to Him, and requests Him to take a stand against Sennacherib's insults for His name's sake, to let all the kingdoms of the earth know that He alone is God. We can therefore conclude that the first story is a history of political events, while the second presents the entire affair as a theological drama: the conflict and combat between a pagan, apostate king and the Lord, God and Ruler of all the kingdoms of the earth.

Yet this distinction itself raises doubts regarding the Documentary Hypothesis in its present form, for whereas blasphemy of God is characteristic of the second story, it is found in the first story as well. It appears in 18:30, 32b–35; 19:4, 6, and probably serves as the reason for the signs of mourning of Hezekiah and his officers in 18:37 and 19:1–2. This blasphemy, as it appears in the first story, is in contradiction to one of the claims of the Rab-shakeh – that it was God who sent Sennacherib to conquer Judah (8:22, 25). This leads us to conclude that the Assyrian blasphemy in the first story is secondary and belongs to the editorial revision of this story. The present sequence of the story was therefore not the result of the merging of two separate documents by an editor, but the work of the author of the second story, who edited the first story, and in doing so significantly altered it.[42]

41   Important material is presented by B.S. Childs, *Isaiah and the Assyrian Crisis* [SBT 2:3] (London, 1967), pp. 80–85.
42   The editor's hand may be detected elsewhere as well; 18:30 is a reworking of 18:29.

In the context of our present discussion, it is the first story which interests us. Its wealth of detail lends it an air of authenticity and indicates that it was not written much later than the events it describes. But the reference to Tirhakah King of Nubia, reveals that at least fifty years intervened between the event and its written form. Tirhakah ascended the throne in 690/89 BCE, at the age of twenty-one, and reigned until 664. He was the adversary of Sennacherib's heirs, Esarhaddon and Ashurbanipal, in their campaigns against Egypt beginning in 675 BCE. The reference to him in this story is an anachronism. Such an anachronism was possible only when the memory of Tirhakah was still fresh, but all the details about him were no longer completely accurate. Therefore, a date of composition of about 650 BCE, shortly after the end of Tirhakah's reign, seems reasonable.

Dating the story somewhat later helps to explain its distorted historical perspective. Sennacherib waged his campaign against Judah in the fourth year of his reign, i.e., in 701 BCE. Hezekiah died shortly thereafter, in 698[43] Sennacherib himself continued to reign until 681. The present narrative, according to which Sennacherib returned to his own land only to be assassinated, joins events which are nearly twenty years apart! The author would have displayed greater historical accuracy had he presented Hezekiah's death as a consequence of the

In the original story Rab-shakeh spoke about Hezekiah's inability to save his people; in the edited version about the Lord's inability. Similarly, for some strange reason, 18:34 and 19:13 were switched. The Kings of Hamath, Arpad and Sepharvaim, who were apparently the subjects of Rab-shakeh's speech, were replaced by the gods of Hamath, Arpad and Sepharvaim, turning the political claim into religious mockery. At first it may seem strange that the editor was also the author of the second story; after all, he could have edited the first story in accordance with his beliefs, without duplicating it. But this option was open to him only theoretically. Working with traditional material – the taunt song (19:21–31) and the oral tradition about Sennacherib's campaign and related incidents – he did not feel free to change it.

43   The view that Hezekiah's reign ended in 686 BCE, thereby allowing time for another campaign by Sennacherib after 689, relies on 2Kgs 18:13, which places Sennacherib's campaign (of his fourth year, i.e., of 701) "in the fourteenth year of King Hezekiah." Since Hezekiah reigned for 29 years, his last year would have been 686. This view is ably presented by S.H. Horn, "The Chronology of King Hezekiah's Reign," *AUSS* 2 (1964), pp. 40–52; "Did Sennacherib Campaign Once or Twice Against Hezekiah?" *AUSS* 4 (1966), pp. 1–28. I have already replied to Horn's arguments elsewhere (above, n. 34), p. 204, n. 37.

heartbreak suffered because of his country's ruin, which was a direct result of his own political adventure.[44] Though the story is indeed based upon reliable historical sources which were available to the author, its intent – to show that prophecies were fulfilled down to their last detail – led to distortions in the dating and sequence of events. There is no reason to doubt the fact that during the Assyrian crisis in the year 701 BCE Isaiah supported Hezekiah and prophesied the deliverance of Jerusalem. Isaiah even predicted a miraculous defeat for the Assyrians (Isa 31:4–9). The essence of his prophecy – a sudden withdrawal of the Assyrians – was even proven true by events. Therefore, there was some justification for historians of the royal court – the quality of their information betrays their origins – to describe events as the fulfillment of the prophetic Word. But it seems that they wished to go even further. In their endeavor to make everything down to the last detail fall into place, they set the prophecy: "I will make him fall by the sword in his land," alongside its fulfillment: "His sons Adrammelech and Sharezer struck him down with the sword." This is the same tendency of involvement with the details of the prophecies which also obtains in the descriptions of the fulfillment of Elijah's prophecies during Jehu's rebellion.

This specimen of prophetic historiography was a self contained story. Why did the editor add his own version of the story, i.e., 19:9b ff?

It seems that he wished to supplement the source he used with other materials at his disposal while emphasizing his own ideas. This material included, first and foremost, the taunt-song against the king of Assyria (19:21–31). The song contains linguistic and stylistic features typical of Isaiah, especially the polemic against the boasting of the pagan king (cf. Isa 10:5–15), the idea that God, as primary cause of all events, determines the course of history far in advance (cf. Isa 22:11) and the assurance that He intends to punish the king of Assyria (Isa 10:12; 14:24–27; 30:27–33; 31:8–9). There is nevertheless a difference: whereas in his other prophecies Isaiah speaks of the downfall of Assyria in the Land of Israel, in the taunt-song he speaks

---

44 An interesting reconstruction of the campaign, which restricts its area of destruction to the Judean Shephelah and the land of Benjamin has recently been proposed by N. Na'aman, "Sennacherib's Campaign to Judah and the date of the *lmlk* Stamps," *VT* 29 (1979), pp. 68–86.

of their enforced retreat. Also incongruous with Isaianic authorship is the hint of Assyria's conquest of Egypt (19:24). That military campaign commenced only in 675 BCE, during Esarhaddon's reign (681–669), and was consummated by Ashurbanipal (669–629) with the sack of Thebes in 663. Thus, the taunt-song could not have been composed by Isaiah himself, but must have been written by one of his disciples, one or two generations later, using the ideas and sayings of the prophet.[45]

There is a dialectical link between the taunt-song and the second prose tale. The former was a response to the taunts and revilements of the Assyrian king (את מי חרפת וגדפת) which it viewed in an original fashion claiming that the king's boasting of his campaigns and victories taunted the Lord because it implicitly denied His supremacy. The narrative tale, however, interprets Sennacherib's taunts and revilements in a simpler manner, as an explicit denial of the Lord's ability to succor, and as a comparison of Him with the gods of the conquered nations (19:10–12, 15–19). This seems to have been derived from the earlier idea, which reflects the bold, penetrating manner of thinking characteristic of the school of Isaiah. The second story, in contrast, cannot conceive of the words חרף and גדף as having any meaning other than simple blasphemy of God. Such a simplistic reading of the taunt-song indicates a late epigonic writer.

The date of composition of the second story is more difficult to establish than that of the first. We may surmise, however, that if the first story and the taunt-song were both written in the mid-seventh century BCE, then the second story must have been composed in a much later period, and by an author who felt that its theological standpoint was not sufficient. Indeed, the question of God's ability or inability to save His people was the foremost issue confronting the Exiles: they were taunted with the claim that the destruction of Jerusalem and the exile of the Jews proved the impotence of their God (cf. Ezek 36:20; Isa 48:11). In reply to these contentions, they presented examples of past events in which the blasphemers of God were punished and His people redeemed, thus offering hope for such salvation in the future. It therefore appears that the author of the

45 See A. Biram, "The Events in Judah and Jerusalem in 701, etc." (Heb.), *S. Dim Memorial Volume* (Jerusalem, 1958), pp.228–250, ad pp. 248–250.

second story, who was the editor of the entire account, should be dated to the middle of the sixth century BCE, sometime after the fall of Jerusalem.

The development of the account of Sennacherib's campaign in Judah is interesting from the perspective of the history of prophetic narrative. The first story included only one short prophecy by Isaiah, which seems to have been slightly edited to reflect subsequent events. And yet Isaiah was the central character of the story. At the height of the crisis, the desperate king turned to him with the request that he "offer up prayer for the surviving remnant" (19:4). Isaiah, in turn, answered with a prophecy encouraging the king to continue his resistance; the prophecy was fulfilled and Jerusalem was saved from surrender and exile. The second story, in contrast, is rooted in much richer Isaianic material, and the place occupied by the prophecy is accordingly much more central. At the same time, Isaiah himself does not dominate the scene here. The king turns not to him, but directly to God, through prayer. Isaiah's prophecy is God's answer to this prayer. But the prophecy is not entirely consistent with later developments. In essence, the three speeches in this story – Sennacherib's (speaking through his messengers), Hezekiah's in the Temple, and God's (through Isaiah) – share one main subject: the struggle between Sennacherib and God for the overlordship of the world, in which God is triumphant; His is the final word and power. Here the prophetic narrative outgrew its original framework. No longer a story concerned with the truth of a prophet alone, it now bears witness to the truth of God' s power as proved through His wars and salvation throughout the history of Israel. In the course of time, prophetic historiography evolved into a soteriology: the account of God's deliverance of Israel.

4. *Merodach-baladan's Delegation*

According to the evidence presented above, it is clear that prophetic historiography written some time after the events in question, was created by the manipulation of the data available to the historian. These data, at least the part concerning political and military matters, were transmitted in the form of royal chronicles, which were preserved for generations in the state archives.

An example of this phenomenon is the account of Merodach-baladan's delegation to Hezekiah and Isaiah's reaction to it contained in 2Kgs 20:12–19.[46] The incident bears the imprint of historical veracity. It apparently occurred towards the end of the first reign of Merodach-baladan in Babylon (720–711 BCE), when he became aware of the increasing Assyrian danger and cast about for possible allies. At the same time, an anti-Assyrian coalition was also formed in the West, to be disbanded by the Assyrian campaign in 712 BCE, which culminated in the conquest of Ashdod. Merodach-baladan's delegation ties in well with these developments. Its date is confirmed by the connection between the delegation and Hezekiah's illness ("For he had heard about Hezekiah's illness," [20:12]), which occurred fifteen years before his death (20:6), i.e., in 713 BCE. Less convincing is the attempt to attribute the mission to Merodach-baladan's second reign, to the year 703.[47] On that occasion Merodach-baladan ruled Babylon for a period of only ten months; it is doubtful whether he would have had time to organize a diplomatic mission to the West.

Isaiah's reaction is consistent with what we know about his political philosophy. He opposed alliance with Assyria (Isa 7:9), with Egypt (Isa 30) and with the Philistines (Isa 14:28–32; 20). It stands to reason that he would also have opposed an alliance with the Babylonians against Assyria. The story, however, does not recount his opposition to an alliance; it is a prophecy of doom foreshadowing the Babylonian Exile. This oracle was fulfilled in 598 BCE through Jehoiachin's exile some 115 years later (cf. 2Kgs 24:12–16). The historicity of such a prophecy is less than likely. It deviates completely from Isaiah's historical perspectives, and lacks his usual argument that Zion must seek refuge in the Lord. In my opinion, this is an excellent example of the way in which prophetic historiography treated its sources. In this episode, it emptied them of most of their contents – the

46 See P.R. Ackroyd, "An Interpretation of the Babylonian Exile: A Study of 2 Kings 20, Isaiah 38–39," *SJT* 27 (1974), pp. 329–352, who contributed several interesting interpretations regarding this story. However, his attempt to link this narrative with the preceding stories using typological exegesis centered on the theme of exile and redemption, failed to convince me.

47 This same conclusion has been recently arrived at by H. Tadmor and M. Cogan, "Hezekiah's Fourteenth Year: The King's Illness and the Babylonian Embassy" (Heb.), *Eretz-Israel* 16 = *H.M. Orlinsky Volume* (Jerusalem, 1982), pp. 198–201.

well-reasoned stand taken by Isaiah – and substituted what the author might have considered the next logical step of such a stand: a vision of the exile of the king's house and his treasures to Babylon. It is to be regretted that in the course of this treatment the prophet's message becomes somewhat diluted. But is this not the usual fate of unusual events, traditions and original ideas when they are forced into the Procrustean bed of general historical theories?

5. The Redaction of the Book of Kings

In the case of Merodach-baladan's mission, the author took an isolated incident from the royal annals of the Kingdom of Judah, reworked it by means of traditions derived from Isaiah, and impressed the entire creation with his own views. What can be done with one fact can, of course, also be done with more extensive historical sources. Such is the case with the Book of Kings: at the authors' disposal were a large number of sources – the annals of the Kingdom of Judah and Israel, chronicles from the temple in Jerusalem, and various collections of prophetical stories: all of these were forged into a work which gave expression to the authors' basic principles.

The basic theological principles of the Book of Kings are of a varied character and origin. Some are of a legal-cultic nature which attests to the influence of the Deuteronomic school, for example, the evaluation of kings by the degree of their dedication to the worship of God and shunning of idolatry or the condemnation of all cult places outside Jerusalem. Other principles – and these are of relevance to our present study – bear the stamp of prophetic literature. This seems to be the case with the violent polemic against the calves at Bethel and Dan, and their condemnation as "the sins of Jeroboam," as if they were pagan idols. The calves, like the cherubs in Jerusalem, were originally considered to represent the thrones of the invisible God, and were common in Israelite sanctuaries.[48] The first to attack them was Hosea, who termed them "that sin of Israel" (10:8), and applied to them the ancient prohibition against making "molten images,

---

48   Cf. H. Th. Obbink, "Jahwebilder," *ZAW* 47 (1929), pp. 264–274; W.F. Albright, *From the Stone Age to Christianity*[2] (Garden City, 1957), pp. 299–301; Y. Kaufmann, תולדות האמונה הישראלית, Vol. 2 (Tel Aviv, 1947), pp. 258–261.

idols . . . the work of craftsmen" (13:2, probably quoting the ancient curse in Deut 27:15). If the Book of Kings denounces the calves throughout its account of the history of the Northern Kingdom and compares them to pagan idols (see especially 1 Kgs 12:28; 14:9; 2 Kgs 17:16), there is no question but that the editor has adopted Hosea's doctrine in cult matters and made it a standard by which all Israelite religious history is to be judged – a classic case of prophetic historiography as we have defined it above.[49] It appears that this editor was not the one who arranged the book in its present form. The final editor, who lived after Josiah's cultic reforms, would have been satisfied with condemning the Kings of Israel for their idolatry and worship at the "high places," the shrines and altars outside of Jerusalem. Our editor, on the other hand, describes their sin more specifically; his relationship with Hosea makes it likely that he lived in an earlier period, i.e., a short time after the destruction of the Northern Kingdom, in the eighth century BCE. Also supporting this date is the fact that he exonerated Hoshea the son of Elah, the last King of Israel, from the sin of the calves. Unlike his usual practice, he does not say of him that "He did not depart from the sins which Jeroboam son of Nebat had caused Israel to commit," but rather: "He did what was displeasing to the Lord though not as much as the Kings of Israel who preceded him" (2 Kgs 17:2). This indicates that the editor had more recent and reliable information of cultic innovations of some sort which had been carried out by King Hoshea.[50]

It is possible that it was this very editor who emphasized the eternal rule of the Davidides despite their sins because God had promised David "to maintain a lamp for his descendants for all time" (2 Kgs 8:19; cf. 1 Kgs 11:36; 15:4). This quotation from a prophecy about the Davidic dynasty resembles the verse in Ps 132:17: "I have prepared a lamp for my anointed one." The fact that in this prophecy there is

---

49 See above, sect. 1.

50 According to the Rabbis, Hoshea son of Elah removed the *praesidia* (garrison troops) who had prevented the Israelites from making pilgrimages to Jerusalem (b Git 88a, b Ta'an 28a, b B Bat 121b). It is doubtful whether these statements reflect a historical tradition. Since Hoshea is not charged with following in the path of Jeroboam son of Nebat, it would seem that he was exonerated of the sin of the calves. Could they have been taken as booty to Assyria during the reign of Pekah? Cf. Hos 10:6: "It too *is being taken* to Assyria as tribute to the great King (Cf. *NJPS*). If so, at any rate, Hoshea son of Elah was not accused of replacing them.

no trace of Deuteronomistic style, as well its being quoted for the last time concerning Joram son of Jehoshaphat, who reigned in the mid-ninth century, may indicate that the editor who included it in his summaries preceded the final editor of Kings by many years. Moreover, this prophecy clearly juxtaposed the Kings of Israel and of Judah: the former were doomed to fail because they clung to the sin of their founder, while the latter were saved despite their personal sins, because of the piety of their ancestor, the founder of the dynasty in Jerusalem.[51] If so, it is possible to surmise the editor's origin identifying him as a refugee scribe who fled the ruins of the Northern Kingdom and lived in Judah during the reign of Hezekiah, towards the end of the eighth century BCE.

Another prophetic idea which found expression in the editing of the Book of Kings was the attempt to demonstrate the infallibility of the predictions of the prophets.[52] This idea is present, as we shall see immediately, in both of the book's recensions.

The material about Northern Israel contains a series of prophecies delivered by *known figures,* all of which are explicitly stated to have come to pass. The circumstances of their fulfillment are documented and are designated by means of the formula: "In accordance with the word of God which He spoke through PN the prophet," or something similar, as in the following list:[53]

---

51   While generally inclined to accept the view of F.M. Cross, "The Themes of the Book of Kings and the Structure of the Deuteronomistic History," *Canaanite Myth and Hebrew Epic* (Cambridge, Mass., 1973), pp. 274–289, I prefer an earlier date for the first edition of the Book of Kings.

52   I accept here, with some modifications, the conclusions reached by G. von Rad, "The Deuteronomistic Theology of History in the Book of Kings," *Studies in Deuteronomy* [Eng. Trans. SBT 9] (London, 1953), pp. 74–91.

53   I have not included in this list two cases: the fulfillment of the Word of God to Joshua (1Kgs 16:34) and the prophecy of Elijah to Ahaziah and its fulfillment (2Kgs 1:16–17). The second case, as we have seen above (chap. 2, sect. 2), was added after the Book of Kings was edited. As for the first instance, it too is not an integral part of the book, interrupting as it does the continuum of the story of Elijah's struggle against Baal (1Kgs 16:29–19:18), as will be seen below (chap. 9). Its report of the fulfillment of a prediction by an ancient "prophet" of the pre-monarchial period is extraneous to this list. The statement in question was originally a curse, not a prophecy. With good reason, this verse is lacking in the Lucianic recension of the Septuagint.

1. 1Kgs 11:31–39: Ahijah the Shilonite to Jeroboam regarding the division of the Kingdom
    - fulfilled in 1Kgs 12:15.
2. 1Kgs 14:12–13: Ahijah the prophet to Jeroboam's wife regarding her son's death
    - fulfilled in 1Kgs 14:17–18.
3. 1Kgs 14:7–11: Ahijah the prophet to Jeroboam regarding the destruction of his dynasty
    - fulfilled in 1Kgs 15:29.
4. 1Kgs 16:1–4: Jehu son of Hanani to Baasha regarding the destruction of his dynasty
    - fulfilled in 1Kgs 16:12.
5. 1Kgs 17:14: Elijah to the widow of Zarephath regarding food
    - fulfilled in 1Kgs 17:16.
6. 1Kgs 21:21–22: Elijah to Ahab regarding the destruction of his dynasty
    - fulfilled in 2Kgs 10:11, 17.
7. 2Kgs 2:21: Elisha regarding the healing of the spring in Jericho
    - fulfilled in 2Kgs 2:22.
8. 2Kgs 4:43: Elisha regarding "eating and leaving over"
    - fulfilled in 2Kgs 4:44.
9. 2Kgs 7:1–2: Elisha regarding the plenty in Samaria and the death of the aide
    - fulfilled in 2Kgs 7:16–17.
10. – – – Jonah son of Amitai, regarding the expansion of the boundaries.
    - fulfilled in 2Kgs 14:25.

It is doubtful whether this series has been preserved in its entirety, and whether its present components are all original. In 1Kgs 22:38 Ahab's death is described: "They flushed out the chariot at the pool of Samaria. Thus the dogs lapped up his blood and the whores rinsed in it, in accordance with the word that the Lord had spoken." This, however, does not seem to correspond with the previous oracles against Ahab. There were apparently many diverse traditions about Ahab which have been only partially preserved. The prophecy fulfilled in 1Kgs 22:38 was either lost, or substituted by a different one.

On the other hand, it is doubtful whether the stories connected with the personal careers of Elijah and Elisha originally formed part of this series. In these tales somewhat different formulae appear, e.g.: "In accordance with the word spoken by Elisha" (2Kgs 2:22), or: "And when they ate, they had some left over, as the Lord had said" (2Kgs 4:44). The impression given is that the series was originally composed of predictions regarding matters of state. In any case, it is surprising that they appear only in accounts of the Northern Kingdom and only up to the time of Jehu's dynasty. This would confirm our earlier suggestion that Jehu's rebellion provided the right atmosphere for the onset of prophetic historiography, which described the course of events as a series of fulfillments of the Word of God. The fact that in some cases (1Kgs 15:29; 16:12; 2Kgs 10:17; 14:25) this series incorporates information from the royal annals or relies on the evaluation of the kings according to their perseverance in the sins of Jeroboam (the calves!) clearly indicates that it too was a product of the first editor of the Book of Kings, from the end of the eighth century BCE.[54]

Alongside the series about Israel, there is another one belonging to Judah. It includes:

1. 1Sam 2:27–35: the Man of God to Eli – fulfilled in 1Kgs 2:27.
2. An anonymous, undated prophecy, stating: "There shall never cease to be a man of yours (before me) on the throne of Israel," in 1Kgs 2:4; 8:25; 9:5, and again in Jer 33:17.
3. Nathan's prophecy to David quoted by Solomon (without mentioning its source) with the intention of pointing out its fulfillment (1Kgs 8:18–20).
4. 1Kgs 11:11: God informs Solomon (no prophet is mentioned) that He will wrest the kingship from him and grant it to his servant.
5. 1Kgs 13:1–10: the Man of God predicts the destruction of the altar at Bethel. This is fulfilled in 2Kgs 23:15–16 (cf. LXX).[55]

---

54 See above in this section. It is somewhat strange that this sequence does not cover the last five kings of Israel: Shallum son of Jabesh, Menachem son of Gadi, Pekahiah, Pekah son of Remaliah, and Hoshea son of Elah. Is it possible that the editor knew no prophet from this period other than Hoshea son of Beeri?

55 The LXX seems to reflect the following Hebrew *vorlage* (cf. BH):

וגם את המזבח אשר בבית אל, הבמה אשר עשה ירבעם בן נבט אשר החטיא את ישראל, גם את
המזבח ההוא ואת הבמה נתץ / וישבר את אבניו/הדק לעפר ושרף אשרה. ויפן יאשיהו,

6. 2Kgs 21:10–15: God announces, through His servants the prophets, that He will destroy Jerusalem because of the sins of Manasseh. In 2Kgs 23:27 God says (= decides) to destroy Jerusalem despite Josiah's repentance.

To these six the following should be added:

7. 2Kgs 10:30: God tells Jehu: "Four generations of your descendants shall occupy the throne of Israel."

Notice the clear similarity to the above in the direct address by God to the king (Nos. 2, 3, 4, above). The phrasing is also similar to the anonymous prophecy to David (No. 2).

In this series, the prophecies are anonymous; they are delivered either by an unnamed Man of God, other unnamed prophets, or proclaimed directly by God. None of the oracles is dated, nor are their circumstances described. From their complete anonymity, we can infer that rather than originating in traditions, these prophecies were derived from the events themselves. From the destruction of Jerusalem, for example, the editor of the series deduced that this event reflected God's will; he considered the time proper for the expression of this will when Manasseh defiled the Temple with idols. In other words this historiographer's theology – and theodicy – was expressed as prophecy. On the basis of 2Kgs 21 and 23, he lived after the destruction of Jerusalem. The earlier, Northern Israelite edition of the Book of Kings was available to him, and he imitated its series of prophecy-fulfillments, though unable to draw on real historical events. Even when sources which would have served his purpose were available to him, such as the prophecies of Isaiah, he did not bother to adapt them to fit his needs. He took exception to the earlier edition, adding an additional pronouncement by God to Solomon (1Kgs 11:11), to supplement Ahijah the Shilonite's prophecy to Jeroboam, since he could not admit the legitimacy of a prophecy to a rebel. What caused him to insert an additional prophecy to Jehu? The fact that this dynasty was of such long duration (five generations), and one of its

---

וירא את הקברים אשר בהר, וישלח ויקח את העצמות מן הקברים וישרף על המזבח ויטמאהו, כדבר ה' אשר קרא איש האלהים / בעמד ירבעם בחג על המזבח. ויפן וישא את עיניו אל קבר איש האלהים / אשר קרא את הדברים האלה.

kings extended his domain to the borders of the Davidic realm, prompted this editor to attempt to explain its strength and stability, which almost rivalled that of the Davidic dynasty itself. The reason for its strength was its extinction of the hated House of Ahab (cf. 2Kgs 21:3, 13 which reflects this attitude).

Both editions of the Book of Kings presented a series of examples in which God's Word was fulfilled in history.[56] This appears to be an interesting case of "quantity becoming quality." When it was demonstrated in the stories cited above, that a particular incident occurred in accordance with a preceding prophecy, this proved only that history follows God's will, i.e., this tells us something about history, not about prophecy. But with a score of such cases from different eras and different prophets we may state the converse: all true prophecy is fulfilled in history.

This principle is forcefully expressed in 1 Kgs 21:28-29, specifically by the idea underlying God's prophecy to Elijah regarding Ahab: "Have you seen how Ahab has humbled himself before Me? Because he has humbled himself before Me, I will not bring the disaster in his lifetime; I will bring the disaster upon his house in his son's time." Ahab's sincere repentance – rending his clothes, wearing sackcloth, fasting, and walking about subdued – cannot cancel the prophetic verdict. At the very most, it succeeds in delaying it temporarily.

The principle of the inviolable fulfillment of prophecies was transmitted by the disciples of the prophets and the prophetic historiographers to later generations. Deutero-Isaiah firmly maintains this position. Fulfillment of the Word is a standard by which the essential difference between God and Man[57] is measured; it also differentiates the true God from the false gods of the nations.[58] A later redactor of

---

56 The Book of Kings includes other prophetic statements besides the ones we have attributed to the two editions. For example, 1Kgs 6:11-13 presents the Word of the Lord to Solomon during his construction of the Temple. It is couched in the language of the Holiness Code, and does not appear in the LXX[B]. It was probably added at a quite late date.

57 Isa 40:6-8: "A voice rings out: 'Proclaim!' And I asked, 'What shall I proclaim?' 'All flesh is grass, all its goodness like flowers of the field: grass withers, flowers fade when the breath of the Lord blows on them. Indeed, man is but grass: grass withers, flowers fade – but the word of our God is always fulfilled!'"

58 Isa 41:21-29: " . . . Let them approach and tell us what will happen . . . foretell what is yet to happen, that we may know that you are gods! . . . Your effect is less than nullity, one who chooses you is an abomination . . . "

Deuteronomy incorporated this principle as an addition to the Law of the Prophet (Deut 18:21–22): "And should you ask yourselves, How can we know that the oracle was not spoken by the Lord? – if the prophet speaks in the name of the Lord and the word does not come true, that word was not spoken by the Lord; the prophet has uttered it presumptuously: do not stand in dread of him." A prophecy which does not come to pass is a false prophecy. The fact that a similar post-script – phrased in almost identical terms and also inquiring how a particular law is to be carried out appears in Lev 25:20–22,[59] proves that these exegetical additions date from the period of the final editing of the Pentateuch, when the various law codes were collated – almost certainly in the fifth century BCE.

At the same time, however, a radically different view was developing – one which claimed that the main purpose of prophecy was to admonish and warn, and that the future predicted was conditioned by the response of the listeners. How and by whom this idea was developed will be discussed below. Here we will only note one example which is relevant to the present discussion. In 2Kgs 17:7–23, after the account of the fall of Samaria, there is a concluding historical summary whose purpose is to justify the destruction of Northern Israel as a result of its sins. It ends (v 23) with the statement: "In the end, the Lord removed Israel from His presence, as he had announced[60] through all His servants the prophets. So the Israelites were deported from their land to Assyria, as is still the case." Here the prophets are the harbingers of the future through the Word of God, as is customary in the Book of Kings. But in v 13, a different role is assigned to the prophets: "The Lord warned Israel by every prophet [and] every seer, saying: 'Turn back from your wicked ways, and observe My commandments and My laws, according to all the teaching that I commanded your fathers and that I transmitted to you through My servants the prophets'." In this verse the prophets are conceived as the transmitters of the Law, admonishers and callers to repentance. Their role as preachers is of far greater importance than their role as prognosticaters. This verse demonstratres the difficulty

---

59 "And should you ask: 'What are we to eat in the seventh year, if we may neither sow nor gather in our crops?' I will ordain my blessing for you in the sixth year, so that it shall yield a crop sufficient for three years . . . "
60 Cf. *NJPS* "warned them"; the distinction is important.

of identifying and classifying coherent literary works in biblical literature. At the very point where the prophetic historiography, here identified, comes to its natural conclusion, its historical viewpoint is contradicted by a completely different outlook. We see the views of opposing schools of thought combined in the formation of ancient Israelite historiography.[61]

---

61 In my opinion, the summary originally included 17:7–12, 16–18 a, 21–23 only. The two interpolations (vv 13–15, 18b–20) are betrayed by resumptive repetition (see chap. 4, n. 13).

12: "... concerning which the Lord said to them, 'You must not do this thing.' "
15: "... which the Lord had commanded them not to do."
18a: "The Lord was incensed at Israel and He banished them from His presence."
20: "So the Lord spurned all the offspring of Israel ... and finally He cast them out from His presence."

These interpolations extend the fate of Israel to Judah, stress the observance of the Torah, commandments and laws, and assign to the prophets the role of transmitting the Torah and admonishing the people regarding its observance. Both interpolations exhibit a linguistic similarity with the Book of Jeremiah.

Chapter Six

PROPHETIC BIOGRAPHY

1. The Biography and the Narrative Portions of Jeremiah

In the courtyard of the Temple, a man stepped up to the prophet, challenged his statements in the presence of the congregation, and broke the symbol which the prophet wore around his neck at the command of God. Astonished by the interruption, the prophet stared at the man who had dared to contradict and dishonor him, and uttered five short words: "This year, though shalt die!" And indeed, less than three months later, his heckler found his way to an early grave.

This story – the tale of Hananiah the son of Azzur, related in Jeremiah 28 – contains all the elements of a *legenda:* an act of sacrilege committed against the Holy Man unleashed his supernatural powers, and these driven by one fateful utterance, speedily find their target – all in accordance with the accepted principles of the interaction between the sacred and the profane.

This story, however, is *not* a *legenda.*[1] Though its author knew of the *legenda*-form, this story develops along entirely different lines. Jeremiah does not respond immediately to the insult; he is thrown into confusion. Hananiah's confident predictions leave him with no ready answer. What a contrast to Elisha who hoisted the mocking aide on his own petard! Jeremiah, on the other hand, instead of a direct reply, commences a learned dissertation on the history of the

---

1 In what follows I disagree with Koch's approach; see K. Koch, *Was ist Formgeschichte? – Neue Wege der Bibelexegese* (Neukirchen, 1964), pp. 222–235, Eng. trans.: *The Growth of the Biblical Tradition* (New York, 1969), pp. 200–210. G. Wanke, *Untersuchungen zur sogenannten Baruchschrift* [BZAW 122] (Berlin, 1971), pp. 151–154, also rejects Koch's view.

prophets. His response to Hananiah is only hinted at: "If a prophet prophesies good fortune . . . " But the provocations only increase: Hananiah takes hold of Jeremiah (can we even imagine such a thing happening to Elisha?), seizes the yoke upon his neck – the symbol worn by Jeremiah at the behest of God – and breaks it, "In the presence of the priests and all the people"; Jeremiah goes on his way, as one thoroughly routed. In the end the situation is somewhat balanced when Jeremiah receives a prophecy, which he conveys to Hananiah not in public, but privately: God's word to Jeremiah remains firm; Hananiah's fate is to be punished by death. The curse is not the result of the violation of Jeremiah's person; the death penalty is incurred solely for having prophesied falsely. Here, God's will is sovereign.

It is the very contrast between this story and the *legenda* which makes it particularly appealing to the modern reader. The tale transcends the limits of prophecy, its subject encompassing the eternal conflict between thought and slogan, between the thinker and the propagandist, between the teacher and the demagogue, between truth and falsehood. The genius of the story lies in its message that it is often difficult to discriminate between truth and falsehood; even the promulgator of truth himself is sometimes confused. It may therefore call Hananiah a prophet, as it does Jeremiah (28:1, 5, 6, 8–10, 11–12, 15, 17). It is thus they appear to the people; thus they appear, momentarily even to Jeremiah himself; and thus they appear to the reader for most of the tale.[2] In this way the story illustrates the difficulty of distinguishing between good and evil, truth and falsehood, when they are presented side by side.

This story, moreover, also differs from the *legenda* in that its intention is not to glorify Jeremiah as a Holy Man, a miracle worker, or an indomitable hero; there is no aura of veneration or awe here. This is also true of other stories in the Book of Jeremiah. He is portrayed as a weak, even pitiful character. A vicious rumor that he was planning to desert to the Babylonians is readily accepted

---

2 In my opinion, there is a degree of atemporal, and therefore ahistorical, literary truth to this situation. From the philological-historical standpoint, on the other hand, the term נביא, "prophet," in this chapter appears to be amphibolous, i.e., it designates a recognized Israelite social institution without making any value judgments.

(37:12–14). Arrested and beaten, no one comes to his aid (37:15). His behavior during that particular incident at the Benjamin Gate is altogether pathetic; he is no more than a ne'erdo-well. On one occasion Jeremiah seems to have realized the ideal of all great prophets: the king will have his counsel, the king believes in him and desires to hear from him the Word of the Lord (37:17). Jeremiah is accepted by the royal court ... but what a court! What a king! Zedekiah is just as weak and pitiful as his prophet, and even more pathetic because of his official status as king. He rules in name only, the true power being wielded by the officials of whom he lives in great fear. He inquires of Jeremiah secretly, furtively, stricken with panic (38:14ff). He weaves schemes to prevent the officials from learning of his conversations with Jeremiah, and draws the prophet into his plots (38:24–27). And in the end – Zedekiah, too, ignores Jeremiah's warnings, and is captured and tried as a rebel against the King of Babylon (39:5–7).

After the destruction of Jerusalem, Jeremiah finds himself in the situation which the past forty years had denied him. His prophecies have been tragically vindicated by the course of events, and the remnant of the people now assemble to enquire of him what the Lord would have them do, solemnly committing themselves to obey (42:1–6). However, immediately upon hearing his message they again decide to act in direct opposition to his instructions. They accuse him of harboring nefarious motives, worse still, they disparage his character, calling him a weakling, a mere tool of his secretary Baruch son of Neriah (43:2–3). The portrayal of Jeremiah in Jer 37–38; 42–43 lacks all religious import and personal dignity. It is the exact opposite of what one would find in a *legenda.*

A further distinction between these stories and the prophetic *legenda* is that they contain fully detailed information on the political events of Jeremiah's time. Unlike in the *legenda,* whose indifferent attitude towards all people other than their main protagonist, the Man of God, finds expression in impersonal titles such as "the King of Israel," "the King of Aram," "the King's aide," etc., here there is a wealth of names and events which make these chapters an outstanding source for the history of Judah on the eve of the Exile. From this standpoint, these stories closely resemble the historiographic genre, sharing a realistic perception of events, an avoidance of miracles and the supernatural, developments being explained on the human level. Declarations such as "the King ordered . . . to arrest the scribe Baruch and the prophet Jeremiah. But the Lord hid them" (36:26) are rarely encountered. The authors of these accounts were skilled in the kind of objective writing that was characteristic of the official bureaucracy. They were apparently involved in political circles and well schooled in the diplomatic and military developments of the period. However, the characteristic features of historiography are lacking here; the main focus of these stories is not a report of the course of national events, nor is the major motivation the desire to explain Judah's fate.[3] The stories are concerned simply with a description of the events occurring in the life of Jeremiah, and as such are most closely related to the biographical genre.

A biography is a narrative account of the stages of a person's life, an account which aspires to authenticity and historical accuracy. It records the actions of a particular individual and his experiences in his struggle to achieve his goals and pursue his principles.[4] An

3 The one exception is 37:2 "Neither he (Zedekiah) nor his courtiers nor the people of the land gave heed to the words which the Lord spoke through the prophet Jeremiah." But this verse, which explains the circumstances in which Jeremiah was consulted in 37:3–10, cannot by itself determine the significance or thrust of chaps. 37–43 in their entirety. Admittedly, 39:1–2, 4–10 describe how Jeremiah's predictions were fulfilled with the fall of Jerusalem. This account, however, was copied by a later scribe from the Book of Kings, or from a historical chronicle which was the source for Kings. The original story of Jeremiah continued directly from 38:28 to 39:3 and thence to 39:14: "When Jerusalem was captured . . . all the officers of the King of Babylon entered, and sat in the middle gate [in judgment, to pass sentence on the inhabitants of the rebellious city] . . . and had Jeremiah brought from the prison compound. They committed him to the care of Gedaliah son of Ahikam," etc. See below, chap. 10, sect. 2. I would therefore conclude that the main significance of the story is not that the destruction of Jerusalem was caused by the people's rejection of the Word of the Lord (as has been suggested by P.R. Ackroyd, "Historians and Prophets" SEÅ 33 (1968), pp. 18–54, and by E.W. Nicholson, *Preaching to the Exiles* [New York, 1971], pp. 103–113). Jer 40:1–6, which expresses this view ("The Lord your God threatened this place with this disaster; and now the Lord has brought it about. He has acted as He threatened, because you sinned against the Lord and did not obey Him"), is a later addition; see below, chap. 10, sect. 2.
4 I prefer this ideational definition, proposed by B. Croce, *Teoria e storia della storiografia* (Bari, 1954), pp. 261–262, to Momigliano's more limiting historical definition: A. Momigliano, *The Development of Greek Biography* (Cambridge, Mass., 1971), p. 11 (and see there for a historical survey and detailed bibliography).

examination of the narrative sections of Jeremiah reveals that they conform to this definition. Describing neither banal nor sensational acts, these stories concentrate primarily on Jeremiah's attempt to transmit the Word of God, and the troubles and danger which beset him because of his dedication. The writing is sober and convincing, detailed and well documented (chaps. 29; 37), and is couched in factual, restrained and impartial language. Though diverse and unconnected incidents in Jeremiah's life are described in these sections, they add up to a unified, authentic portrait of the prophet.[5] Weak, despised, a victim of false accusations, beaten, jailed, and despairing of his life, yet Jeremiah always remains a man of truth, refusing to yield, to forbear, or abandon his mission, because of either fear, or pity.

Unlike a biography, however, the narratives in Jeremiah do not form a continuous sequence. The episodes described in chaps. 26–36 are entirely disconnected (with chaps. 27–28 a possible exception).[6] Though chaps. 37–43 do present a continuous account, beginning with Zedekiah's inquiry of Jeremiah during the siege and ending with Jeremiah's enforced journey to Egypt, they cover only a period of one to three years in the prophet's life. However, the intention of constructing a continuous narrative out of these individual episodes can be discerned here; we may ask why it was not realized. The answer probably lies in the arrangement of the Book of Jeremiah. Some of the prophet's speeches are arranged in chronological order, indicating that there was an attempt to produce a biographical sequence; the inaugural prophecy at the beginning of the book (1:4–10) is followed by speeches attributed to the Assyrian period (2:36) and Josiah's reign (3:6), etc. We may thus infer that Jeremiah's "biographer" – the disciple whose account of Jeremiah's life can be traced in 37–43 – at some stage encountered the original records of 1 ff and 26–36, and out of reverence to the existing traditions, did not construct a continuous biography from this early material but merely added to it a biographical account of Jeremiah's later days. We can therefore assume that it was an early trend towards canonization which

---

5   *Pace* S. Mowinckel, *Zur Komposition des Buches Jeremia* (Kristiana, 1914), pp. 24–28.

6   See the discussion in W. Rudolph, *Jeremia* [HbzAT] (Tübingen, 1968), 172–173.

prevented the composition of a homogeneous record of the prophet's life.[7] It thus seems that there is sufficient justification to define the narrative chapters in the Book of Jeremiah as Prophetic Biography.

2. The Biographical Chapters in Jeremiah: Structure, Composition and History

The study of the structure and composition of the biographical chapters in Jeremiah can contribute to the understanding of the history of this biography. We should not, however, examine these chapters out of context,[8] but must take into account the entire problem of the Book of Jeremiah while considering the principles of literary organization which dominate the Hebrew Bible in general.

A common principle of arrangement in the Hebrew Bible is the concentric organization, i.e., in a given compound unit the homogeneous sections are not arranged successively, but are placed on either side of a nucleus, sometimes even at both the beginning and end of the unit, in a way that has been defined as *inclusio*.[9]

Such a concentric arrangement is evident in the appendix to the Book of Samuel (2Sam 21–24), as is shown by the following:[10]

a. 2Sam 21:1–14: A calamity, the famine, ending: "And God responded to the plea for the land . . ."
b. 2Sam 21:15–22: Tales of David's heroes.
c. 2Sam 22: David's Psalm.
c. 2Sam 23: 1–7: David's last words (a psalm).
b. 2Sam 23:8–32: Tales and list of David's heroes.
a. 2Sam 24: A calamity, the plague, ending: "And the Lord responded to the plea for the land . . ."

---

7 See A. Penna, "Le parti narrative in Isaia e Geremia," *RiBib* 13 (1965), pp. 334–335, who presents a similar argument. In his opinion, the emphasis on prophecies rather than personalities prevented the formation of prophetic biographies.

8 As was done in the first Hebrew edition (1982) of the present work, pp. 86–100.

9 Cf. S. Talmon-M. Fishbane, "The Structuring of Biblical Books – Studies in the Book of Ezekiel," *ASTI* 9 (1976), pp. 129–153.

10 See M. Z. Segal, ספרי שמואל (Jerusalem, 1956), p. 364. Ms. Leah Mazor (Jerusalem) pointed out to me that he was preceded by J. Wellhausen, *Die Composition des Hexateuch* etc.[3] (Berlin, 1899), pp. 260–261; K. Budde, *Die Bücher Richter und Samuel* (Giessen, 1890), pp. 255–6. Their explanations of the origin of this addendum, however, differ from the one presented here.

The origin of this type of arrangement probably lies in ancient Israelite scribal practice. Throughout the entire biblical era up to the end of the Second Commonwealth period, scrolls, not *codices,* were used. To expand a text, the scribe would append his additions at both ends of the scroll. This was easily accomplished by writing on new pieces of leather or papyrus and stitching them on to the edges of the extant scroll. Thus the concentric order came into being; and once it was employed it became the fashion, even when not required for technical reasons. Hence, one does not necessarily always find the older material in the center of a compound unit, and the more recent at its edges.

This kind of concentric order, with its most salient feature the *inclusio,* dominates, as far as I can see, the internal organization of the various collections in the book of Jeremiah. The book is composed of the following collections:

I. Chapters 1–24: Undated visions, prophecies of judgment, laments.

II. Chapters 25–36: Speeches of Jeremiah and stories about him, all dated. This collection in turn includes:

    III. Chapters 30–33: Words of consolation – a collection organized around the restoration story and speech of chapter 32.

IV. Chapters 37–45: A continuous biographical account of Jeremiah, ending with a prophecy on Baruch.

V. Chapters 46–51: Prophecies about the nations.

VI. Chapter 52: Appendix – the fall and exile of Jerusalem.

The first collection, following the inscription and the prophet's consecration (Jer 1:1–10), opens with a vision (the almond rod), introduced by the words: "What do you see, Jeremiah?" (1:11); it concludes with another vision, the two baskets of figs (chap. 24), its interpretation being introduced by the same question: "What do you see, Jeremiah?" (24:3).

The same pattern appears in the fifth collection. It opens with a great power, Egypt (chap. 46), followed by its neighbors, the Philistines (chap. 47); at the end stands the other great power, Babylon (chaps. 50–51), preceded by its neighor, Elam (49:34–39). All the other peoples are included within this frame.

The same order appears in collections II, III, and IV, which are of relevance to our subject. The second collection begins with a speech from the fourth year of Jehoiakim (chap. 25), and ends relating an episode from the same year (chap. 36), although its conclusion took place only in the following year (36:9 ff). To this *inclusio* corresponds the concentric order of the entire collection:

Chapter 25:   Jehoiakim's reign – the speech about the Babylonian conquest.

Chapter 26:   Jehoiakim's reign – the Temple sermon and Jeremiah's trial.

Chapter 27:   Zedekiah's reign[11] – the reins and the yoke against the anti-Babylonian conspiracy.

Chapter 28:   Zedekiah's reign – clash with Hananiah son of Azzur.

Chapter 29:   Zedekiah's reign – letters to the exiles in Babylon.

Chapter 32:[12] Zedekiah's reign – purchase of Hanamel's field.

Chapter 34:   Zedekiah's reign – release of the slaves and their re-enslavement.

Chapter 35:   Jehoiakim's reign – Jeremiah offers wine to the Rechabites.

Chapter 36:   Jehoiakim's reign – reading of the scroll, its burning and rewriting.

There are thus five episodes from Zedekiah's reign framed by four episodes from Jehoiakim's reign, two at the beginning and two at the end.

11   The title erroneously states: "At the beginning of the reign of King Jehoiakim . . ." (27:1). But there is no doubt that this is a secondary corruption (cf. vv3 and 12) which could hardly have affected the order of the chapters.
12   For chaps. 30, 31 and 33, see below.

This order was disrupted by the insertion of chaps. 30–31 and 33 which are not dated. This insertion was due to a secondary reworking, carried out by a later editor who, again according to the concentric pattern, arranged a small collection of restoration prophecies (chaps. 30–33) on either side of the consolation episode of Hanamel's field (chap. 32). Its contents are defined at the beginning: "Write down in a scroll all the words that I have spoken to you. For days are coming – declares the Lord – when I will restore the fortunes of My people Israel and Judah . . ." (30:2–3). Thus the third collection came into being.

The arrangement of the second collection is a key to the structure of the fourth. The main problem here is that the continuous biography of Jeremiah during and after the fall of Jerusalem ends in chap. 45 with a prophecy to Baruch dating from the fourth year of Jehoiakim, more than 18 years earlier! However, once the principle of *inclusio* is recognised, the problem can be resolved: the editor put Baruch's prophecy at the end because of its analogy with the episode directly preceding this collection in which Baruch committed to writing the prophecies in the fourth year of Jehoiakim (cf. 36:1–4; 45:1)! The fourth year of Jehoiakim, on the eve of Nebuchadnezzar's first campaign to the west, thus stands at the beginning of all the dated prose passages of Jeremiah (chap. 25), at its end (chap. 45), and in the middle (chap. 36), where the single episodes give way to the continuous narrative.

Turning now to the history of these two "biographical" collections in the book of Jeremiah, it appears that the second collection was organized according to a single concentric plan. Its various episodes, however, are not of one piece, but belong to two distinct literary types: biographical tales (e.g., 26; 28; 36) and speeches (e.g., 25; 27; most of 34). On account of their lively descriptions, the stories appear to be contemporaneous with the events. This is also attested by the fact that they open with the reign of Jehoiakim. A late writer would not have chosen this point for the beginning of his story, but would have begun his account as early as Jeremiah's birth or from the time of his consecration. It is thus plausible that their author became acquainted with Jeremiah in the first years of Jehoiakim's reign, after the battle of Carchemish and before the subjugation to Babylon. Since Baruch son of Neriah appears at Jeremiah's side exactly at this time, in the fourth year of Jehoiakim, and because of his dominant role as secretary to the prophet in two of the stories, it is very likely that Baruch himself was the author of the biographical tales in their presumed original form. The speeches, however, are from a much later date. Some of them can be proved to be Deuteronomistic elaborations on earlier biographical narratives, such as chap. 25 which is a reworking of chap. 36.[13] An examination of their ideology proves that they were not written before the Restoration, at the end of the sixth century BCE, some three generations after Jeremiah's activity.[14] If so, the conclusion must be that the collection itself, which represents a combination of the two literary genres, was compiled at a very late stage, in the fifth century. However, this was not the final phase of the book's formation, since we have seen that the collection of consolation prophecies (chaps. 30–33) came into being at a still later stage.

The order of the various episodes in the second collection indicates that they were first written down in order to record individual events significant in the prophet's life. No attempt was made at first to join them into a continuous biography. Indeed, two episodes from Jehoiakim's reign (35; 36) and two from Zedekiah's (32; 34) are not in chronological order. It thus appears that there was no intention of constructing a comprehensive biography here.

The fact that the second collection was compiled after the composition of the Deuteronomistic speeches suggests how the fourth collection (chaps. 37–45), which contains a continuous biography of Jeremiah during and after the fall of Jerusalem, came into being.[15] In this collection Deuteronomistic speeches appear only towards its end (most of chaps. 42 and 44), and were it not for the analogy from the second collection, which indicates that the collections were compiled after the composition of the Deuteronomistic layer, the speeches

13 Cf. Mowinckel (above, n. 5), pp. 7–10, and recently: A. Rofé, "Studies on the Composition of the Book of Jeremiah" (Heb.), *Tarbiz* 44 (1975), pp. 1–29 (English summary, pp. I-II).
14 The evidence cannot be adduced here. Cf. Rofé, *loc. cit.*
15 The history of this story has recently been discussed by Wanke (above, n. 1), and K.-F. Pohlmann, *Studien zum Jeremiabuch* [FRLANT 118] (Göttingen, 1978). In my opinion, both these works offer a somewhat hypercritical analysis and simplistic synthesis (Wanke distinguishes three compositions; Pohlmann – three strata).

could have been considered merely a secondary expansion of the biography. However, the date and manner of composition of the fourth collection can be clarified by examining three other points: the relation between chaps. 37 and 38, the presence of a Judean state chronicle in 40:7–41:18, and the juxtaposition in 39:3– 40:6 of two accounts about Jeremiah's release, one of which (39:11–12, 40:1–6) exhibits features of late martyrology.

The two parallel stories concerning the release of Jeremiah will be further discussed below;[16] here we shall examine two other questions, the first being the Judean chronicle of the fall which is preserved in Jer. 40:7–41:18. The existence of the chronicle is attested by the following facts:

(1) The same document is quoted at the end of the Book of Kings, in the story about Gedaliah son of Ahikam; cf. 2Kgs 25:23–24–Jer 40:7–9; 2Kgs 25:25 – Jer 41:1–3; 2Kgs 25:26 – Jer 41:16–17; 43:5–7. The chronicle as presented in Jeremiah is even in tone and displays no signs of having been expanded from the brief account in Kings. On the other hand, since Kings does not mention the prophet Jeremiah, nor quote from his book, it should not be considered a condensation of Jer 40–41. We may therefore conclude that Kings and Jeremiah – each in its own way – both drew on a third, independent source.

(2) In the story in Jer 40:7–41:18, Jeremiah himself is nowhere mentioned, nor is there any indication of his whereabouts during the massacre carried out by Ishmael at Mizpah. It is inconceivable that Ishmael would have overlooked the prophet from Anathoth, who was known to be one of the foremost advocates of surrender to the Babylonians.

(3) A yet more important consideration is that the warnings which Gedaliah received regarding Ishmael's nefarious intentions came from Johanan son of Kareah, while Jeremiah, the prophet of God who dwelt with Gedaliah at Mizpah, former adviser to King Zedekiah, played no role in these events and is nowhere mentioned as offering counsel to one who had been his friend and ally (cf. Jer 26:24).

In the light of these factors we must conclude that this story did not originate within Jeremianic tradition.[17] It is derived from a chronicle

16 Cf. below, chap. 10, sect.2.
17 See P.A.H. de Boer, "Some Remarks Concerning and Suggested by Jeremiah 43:1–7," *Essays in Honor of H.G. May* (Nashville, 1970), pp. 71–79, who has

of the kind written by royal scribes, which in this case recorded the events of the Destruction of Judah. Parts of it are quoted in the Book of Kings, and a more extensive section is reproduced in the Jeremianic biography. The fact that Jeremiah's biographer chose to quote the description of these events from the royal chronicle and not to relate them in his own words would seem to indicate that he lived later than the Exilic era, did not know of its events firsthand, but did know of the literature produced by other, non-prophetic circles contemporary with the Exile. It therefore seems reasonable to date him not earlier than the mid-sixth century.

A similar conclusion can also be reached on the basis of a comparison of 37:12–21 with 38. These stories seem to duplicate each other. Both tell of Jeremiah's arrest for treason or incitement to treason (37:13–15/38:1–6); in both the courtiers cast him into the pit or the pit-house (37:16/38:6); in both King Zedekiah intervenes on his behalf and delivers him from danger (37:17/38:7b–13); in both the king seeks advice from Jeremiah after saving him, and Jeremiah advises him to surrender (37:17–19/38:14–23); in both Jeremiah requests not to be returned to the House of Jonathan the Scribe (37:20/38:26); and both end at the same point: Jeremiah lodged in the prison compound (37:21/38:28, 38:13). Moreover, 37:21 foreshadows the end of the siege and the city's fall, when "all the bread in the city was gone"; cf 2Kgs 25:3; Jer 52:6.

One may, of course, explain the duplication by maintaining that the courtiers who cast Jeremiah into the pit (38:6) took him from the prison compound. One may also note the contentual difference between the two stories. While the first describes Jeremiah's long and difficult imprisonment in the House of Jonathan the Scribe, the second story tells of his drowning in a mud pit which could have led to his death. But such a distinction would not be very helpful either. First of all, would Jeremiah have been allowed to carry out a peace campaign from the prison compound in the presence of the army (37:2/38:4, but cf. also 32:1:–15)? Secondly, the courtiers are not said to have taken him from the prison compound; quite the contrary – 38:6 sounds as though he was brought there for the first time. Thirdly, the stories themselves seem to give the impression that the two places

examined the connection between the story of Jeremiah and the Exilic Chronicle.

in which Jeremiah was in danger were identical. According to
37:15–16: "The officials were furious with Jeremiah; they beat him
and put him into prison, in the house of the scribe Jonathan – for it
had been made into a jail. Thus Jeremiah came to the pit-house and
the cells, and Jeremiah remained there a long time." But 38:9 runs:
"Those men have acted wickedly in all they did to the prophet
Jeremiah: they have put him down in the pit, to die there of hunger.
For there was no more bread in the city." Thus it appears the pit held
no danger of death by drowning, but was rather a place of confinement
(cf. Gen 40:15; 41:14; Exod 12:29), like the one mentioned in 37:16.

It is therefore apparent that Jeremiah's confinement took place in
Jonathan the Scribe's house, also called "the pit" or "the house of the
pit." Two versions of this story are extant. The version in 37:12–21
reported the events as they happened. The version in chap. 38, on the
other hand, added a dramatic touch, relating how Jeremiah, cast into
a mud pit to drown, was rescued at the last moment by one of the
king's servants. This is a late anecdotal development. Its presence here
implies, however, that the continuous biography was also not an
eyewitness account of events by a contemporary observer such as
Baruch son of Neriah, but the result of a long history of development.
Its composition was preceded by oral traditions and variant versions
which evolved over at least a generation. Also contributing to this
conclusion is the fact that Baruch is mentioned only towards the end
of this account (43:3–6). Our conclusion is that this part of the
biography as well was not written before the mid-sixth century.[18]

The history of the biographical material on Jeremiah can be
summarized as follows: isolated episodes from the prophet's life were
written down relatively early, probably soon after the events occurred.
These episodes, and later versions of them, were subsequently
compiled in one scroll, but no attempt was made at that time to
synthesize them into a continuous account. The history of chaps.
37–45 is somewhat different. An editor, working with various stories
available to him – some historical, some anecdotal – and with an
official chronicle from the time of the Exile, composed a continuous

---

18 The popular view that the biographical chapters of Jeremiah were written by
Baruch son of Neriah has therefore no foundation. The simple appeal of this view,
however, has made some scholars reluctant to abandon it. For a survey of critical
opinion on this question, see my article (above, n. 13), p. 3 and n. 10.

biography of the prophet dealing with the period around 586 BCE. He did not touch the earlier part of Jeremiah's life, possibly because a collection of stories about the prophet and a collection of his words and oracles during that period had already been assembled.

3. Factors Leading to the Rise of Prophetic Biography

As mentioned above, the Jeremiah narratives, inasmuch as they provide a convincingly faithful description of his life and his role as a prophet should be considered the beginning of biography, even if they do not present a complete account of his life. In attempting to isolate the factors that led to the creation of this literary genre we should ask ourselves in what way Jeremiah differed from Elisha, in other words, why Elisha was made a hero of *legenda* while Jeremiah became the subject of biography.

It seems that this difference was not solely one of personality. Elisha is indeed portrayed as a respected figure who was admired by the king, his ministers and the elders (2Kgs 4:13; 6:32), and as the center of a large coterie of disciples and admirers (4:38–44), whereas Jeremiah, in the stories related about him and in his own confessions (Jer 8:18/20:18), is revealed as a lonely, persecuted and tormented, figure. Nevertheless, Jeremiah too, possessed influential allies and admirers – princes, priests, as well as the king himself (Jer 26:24; 29:25–29; 36:11–25; 37:17–38:27). He too, vanquished his adversaries through the power of the Word of God vested in him (28:15–17), and his survival of the many attempts on his life proves that he possessed immunity to any direct harm inflicted by his enemies.[19] Had he not won the respect and awe of his contemporaries, Jeremiah could not have endured the twenty-two years of harassment at the hands of the king, priests and prophets during Jehoiakim's reign, and by the princes during Zedekiah's reign. The story of Hananiah demonstrates that the differences between the ways in which Elisha and Jeremiah were

---

19 Cf. Y. Kaufmann, *The Religion of Israel,* trans. M. Greenberg (Chicago, 1960), p. 412. The nature of Jeremiah's predicament during the siege is stressed, in a poignantly anecdotal fashion, in 38:1–13. The nobles want him dead, but dare not slay him; they cast him into the mud pit, expecting him to die there: "But let us not do away with him ourselves," as Joseph's brothers said . . .

portrayed lay more in the eye of the beholder than in the personalities of the prophets.

We could, of course, attribute the difference to the manner in which the stories were transmitted; that is, assume that the Elisha narratives had evolved through a long period of oral transmission and were thus transformed into *legenda,* while the Jeremiah narratives had been early recorded in writing, so that they never acquired the accretion of miracle and wonder stories and remained factual biographical descriptions.[20] Such an assumption, however, cannot be correct for we have already seen that the author of the continuous narrative of 37–45 lived several generations later than Jeremiah and had at his disposal a number of sources, some of which were oral, or at least had been so for part of their history of transmission. Nevertheless, these were not transformed into the *legenda* such as those which had developed around Elisha. Thus, it seems that the manner of transmission does not necessarily affect the formation of a literary genre.

Most determinative was, in my opinion, the origin and characteristic of the authors and transmitters of these stories. Something about these people and their circles can be gleaned from the rather meager information scattered throughout the narratives themselves. We mentioned above that Gehazi was not the sole narrator of the tales of Elisha's exploits, just as Baruch was not the sole author of the biographical chapters on Jeremiah. Nevertheless, these two may be considered as typical representatives of the authors and transmitters of these traditions. Gehazi is of unknown family and place of origin. He is apparently of poor extraction – hence his taste for easy wealth (2Kgs 5:20) – and he relates stories about Elisha in the popular style, orally, even when in the king's court (2Kgs 8:4–5). Baruch son of Neriah son of Mesheiah, on the other hand, is the scion of a distinguished Jerusalemite family. His brother Seraiah was a member of Zedekiah's court (Jer 51:59). Baruch himself was a scribe (Jer 36:26,32), and his scholarly attainments enabled him to fill administrative posts in the king's service. He committed to writing Jeremiah's prophecies at his dictation (Jer 36:4ff) and kept his legal documents (32:12ff). It seems safe to conclude that the classical prophets, starting from the time of Isaiah (Isa 8:2), had disci-

---

20 Thus M. Kessler, "Form Critical Suggestion on Jer. 36," *CBQ* 28 (1966), pp. 389–401.

ples and allies among the enlightened circles in the kingdom. These groups preserved a generations-old tradition of objective factual writing, developed in the royal service, which was used in official records, edicts, correspondence and the royal chronicles. When, in the Exilic period, these scribes of Jerusalem and their disciples realizing the importance of Jeremiah and the other prophets, undertook the descriptions of their lives, they adopted the conventional forms of writing to this new subject.[21]

This may explain why Jeremiah's political outlook and advice occupy such a significant role in these stories. Chaps. 25, 27–29, 32, 36 and the entire complex of chaps. 37–43 deal almost exclusively with this aspect of Jeremiah's message and almost entirely omit his religio-moral teachings (29:23 being the exception).[22] If, as we claim, the Jeremiah narratives were handed down by government officials, it is understandable that the writers would concentrate on matters relating directly to their own occupation and interest.

This also suggests how the classical prophets – especially Jeremiah who was apparently not particularly effective or impressive – were able to attract supporters from political circles. The classical prophets viewed world history as the arena of God's revelation. Details of events – dates, names, places – held great significance for them, because these expressed the universal fulfillment of God's plan: "The plan that is planned for all the earth; that is the arm poised over all the nations" (Isa 14:26).[23] This interest in history was in perfect accord with the education and interests of the political circles – the ministers and officials. Moreover, these men, whose education and occupation had prepared them to understand the importance of detail, received from the prophets the much-desired answers to the great questions of the day – why the ascent of Assyria and Babylon and the decline of Egypt; why surrender, enslavement, exile and destruction?

---

21 Here I have accepted and attempted to develop H. Gunkel's description presented in *Elias, Jah. und Baal* (Tübingen, 1906), p. 40.
22 *Pace* G. Fohrer, "Erzählung und Geschichtsbericht in Prophetenerzählungen," *I.L. Seeligmann Volume*, Vol. III (Jerusalem, 1983), pp. 171–192 who considered the Jeremiah stories to faithfully render his words. In any case, it is a one-sided version, like that of Isaiah's speeches (above, chap. 5, sects. 3–4).
23 Cf. *NJPS,* slightly differently.

The rise of classical prophecy also witnessed a change in the self-perception of prophets and their prophecies, a change that appealed to the more sophisticated nobles and officials. Elisha and Elijah had been "Holy Men of God" upon whom the spirit of God rested and who thereupon performed miracles and wonders. Now, however, a new concept is introduced: the prophet as a human messenger, who receives the Divine Word and transmits it using the messenger's formula "Thus says the Lord."[24] The prophet is a "son of man" for Ezekiel; a "man of unclean lips" for Isaiah; and a "youth . . . I don't know how to speak" in Jeremiah's plaint. What has occurred here is the secularization of the nature of the prophet. The prophet has now become a man of flesh and blood, who no longer performs breath-taking miracles, but who, now and then, receives a message from God. This approach, which diminishes the prophets' holiness, limiting their contact with God to specific points and times, certainly was more acceptable to the official circles of the kingdom.

Thus we can trace the development of the prophetic biography. The beginnings of this literary genre may be discerned in Amos 7:10–17 and Isa 7:1–3; 20; it reached its height with Jeremiah. The changes which took place with the appearance of classical prophecy – namely, the secularization of the prophetic office and the prophets' association with the intellectual circles – are the very factors which contributed to the development of this new genre. It attempts to present an accurate picture of the prophet, portraying him in all his loneliness and suffering, weakness and degradation, yet at the same time, in all his courage and spiritual greatness.

---

24 Cf., for example, C. Westermann, *Basic Forms of Prophetic Speech* (Engl. Transl.; Philadelphia, 1967), pp. 90–128.

PART THREE

FROM *LEGENDA* TO MARTYROLOGY

Chapter Seven

THE ETHICAL *LEGENDA*[1]

1. *Legenda* and Ethical *Legenda*

In the earlier chapter on the *legenda* we observed that this genre usually displayed a morally neutral tendency. Miracles were often performed not necessarily for the morally deserving, but rather for those whose merit lay solely in their close relationship with the Man of God. At other times, as in the case of the bears and the youths, the miracle was a harsh response completely out of proportion to the provocation which induced it. Moreover, we have seen that these *legenda* originally expressed a primitive religious outlook, the miracles described being performed not in response to the believer's prayers, nor through divine intervention, but as magical acts that were a manifestation of the prophet's supernatural powers.

These qualities of the *legenda,* which are surprising when viewed from the perspective of the more profound and theologically more advanced strata of biblical thought, were assuredly displeasing to the ancient reader as well. Hence our suggestion that in two such *legenda* (2Kgs 2:19–22; 4:42–44),[2] one of the editors of the Book of Kings inserted into the descriptions of the miracles the notion that they were God's behest. Similarly, in the story of the resurrection of the Shunammite's son, a later hand apparently appended the words, "and prayed to the Lord" (2Kgs 4:33b), the original version having portrayed the miracle as a magical transference of life-force

---

1 This chapter is an expanded and revised version of my article "Classes in the Prophetical Stories: Didactic Legends and Parables," *SVT* 26 (Leiden, 1974), pp. 143–164, ad pp. 145–153. See there for references to earlier literature.
2 See above, chap. 1, sect. 1; chap. 5, sect. 5.

accomplished by the Man of God's powers: "He went in, he shut the door behind the two of them . . . Then he mounted (the bed) and placed himself over the child. He put his mouth on its mouth . . ." (vv 33–35). But what the editors could do could also have been done by the authors, i.e., they could have formulated the *legenda* in such a way as to elevate and refine its religious level. The *legenda*, furthermore, could also serve as a vehicle for the expression of other cherished beliefs and ideas. In such cases, principle would dominate plot, the miracle would become secondary and the homily primary – in other words, the *legenda* would be transformed into an ethical *legenda* – a genre in its own right.

In this chapter we shall examine several of these ethical *legenda*, discuss their main ideas, and investigate the manner in which the form and substance of the *legenda* evolved into an ethical *legenda*.

2. *Elisha, Naaman and Gehazi*

The well known tale related in 2Kgs 5 is in fact composed of two separate stories: the curing of Naaman's leprosy (5:1–19) and Gehazi becoming afflicted with Naaman's illness (5:20–27). Since the latter episode presupposed the former – which can stand independently – some scholars have assumed that the story of Gehazi's affliction was a secondary stratum added to the original tale of Naaman's illness.[3]

In addition to the independence of the first story, there are several other factors which have been presented in support of a two-strata theory. Gehazi, for example, the main figure in vv 20–27, is not even mentioned once in the first story, in which Elisha is served merely by an anonymous "messenger" (v 10). Furthermore, Naaman' s great host, referred to in the first story (v 15) is never mentioned again and only his chariot is specified (vv 21, 26). In my opinion, it is doubtful whether these considerations are sufficient to warrant the identification of two distinct literary strata here. In the first place, Gehazi's appearance in the first story would have been inappropriate: an anonymous messenger was intentionally sent (v 10) in order to

---

3   Cf. e.g. J. Gray, *I & II Kings: A Commentary*[2] (OTL; London, 1970), *a.l.* The unity of the story is now vigorously defended by Y. Zakovitch, *Every High Official Has a Higher One Set over Him: A Literary Analysis of 2 Kings 5* (Tel Aviv, 1985).

deny the existence of any personal contact between Elisha and Naaman, which might have led to the healing being understood as a magical "laying on of hands"' performed either by Elisha or through his servant (cf. 4:29). Furthermore, Naaman's host is not mentioned in the first story either, not before v 15 (cf. v 9: "So Naaman came with his horse and chariot");[4] and then only for the purpose of magnifying the significance of Naaman's public confession: "Now I know that there is no God in the whole world except in Israel." Tangible links, on the other hand, can be discerned between the two stories: the clothes and silver in v 5 become significant in the light of Naaman's gift in vv 22–23. A more substantial connection is the development in Naaman's character following his change of faith. The swaggering Aramean conqueror, proud and quick to anger, who makes his appearance before Elisha's house in all his splendor in the company of his horses and chariots (vv 9–12) is transformed into a man of humility, solicitous of the welfare of others (vv 21–23). This story is another interesting example of the ability of the narrators of the *legenda* to portray characters in a dynamic fashion.[5] Moreover, one of the central features of the first story – Elisha's refusal to accept Naaman's proffered gift – is highlighted by the second story. In general, it seems that considering the two stories as a single unit contributes to our understanding of the meaning of the narrative as a whole and of its separate parts as well.

The tale of Naaman contains an underlying idea that is not encountered in *legenda*: the miracles performed by the Holy Man are not intended to benefit any particular person or persons, but to increase and spread the belief in God, even among other nations. From this perspective, the miracle succeeded beyond Elisha's expectations. He had said: "Let him come to me, and he will learn that there is a prophet in Israel" (v 8), but Naaman, when healed, acknowledged much more than that: "There is no God in the whole world except in Israel" (v 15). That this declaration was a confession of monotheistic belief is clear from what follows: Naaman decides to serve the Lord alone, even in Aram (v 17), and requests His pardon

---

4 Contra *NJPS* which vocalizes differently.
5 See, e.g., chap. 2, sect. 1 (on the Shunammite's transition from barrenness to fertility) and chap. 3, sect. 1 (on Elisha's transition from disciple to master).

for the times when his official duties will require him to participate in the worship of another god (v 18).

Since the purpose of the miracle was to demonstrate the greatness and uniqueness of the Lord God of Israel – whose uniqueness lay in that no other god possessed His power of deliverance – the miracle could not be accomplished through magical means, usual in the *legenda*. Indeed, Naaman only expected a magical feat: "'I thought' he said, 'he would surely come out to me, and would stand and invoke the Lord his God by name, and would wave his hand toward the spot,[6] and cure the affected part'" (v 11). He had anticipated the use of divine names, and the gesticulation practised by sorcerers and magicians. But Elisha sent him to bathe in the Jordan, a "cure" which because of its simplicity disappointed Naaman (v 12). This proved convincingly that Naaman was cured not through magic, as practised by the pagan nations, but through contact with the Lord's holy land. He alone has the power to heal, and He alone should be worshipped.[7] The miracle constitutes proof of God's power and uniqueness, and as such it must be unambiguous and emphatic.

For the same reason, the miracle should not be an occasion for personal gain. It may serve only one exalted purpose – the spread of the belief in God. Therefore the prophet adamantly refuses to accept any gift as recompense. Elisha's refusal, in which he stresses his role as God's servant – "As the Lord lives, whom I serve" (v 16) – forces Naaman to acknowledge God directly in order to express his gratitude: "Then at least let your servant be given two mule-loads of earth; for your servant will never again offer up burnt offering or sacrifice to any god, except the Lord." Here, the service of God is portrayed as an alternative to offering a gift to the prophet.[8] This is the reason for the terrible punishment inflicted upon Gehazi. He made use of Naaman's cure as an opportunity (v 26) for acquiring

6 This no doubt refers to the affected spot, as was noted by Targum, Rashi, and Kimhi. Gersonides, on the other hand, who interpreted המקום as "the place where he [Elisha] worships God," has even the Aramean general expecting to be cured by nonmagical means, and turns Elisha into an advocate of the unification of worship in Jerusalem!

7 Cf. H. Gressmann, *Die älteste Geschichtsschreibung und Prophetie Israels*² (SATA) (Göttingen, 1921), p. 298.

8 For the use of expression ולא "at least" in conversational prose to introduce an alternative, see 2Sam 13:26.

wealth. By doing so he negated – or at least endangered – the aim of the miracle: recognition of the Lord. In this respect as well the account of Naaman's cure is significantly different from the other prophetic tales in which gifts were routinely offered to prophets by their followers, admirers, and those who sought their oracles (Samuel, 1Sam 9:7–8; Ahijah, 1Kgs 14:3; Elisha, 2Kgs 4:42).

The transformation of the simple *legenda* into a value-laden ethical *legenda* was accompanied by a number of changes in structure. In the ethical *legenda* there is no tension, no question as to whether the miracle will indeed be accomplished. Even "a young girl from the Land of Israel" (2Kgs 5:2) knows that Elisha has the power to heal Naaman. Elisha himself is similarly confident of his ability: "Let him come to me ... " Compare his perplexity in 2Kgs 4:2. The only despair in this story is that of the king, who is far removed from the prophet's sphere of influence. The king's despair is portrayed in order to contrast his helplessness with Elisha's unlimited power and to stress that it is the prophet, not the king, who possesses divine charisma.[9] Tension in the narrative only revolves around the question of Naaman's compliance with Elisha's instructions. This difference is consistent with the nature of the ethical *legenda,* where the principle itself is of greater importance than the performance of the miracle. The problem was not the miracle but whether the message expressed by it would be heard and understood. A new element introduced into this story (which we will encounter in another tale of the same type) is the meeting between the deliverer and the delivered after the act of deliverance (vv 15–18). This meeting enables the recipient to make his confession and to formally proclaim his recognition of the Lord and His prophet. The purpose of the miracle – the recognition of God's universal power – is first hinted at by the narrator at the beginning of the story: "Naaman ... was important to his lord and high in his favor, *for through him the Lord had granted victory to Aram*" (v 1). A further indication of the special nature of this ethical *legenda* is the spirit of brotherhood transcending national boundaries which pervades the story. The captive girl from Israel was a servant

---

9   This was noted by Gressmann (above, n. 7), p. 297. One may add to his examples of royal charisma the story of Dr. Johnson, who as a child, at the beginning of the eighteenth century, was brought to Queen Anne to be healed by her touch: J. Boswell, *The Life of Samuel Johnson* (New York, 1930), p. 6.

of Naaman's wife, but the difference in their national origin and position did not prevent the two women from becoming friendly, sharing their cares and concerns, and exchanging advice (vv 2–3). The king of Israel's suspicions (v 7) and Naaman's initial zealous patriotism (v 12) are both exposed as being senseless. Elisha's greatness breaks down all barriers and brings about Naaman's conversion. But Gehazi's covetousness reawakens the old biases: "My master has let that Aramean Naaman off... " (v 20), a cogent example of the pursuit of personal gain masquerading as patriotism.

Where should the source of the views expressed in this story be sought? This is undoubtedly one of the central questions for the understanding of the history of prophecy. Our initial inclination is to attribute their origin to the influence of classical prophecy. All these views – the anticipation of the nations' recognition of God, the repudiation of sorcery in prophecy, and the condemnation of accepting rewards for the performance of the prophetic office – are clearly part of the prophetic theology of later generations. Since Elisha is indeed portrayed elsewhere as indulging in magic and accepting gifts, we may conclude that the account of Naaman's cure was a later composition inspired by the prophecies of Amos, Hosea, and Isaiah. We must admit on the other hand, that very little is known of the ideology of Elisha and his band of disciples. The analogy with the Hassidic שבח – whose importance for the understanding of the legenda was noted above –[10] testifies that even within the framework of a religious movement espousing noble ideals, common and somewhat crude legenda could be propagated at the same time. Legenda about the צדיקים rarely reflected the ideology present in their teachings.[11]

Some conception of the origins of the story of Naaman can be gleaned not only from the ideas preached by the author, but also from those that are taken for granted. Firstly the idea of the sanctity of the Land of Israel. What is found here is not the ancient view of the Land of God being the only suitable place for His worship (1Sam 26–19; Hos 9:3–5). The comparison between the Jordan and the rivers of

10   In chap. 1.
11   Cf. J. Dan, הנובלה החסידית (Jerusalem, 1966), pp. 8–9.

Aram in the cleansing of Naaman, whose purpose is to ascribe wondrous curative powers to the Land, signifies an idealized conception of the Land reflecting the longings of the descendants of exiles living far from their coveted homeland. Related to this issue is the problem of Naaman's altar. In the present form of the story in the Book of Kings, Elisha does not respond to Naaman's offer to build an altar with the two mule-loads of earth taken from the Land of Israel. His silence is in keeping with the Deuteronomistic redaction of Kings, which forbids sacrifice to God anywhere outside Jerusalem, even in the Land of Israel, not to mention in foreign lands. But, according to all indications, in the original story Elisha explicitly agreed to this initiative. This is clearly the thrust of the story's internal dynamic.[12] Naaman surely would not have required Elisha's permission to carry off some earth from the Holy Land on a pair of mules![13] It was rather Elisha's agreement to his cultic initiative that he desired.[14] This request, following upon the declarations that "There is no God in the whole world except in Israel" and "Your servant will never again offer up burnt offering or sacrifice to any god, except the Lord" (vv 15, 17), could not have gone unrequited. The story, in its original form, seems to have sanctioned Naaman's proposal, not because of the needs of some anonymous pagans who wished to serve God, but because of specific historical circumstances, namely the situation of the Israelite exiles, beginning in 731 BCE. Scattered throughout the Assyrian empire, these exiles would be permitted to erect altars and sacrifice to God on foreign soil, following a procedure attributed to Elisha for overcoming the problem of the "unclean land": the altars were to be erected upon earth imported from the Land of Israel. In the light of these historical considerations, the story should most likely be attributed to the end of the eighth, beginning of the seventh century BCE, at the start of the Israelite exile.

---

12 In employing this term I have followed I.L. Seeligmann, "Aetiological Elements in Biblical Historiography" (Heb.), *Zion* 26 (1961), pp. 141–169, esp. pp. 155–157.

13 Gersonides therefore explained that Naaman had asked Elisha for earth from property belonging to the prophet, and Abrabanel – from the ground upon which Elisha stood.

14 Thus, correctly, David Altschuler's מצודת דוד: "He was unwilling to take it without the prophet's permission."

3. *Elijah at Zarephath*

It is at times possible to demonstrate that an ethical *legenda* was created by the revision and reshaping of a story which had previously existed as a simple *legenda*. This can be illustrated by the comparison of two largely similar stories, as for example the tale of Elijah at Zarephath (1Kgs 17:8–24) and a parallel tale of Elisha (2Kgs 4:1–7, 18–37).

The first story tells of Elijah's sustenance at Zarephath by a widow; because of his miracle her jar never ran out of flour and her jug never lacked for oil, until the famine passed (17:8–16). Although it is impossible to prove that this story about Elijah is directly dependent on the parallel tale of Elisha's multiplication of the widow's oil (2Kgs 4:1–7), it should be noted that the latter tale is a short, self-contained *legenda,* unrelated to any of the other stories told about Elisha. It appears here in its original form, as it was related by the prophet's band of disciples. The story about Elijah, on the other hand, is well-integrated into the larger literary unit of the account of Elijah's struggle against Baal (1Kgs 16:29 –19:18).[15] It relates how Elijah lived during the drought. God had told Elijah: "I have designated a widow there to feed you" (17:9), and Elijah explains to the widow that the miracle will last "until the day that the Lord sends rain upon the ground" (17:14). Accordingly the story is synchronized chronologically with the struggle against Baal. The first year Elijah hid in Wadi Cherit (17:7), the second year he spent with the widow in Zarephath (17:15), and in the third year God sent him to appear before Ahab so that He could send rain upon the earth (18:1). Thus from a literary-historical perspective, the *legenda* describing Elijah's miracles of the food at Zarephath reflects a later stage of development than the parallel story of Elisha's miracle of the oil.[16]

The story in 17:8–16 underwent a process of moral development. The widow was the object of a miracle, not because of her husband or her closeness to the Man of God, but because she had proved in

---

15 This narrative will be discussed below in chap. 9.
16 It has already been noted that the Elijah cycle is more developed from a literary standpoint and loftier on a religious level than the Elisha stories, so that apparently more of the original material associated with Elisha was transferred to Elijah than the opposite; see C. Alcaina Canosa, "Panorama critico del ciclo de Eliseo," *EsBib* 23 (1964), pp. 217–234.

two trials to possess an excellent moral character. In one, she showed her concern for a passing stranger by offering him a drink (10b–11a) – which is a recurring theme in the test of women's character (Gen 24:14). She next proved her faith in the Word of God by letting a stranger share her last meal. After having passed these two tests, she received the prophet's miraculous gift of plenty. Furthermore, here, unlike in the story of Elisha's oil-wonder, the miracle is accomplished not by magic, but through the Word of God communicated by His prophet. This, too, is in keeping with the general tenor of this *legenda,* and of the preceding one about Elijah in Wadi Cherith, as both of them demonstrate Elijah's dependence on an obedience to God's command (17:2, 5, 8). All this supports the claim that this *legenda* is a revised, expanded, and morally superior version of a simple *legenda* present in or represented by the Elisha cycle.

Somewhat different is the account of Elijah's resurrection of the widow's son. This *legenda* (1 Kgs 17:17–24) is not an integral part of the account of God's struggle against Baal (1 Kgs 16:29–19:18), and its absence would detract nothing from the general meaning. Moreover, it plays no part in the above-mentioned chronology of the drought. The widow's declaration: "Now I know that you are a man of God and that the word of the Lord is truly in your mouth" (v 24), is announced as if the miracle of the flour and oil, which was related in the previous *legenda,* has not occurred. The story thus appears to have been inserted into its present position by a later author; in its present context the story is even later than the one preceding it. While we could perhaps claim that this *legenda* is in itself an early one, it nevertheless displays signs of a late composition; only here (vv 18, 24) and in the tale of Ahaziah's illness (2 Kgs 1:9, 10, 11, 12, 13) is Elijah called "Man of God," and we have already shown that the latter story should be assigned a late date. It appears that the title "Man of God," so common in the Elisha stories,[17] was a typical appellation of that prophet, and was only secondarily assigned to Elijah. The transfer of qualities and acts of minor characters to more eminent figures is an accepted feature of folkloristic literature.[18] And thus *legenda* that were

17 Elisha is called "Man of God" no less than 27 times in eleven different stories: 2 Kgs 4:7; 4:9, 16, 21, 22, 25 (twice), 27 (twice); 4:40; 4:42; 5:8, 14, 15, 20; 6:6; 6:9, 10, 15; 7:2, 17, 18, 19; 8:2, 4; 8:7, 11; 13:19.

18 Similarly the title: "Father, father, Israel's chariots and horsemen" was transferred from Elisha to Elijah; see above, chap. 3, sect. 1.

not firmly anchored in the narrative flow were transferred from Elisha to the more illustrious Elijah.

Upon examination, the story of the resurrection of the Zarephathite widow's son is found to be not only later than, but dependent upon, the story of the Shunammite. Two details of the story demonstrate this dependence. Firstly, the boy's condition. The Shunammite's son was dead, and Elisha resurrected him – a wondrous act without equal. The condition of the Zarephathite child is somewhat ambiguously described. The widow protests that Elijah has come to "cause the death of my son"; Elijah passes on her complaint to God. But the boy is not explicitly said to have died: the expression "until he had no breath left in him" (v 17), and similar ones, merely indicate a coma or unconsciousness (Dan 10:17; cf. Judg 15:19 1Sam 30:12; 1Kgs 10:5). Even the word ויחי "revived" (v 22), which sounds like "resurrection," is often used to denote healing (Num 21:8–9; Josh 5:8; 2Kgs 1:2; 8:8, 9, 10, 14; 20:1, 7). The author apparently intended merely to describe a miraculous cure by Elijah, and he seems to have employed terms reminiscent of death and resurrection because he was influenced by another tale which told of such a miracle. Further proof of the story's dependence is the statement that the prophet resides in the woman's house. The Shunammite, who was a wealthy woman, had the resources necessary for the addition of an upper chamber to her house in order to provide accommodation for Elisha. The widow of Zarephath, on the other hand, was completely destitute, yet she is also described as having an attic in which the prophet lived. How could such a needy woman have an attic, unless this detail was also borrowed from the story about the Shunammite?

The character of the *legenda* describing Elijah and the Zarephathite boy is further clarified by a comparison of the treatment given the child in the parallel story in 2Kgs 4:18–37. In the case of Elijah, the magical transference of the Man of God's supernatural powers to the child is kept to a minimum (v 21a: "He stretched out over the child three times") and, instead, the emphasis is placed on the act of Elijah's prayer (vv 20, 21a–b) and God's acceptance of this prayer (v 22). The author of this *legenda* had his own clear notion of actions proper or improper for prophets, and he portrayed the Man of God accordingly. "His" Elijah uses the proper means to cure the child, and is thus revealed as a great master of prayer, a worthy successor to Moses and

Samuel (Jer 15:1; Ps 99:6). The miracle here acquired ethical value, as is evident from its effect. Whereas the Shunammite responded to her miracle with a spontaneous gesture of mute adoration, the widow of Zarephath responds with a declaration of faith: "Now I know that you are a man of God and that the word of the Lord is truly in your mouth" (v 24).[19] – which echoes the belief expressed in the story of Naaman.

Conversely, the Elijah version of the *legenda* is weaker in its development of the story's characters. Compare the primitive accusation the Zarephathite hurls at Elijah (1Kgs 17:18) – primitive in its irrational dread in the presence of the holy,[20] characteristic of the simple masses – with the noble, yet poignantly tragic reprimand of the Shunammite (2Kgs 4:28). While the Zarephath *legenda* may display a greater moral refinement, it still retained several traits characteristic of the simple popular *legenda*. Not always do theological sophistication and literary perfection go hand in hand.

4. *Moses at the Waters of Meribah*

The accounts of Moses' attempts to extract water from the rock at Massah and Meribah (Exod 17:1–7) and at the Waters of Meribah (Num 20:1–13) provide a striking example of the transformation of a simple *legenda* into an ethical one. As the medieval Jewish commentator R. Joseph Bekhor Shor noted,[21] these two stories are merely two versions of the same incident – or, as we would put it, of the same tradition. This can be seen in numerous points of similarity: the people, suffering from thirst, complain to Moses, who in turn beseeches God for assistance.[22] God shows Moses a rock from which he is to extract water. Moses strikes the rock, the water flows, the people drink, and thus the place receives its name. Furthermore, the version appearing in Num 20:1–13, bearing the mark of the Priestly

---

19 See: A. Schmitt, "Die Totenerweckung in Kön xvii 17–24. Eine form- und gattungskritische Untersuchung," *VT* 27 (1977), pp. 454–474, ad pp. 462–464.
20 Cf. R. Otto, *The Idea of the Holy*[2] (Engl. trans.), (London, 1959).
21 In his commentary on Leviticus and Numbers (Heb.), ed. J. Gad (London, 1960), pp. 98–99.
22 In Num 20:6 the appeal is made not by crying out to the Lord, but by falling prostrate before the Tent of Meeting.

document (P),[23] is clearly a later secondary adaptation of Exod 17:1-7. The evidence lies in the function of Moses' staff. Whereas in Exodus 17 God commands Moses to take his staff in order to strike the rock (vv 5-6), in Numbers 20, though He still tells Moses to take his staff, He commands him to *speak* to the rock. Moses' staff plays no active role in the miracle.

What was the purpose of this later version? Why was the story retold with these minor changes? In my opinion, the author's intention was to introduce theological changes into the story, i.e., to transform it into an ethical *legenda*. In the simple *legenda* in Exodus 17 there is nothing wrong with the magical methods used by Moses to produce water. The ethical *legenda* in Numbers 20, on the other hand, requires that the miracle occur in response to God's command pronounced by His servant Moses. Thus God's Name would be sanctified in the eyes of the Israelites, by demonstrating the scope of His power. When Moses struck the rock with his staff, he used magic, and lost an opportunity to "sanctify God through water" (cf. Num 27:14 and Deut 32:51). For this reason he and Aaron were punished – and condemned to die in the desert. This ethical *legenda*, like those of Elijah in 1Kgs 17:8-24, takes a firm stand against magic, substituting it with the power of the Word of God. However, instead of changing the details of the story to achieve this end (possibly because the tradition was too firmly established to permit any editorial freedom), this story merely reinterprets them: Moses did strike the rock, he performed a magical act, but this was a sin and he was severely punished for it.

The fact that two tales about Moses are in fact a simple and an ethical revised version of one and the same *legenda* indicates that the literary genres characteristic of the prophetic narratives are also contained in the Pentateuchal literature. This realization helps to illuminate many portions of the Pentateuch and assists in determining their date of composition and provenance.[24]

---

23   Cf. the critical commentaries and introductions.

24   A similar comment was made by M. Buber, *Moses: The Revelation and the Covenant* (New York, 1958), p. 58: "I suppose that the expansion of tradition into the legendary cycle of the Egyptian Ten Plagues took place among the disciples of Elisha, who sang the legends of the Father of the *nebiim* together with those of their own master."

5. Isaiah and the Healing of Hezekiah

The transformation of a simple *legenda* by a later author, redactor or editor into an ethical *legenda* can explain problems of content and continuity as, for example, in the story of Isaiah and the healing of Hezekiah (2Kgs 20:1–11).

Two miracles are described in this story: Hezekiah' s cure (vv 1–7) and the recession of the shadow on the dial of Ahaz (vv 8–11).[25] According to all indications these miracles were not related by the same author, or at least did not form a narrative sequence; there is no sense in Hezekiah asking for a sign (v 8) if he had already been healed (v 7). On the other hand, vv 8–11 do not constitute an independent story, but presuppose the existence of vv 1–7; it seems most likely that the incident of the sign was a later expansion of the story of the cure. The incongruity between the two sections was noted by a later biblical writer, the author of Isaiah 38.[26] Not only did he add the poem attributed to Hezekiah (Isa 38:9–20); he also transferred the verse describing Hezekiah's recovery from its original place preceding the sign (2Kgs 20:7) to a position following it (Isa 38:21). The rearrangement of problematic verses is a characteristic solution of late biblical authors and editors.[27]

But the first story in itself (2Kgs 20:1–7) is not entirely problem-free. The cure through the agency of Isaiah is quite unexpected, and contradicts the previous prophecy (which had promised that the recovery would be accomplished by God, v 5). Who is the real healer? God, by answering the supplicant's prayer, or the prophet, who, using his knowledge of wonder-cures, prescribes a cake of figs? From a different perspective, this story lacks the element of suspenseful anticipation of the miracle so characteristic of the simple *legenda*. There is no tension in this story, because here the prophetic Word *precedes* the performance of the miracle, rather than accompanying or following it.[28]

---

25 For the realia, see Y. Yadin, "The Dial of Ahaz" (Heb.), *Eretz Israel* 5 (*Mazar Volume*; Jerusalem, 1959), pp. 91–96.
26 The lateness of this author is evident from his language: וימרחו "and let them spread it" (v. 21) reflecting not biblical, but rabbinic diction.
27 Cf. A. Rofé, "The Composition of the Introduction of the Book of Judges" (Heb.), *Tarbiz* 35 (1966), pp. 201–213.
28 Comparing the story of Elisha and Joash (2Kgs 13:14–19), we see that Elisha's

A form-critical approach may offer the best solution to the problem of this story's literary discontinuity. The original was a simple *legenda* which told of Hezekiah's nearly fatal illness and his miraculous cure by Isaiah. A later hand expanded the tale with an additional *legenda* (2Kgs 20:8–11), in which the miracle was accomplished not by the prophet, but through God's response to his prayer: "So the prophet Isaiah called to the Lord and He made the shadow . . . recede" (v 11).[29] This author assigned particular importance to prayer, so it can be easily understood why he was dissatisfied with the existing story of the king's illness and recovery. He therefore expanded it with a description of the king's prayer and God's response.[30] As in the story of Elijah's cure/resurrection of the Zarephathite widow's son, the moral expressed here is that prayer, not magical acts, has the power to perform miracles. The present story, however, differs somewhat in that the prayer here is not that of the prophet, but of the king, a temporal figure. It is possible that the author wished to stress that "The Lord delivers[31] *all* who call him with sincerity" (Ps 145:18; cf. also Ps 86:5). Thus he attributed the main prayer to the king whereas the prophet had already abandoned all hope (2Kgs 20:2).

statement: "An arrow of victory over Aram, etc." (v 17) was made after the arrow had been shot, as if to accompany it on its flight. The story of the spring of Jericho is similarly constructed (2Kgs 2:19–22), even though the Word of God is a secondary element. First Elisha threw the salt into the spring and only then did he proclaim: "Thus said the Lord; I heal this water, etc."

29 So R. Kittel, *Die Bücher der Könige übersetzt und erklärt* (GHAT; Göttingen, 1900), and J.A. Montgomery, *Commentary on the Book of Kings* (ICC; New York, 1951).

30 A diametrically opposed interpretation was proposed by Y. Zakovitch, "2Kings 20:7 – Isaiah 38:21–22" (Heb.), *Beth Mikra* 50 (1972), pp. 302–305. In his opinion, the foreign element which was introduced and interrupted the flow of the story is the description of the cure using the fig cake (2Kgs 20:7). This insertion was made "in order to attribute to Hezekiah's recovery as well an element of prophetic magic" as in the Elisha stories. But in the light of what we have noted in this chapter of the tendency to reject magic in favor of a more exalted conception of the prophet's role, it would seem that the cure was the older element in the story, and the prayer (which eventually dominated the story) was added later. Similar to the late biblical legendary development, which turned the miracle-working prophet into a master of prayer, the later rabbinic legendary trend transformed wonder workers such as Honi Ha-Me'aggel and R. Hanina b. Dosa into masters of halacha! See G.B. Sarfatti, "Pious Men, Men of Deeds, and the Early Prophets" (Heb.), *Tarbiz* 26 (1957), pp. 142–144.

31 קרוב in Ps 145:18 is synonymous to מושיע; cf. the following verse as well as Ps 34:19.

* * *

The common denominator of all the *legenda* discussed in this chapter is that they stress the power of prayer and the Word of God, minimizing the value of magic in the performance of miracles. We have explained this as the total rejection of magic in the transition from the simple to the ethical *legenda*. And at the same time the miracles themselves lose much of their earlier significance. God's dominion over all things leaves little room for doubt as to whether the miracle will or will not occur. In the Naaman story (2Kgs 5), for example, the miracle is "in the bag" from the very beginning. Its occurrence is no longer the issue, interest now being focused on the purpose of the miracle (the Sanctification of God's Name), the impetus for God's intervention (prayer), or the means of God's intervention (the "Word"). The miracle is shunted aside; it is the meaning, the significance of the miracle, which concerns the ethical *legenda*. This turning point in the evaluation of the miracle is aptly expressed in the following hassidic teaching:

> "Miracles," repeated R. Yaakov Yitzhak, "Miracles are not really important." "Then what is important?" asked R. Naftaly, "The Rabbi himself has said that a miracle bears witness to the presence of the Schechinah among us!" R. Yaakov Yitzhak replied: "The miracle merely witnesses; therefore it is unimportant. Tears are important! Repentance is important! Love is important! That the Rabbi separates Good from Evil and helps the Schechinah rise out of the dust – that is important! How do you know – maybe the Rabbi does wonders to disguise his true nature so that no one will understand what it really is?"[32]

---

32   Cf. Martin Buber, *For the Sake of Heaven,* trans. Ludwig Lewisohn, Philadelphia, 1945, p. 37 for a slightly different translation.

Chapter Eight

EXEMPLUM AND PARABLE[1]

1. *Definition of the Literary Genres*

Our analysis of the ethical *legenda* has shown clearly that the primary aim of this narrative type was to impart a truth of some kind. Accordingly, the biblical authors took existing *legenda* and adapted them to teach a moral lesson. In such cases, the miracle, which had been the central feature of the *legenda* in its simple form, was shunted into the background, and the ethical issue became the main focus of the story. However, it was also possible to present ethical teachings through stories about prophets who had not performed wonders or miracles. In such stories the behavior and beliefs of the prophets which corresponded with the author's conceptions of truth were stressed. This is the paradigm or *exemplum*: a story in which a historical character or event is described in such a way as to edify and inspire. An *exemplum* about a historically recognized prophet, or prophet-like figure among the ancestors or leaders of the nation, would teach proper opinions or conduct by positive example. But *exempla* could also be composed about sinful personages in order to demonstrate the importance of avoiding evil deeds.

Related to the paradigm or *exemplum* is the parable which instructs by means of an imaginary incident. The least historical of all the prophetical narratives, it is also the most ingenious. Completely free

1   On this subject, see my article "The Betrothal of Rebekah (Genesis 24) – A Historico-literary Study" (Heb.), *Eshel Beer-sheva* 1 (1976), pp. 42–67, esp. pp. 54–59. An earlier version of sect. 2 was published as "The Story of Micaiah Son of Imlah and the Classes of the Prophetic Narratives" (Heb.), *Reflections on the Bible . . . Yishai Ron,* Vol. II (Tel Aviv, 1977), pp. 233–244.

from the strictures of historical tradition, it creates characters and events in whatever fashion will best suit its point. It is obviously difficult at times to distinguish between an *exemplum* and a parable. The distinction is easier when the context of the story is familiar or when it relates to historical events known from other sources. For example, Joab's reference to the death of Abimelech under the tower of Thebez in his attempt to guess David's response, in 2Sam 11:20-21,[2] is clearly a paradigm, a historical event cited in order to convey some truth; whereas the story of the poor man's lamb, related by Nathan in 2Sam 12:1-4 is clearly a parable, invented by the prophet in order to admonish David. In other prophetical stories it is not always possible to distinguish between historical elements and imaginary incidents. The decision as to what is authentic historical fact or traditions accepted as authentic history, and what was sheer imagination recognized as such already in antiquity, is largely a subjective one.

Nevertheless, we must ask what led to the creation of parables. From earliest times, Israelite history was rich in heroes and villains who provided excellent material for *exempla*. If these characters were, nevertheless, insufficient for the biblical authors who created new, imaginative stories, it was because simple "black-and-white" historical judgments could not serve their purposes. They wished to describe more complex situations which would enable them to address themselves to more complex issues. Such situations and issues could arise most naturally within the context of prophecy, because of its irrational nature. And, indeed, the parables about prophecy deal with its enigmatic aspects: the fulfillment of God's prophecy and the status of the prophet as the messenger of the Lord. In other words, these parables concentrate on the complex relationship between the prophet and God.

In this respect, the prophetic parable differs from the prophetic *legenda*. The *legenda*, which as we have seen illustrates the people's veneration of the prophet, centers around the prophet's activities in relation to the people. The parable, on the other hand, is concerned with the relation between the prophet and God. There is no room in

---

2   Indeed, in the LXX to 2Sam 13:22 David speaks according to what Joab expected him to say. This, in my opinion, is an addition, the original text being the one preserved in MT.

the parable for veneration of the prophet, dwarfed as he is in comparison with the Lord. While in the *legenda* the miracle is initiated by the prophet, in the parable he is a passive witness, sometimes even the object of the miracle, which is performed exclusively by God. God brings about a miracle involving the person of the prophet in order to teach a truth hidden from all, the prophet included.[3]

In this chapter we shall examine the prophetical *exempla* and parables and attempt to ascertain the moral conveyed by them, against their theological background, and attempt to establish the date of the appearance and flourishing of this literary genre.

2. *Micaiah Son of Imlah and the Prophets*

The examination of the contents and meaning of the story of Micaiah is 1Kgs 22:1–28[4] indicates that it is a paradigm. To briefly summarize its plot, the king of Israel (identified as Ahab only in v 20) and Jehoshaphat king of Judah decide to wage war against Aram in order to liberate Ramoth-gilead. Jehoshaphat urges the king of Israel to inquire of them whether he should embark on this campaign. There is no doubt that these were prophets of the Lord, speaking as they do in His name (vv 6, 11, 12, 14, etc.). They answer in the affirmative, assuring the king of complete success. Jehoshaphat, nevertheless, is still dissatisfied and wishes to consult yet another prophet of the Lord. At his request, Micaiah son of Imlah is brought on the scene.

Initially, Micaiah concurs with the other prophets: "March and triumph! The Lord will deliver (it) into Your Majesty's hands" (v 15). But when the king adjures him to speak only the truth in the name of the Lord, Micaiah responds by describing a vision of the heavenly council in attendance upon the Lord, who wishes Ahab to be defeated in Ramoth-gilead. Various suggestions of how this can be accomplished

---

3 See my article "Classes in the Prophetical Stories: Didactic Legenda and Parable," *SVT* 26 (1974), pp. 142–164 ad p. 154.
4 This story is repeated (with minor changes) in 2Chr 18:1–27. That this alone of all the prophetic stories is included in the Book of Chronicles seems to be due to its martyrological tendencies; see below, chap. 10. Or did the Chronicler intend it as a comparison between the righteous kings of Judah and the evil ones of Israel? See 2Chr 19:1–3, and below, n. 11.

are proposed and rejected, until "the spirit" offers to be a false spirit in the mouths of the prophets. The Lord agrees: "So the Lord has put a lying spirit in the mouth of all these prophets of yours; for the Lord has decreed disaster upon you" (v 23). Zedekiah son of Chenaanah, one of the four hundred, approaches Micaiah, strikes him on his cheek, asking ironically: "Which way did the spirit of the Lord pass from me to speak with you?" (v 24). Micaiah answers sarcastically[5] that Zedekiah will discover how on the day he hides, humiliated by the belying of his prophecy. So ends the confrontation. The king of Israel orders Micaiah handed over to two officials, the city's governor and the "King's son" to be imprisoned until Ahab's safe return. Micaiah retorts with confidence that the king will not return safely from this or any other venture.

The story continues, but Micaiah is not mentioned again, neither is the fulfillment of his prediction nor the failure of his opponents. The details of Ahab's death, how his blood drained into the chariot, how it was washed at the pool of Samaria where "the dogs lapped it up and the whores bathed [in it]" (vv 35, 38) are described in regard to another prophecy (which apparently has not been preserved in its original form (cf. 1Kgs 21:19).[6] The ambience of the story changes at this point from the sober historiographical tone of vv 1–28 to the folkloristic character of the events of v 29 ff: Ahab's disguise, the Aramean strategem, the arrow accidentally striking Ahab. There is thus a change in both the subject and the sources of the tale.

The story presented in vv 1–28 seems monolithic, except for an interruption in its continuity in vv 16–19:

---

5 Since the essential difference between Micaiah's inspiration and that of the other prophets was that they prophesied by "the spirit" while he was granted a vision, Micaiah's reply in v 25 can only be understood as sarcasm (see below). His ironic tone is also clearly perceived in his prophecy in v 15: "March and triumph! The Lord will deliver [it] into Your Majesty's hands."

6 The existence of another oracle of doom against Ahab explains why he disguised himself before entering into battle in an attempt to evade his fate. The disguise, therefore, was not necessarily a result of Micaiah's prophecy. Nor do the contents of this chapter agree with Elijah's prophecy against Ahab in 1Kgs 21:19. Ahab's blood was lapped up by the dogs not in Naboth's field but in Samaria, and the whores' bathing in his blood was not mentioned by Elijah. There may have originally been complete consistency between the prophecy and the fulfillment of Ahab's fate in this chapter, but this was disrupted when the first part of the story was reworked into an *exemplum*.

(16) The king said to him: "How many times must I adjure you to tell me nothing but the truth in the name of the Lord?"
(17) Then he said, "I saw all Israel scattered over the hills like sheep without a shepherd; and the Lord said, 'The masters of these people[7] will not return safely to their homes.' "
(18) "Didn't I tell you," said the king of Israel to Jehoshaphat, "that he would not prophesy good fortune for me, but only misfortune?"
(19) But Micaiah said, "Then hear the word of the Lord! I saw the Lord seated upon His throne . . ."

Verse 19 clearly serves as a direct continuation of v 16 . Ahab says: "How many times must I adjure you to tell me nothing but the truth in the name of the Lord." And Micaiah answers: "Then hear the word of the Lord!" On the other hand, there seems to be no connection between v 18 and v 19, which caused the Septuagint to render it as: "Not so; listen etc.", as if they read: לא כן שמע דבר ה'. Further evidence that vv 17–18 were not part of the original text but a later insertion is the resumptive repetition of v 17 in v 19. "He said: 'I saw . . . '"; "He said . . . 'I saw . . .'." We have already noted above other examples of resumptive repetition marking an interpolation.[8] In my opionion, vv 17–18 were added by an early reader of the story who found it offensive that God was portrayed as a devilish plotter seeking to entice Ahab to his death at Ramoth-gilead,[9] and who sought to justify God by asserting that Ahab deserved punishment because he had deserted his people – just as an unfaithful shepherd neglects his flock. This is a common complaint against kings often voiced by the classical prophets.[10] The interpolator attributed to Ahab the same offense.[11]

---

7   Taking the ל of לאלה as a possessive (see dictionaries for numerous other examples). Here the negation precedes the subject for added emphasis, as in Num 16:29; see P. Joüon, *Grammaire de l'Hébreu Biblique*[2] (Rome, 1947), p. 490, par 160e. In this and several other less significant details, our translation of this section differs from *NJPS*.
8   See above, chap. 4, sect. 3, on Elisha at Dothan.
9   The reader predated the author of Chronicles; see below, n. 11.
10 On irresponsible shepherds and scattered flocks, see Jer 10:21; 23:1–4; 50:6–7; Ezek 34: 1–16; Zech 11:4–17; 13:7. The ideal king, in contrast, is compared to a faithful shepherd: 2Sam 5:2; Ps 78:70–72. Hammurabi similarly describes himself as a shepherd, a shepherd of men, a shepherd who grants peace: *re'um, SIBA niši,*

Though the rest of the story reads as a continuous sequence, it is not completely free of difficulties. A serious problem is presented by Jehoshaphat's dissatisfaction with the four hundred prophets. Why did he feel the need for additional prophetic approval? The Rabbis, aware of this difficulty, commented: "And Jehoshaphat said, 'Is there not here a prophet of the Lord besides, that we may enquire of him?' Thereupon he [Ahab] exclaimed, 'But behold all these!' 'I have a tradition from my grandfather's house that the same communication is revealed to many prophets but no two prophesy in the identical phraseology,' " (bSanh 89a, trans. H. Freedman, ed. Soncino; London, 1969). In other words, true prophets may receive the same revelation, but they convey it in their own personal manner, which is then demonstrated by the talmudic discussion in which two versions of an oracle against Edom appearing in Jer 49:16 and Obad 3 are compared.

There is some textual basis for the rabbinical interpretation. The messenger sent to fetch Micaiah entreats him to "speak a favorable word" as did the other prophets, whose words are "with one accord favorable to the King." It should be noted that the messenger did not mean that Micaiah's speech should be identical with that of the other prophets, but that it should be likewise favorable. Indeed, not all four hundred prophets really speak in the exact same manner. Zedekiah son of Chenaanah, for example, made himself a pair of iron horns, and announced to the king: "Thus said the Lord: With these you shall gore the Arameans till you make an end of them" (v 11). None of the other prophets expressed himself in this fashion. There is, furthermore, a

SIBA mušallimum. Cf. G.R. Driver and J.C. Miles, *The Babylonian Laws,* Vol. II (Oxford, 1955), pp. 6 (ia, 51), 12 (iva, 45),96 (xxivb, 43). The other elements of this interpolation were borrowed from Micaiah's statement in v 28: "If you ever come home safe, the Lord has not spoken through me," and Ahab's claim in v 8: "He never prophesies anything good for me, but only misfortune."

11 The Chronicler already seems to have understood v 17 as an indictment of Ahab, as he adds in his own version of the story: "King Jehoshaphat of Judah returned *safely to his palace,* to Jerusalem" (2Chr 19:1). Ahab, the sinful king, did not return home safely; Jehoshaphat the good king did.

We thus have four reasons for assuming that vv 17-18 were interpolated into the original story: disruption of the continuity, resumptive repetition, identification of the motives of the interpolator, and recognition of his sources. Without these criteria, the existence of documents, strata, or interpolations cannot be assumed, contra Würthwein (below, n. 15) and H. Schweizer, "Literarkritischer Versuch zur Erzählung von Micah ben Jimla (1 Kön 22)," *BZ* (N.F.) 23 (1979), pp. 1-19.

stylistic difference between v 6: "March and the Lord will deliver [it] into Your Majesty's hands," (the Lucianic recension has the equivalent of "March and the Lord will surely deliver [it] into Your Majesty's hands") and v 12: "March upon Ramoth-gilead and triumph! The Lord will deliver it into Your Majesty's hands." This brings us back to our original question: Why did Jehoshaphat distrust the four hundred prophets? There must have been some directly perceivable characteristic which distinguished them from Micaiah. What then was it?

Micaiah himself notes an essential difference between himself and the four hundred. He participated in the heavenly council (v 19: "I saw the Lord seated upon His throne, with all the host of heaven standing in attendance to the right and to the left of him. The Lord asked . . ."), observed its discussions, and now, with the permission of the "chairman" (v 19: "Then hear the word of the Lord"), he "leaks" some of the proceedings to those who had not been present. The four hundred, on the other hand, were not privileged to participate. They were merely visited by "the spirit" sent by the council, and prophesied through its agency. Zedekiah, when he approached to strike Micaiah, merely confirms that his prophecy came through the spirit (v 24): "Which way did the spirit of the Lord pass from me to speak with you?"[12] He innocently believes that all prophecy comes through the spirit; Micaiah does not trouble to correct him.

Is there a manifest difference between prophecy through the spirit and prophecy derived through audio-visionary experience? There indeed, seems to be. We know of bands of prophets who behaved frenziedly when the spirit of the Lord descended upon them, as described for example in 1Sam 10:5–13; 19:20–23. There, as here, prophecy is a *collective,* nearly contagious experience. Its signs are lyres, timbrels, flutes, harps, singing, dancing, running, jumping, wild gesticulation and disrobing. Such behavior is also displayed by the prophets of Baal in 1Kgs 18:26–29: collective prophesying, screaming, jumping on the altar, and the self-infliction of knife-wounds until blood ran.

A similar phenomenon is mentioned in Wen-Amon's description

---

12 The "spirit" (v 12) is a reification of "the spirit of the Lord" (v 24) which speaks through the prophets. This time, however, it purposely lies to them (v 22) and is therefore called "a lying spirit" (vv 22–23).

of his journey to Byblos in the eleventh century BCE,[13] and it is also known in the classical world as Dionysian prophecy. The word enthusiasm, from the Greek'εν θεός means that a god has entered a person and driven him to frenzied behavior. This is the opposite of ecstasy – from the Greek verb'εξίστημι "to leave, to exit" – which means that the person's soul leaves his body and travels in distant realms. While enthusiasm is marked by an increase in bodily activity, ecstasy involves stillness and loss of consciousness.[14] We find clear cases of ecstasy in the Bible: Balaam, who is portrayed as falling on his face and seeing visions (Num 24:4, 16, although the framing verse 2:2 describes him as a "spirit"-prophet), and later Ezekiel and Daniel (in his portrayal as apocalyptic seer, Dan 7–12).

These distinctions make it clear why Jehoshaphat was dissatisfied. The sight of the enthusiastic prophets whom Ahab had assembled aroused his suspicion. It is thus also clear what the author of this story wished to convey through Micaiah's speech. Two grades of prophecy exist. The highest is that of the prophet who sees, hears, and speaks the Word of God. This kind of prophecy is completely reliable. On a lower level stands the enthusiastic prophecy, achieved through "the spirit of the Lord." It may be true prophecy – the spirit is not always lying – but it is occasionally used as a misleading diversion in order to serve as a just punishment. The purpose of the Micaiah story was to teach a lesson about the various kinds of prophecy; thus it should be considered an *exemplum*.[15]

Confirmation of this interpetation of the story can be found in the classical prophets. Several scholars have already noted that most of the classical prophets, from Amos to Jeremiah, and later, Haggai and Malachi, do not attribute their prophecies to the Spirit of the Lord.[16]

13 See J.B. Pritchard, *Ancient Near Eastern Texts*[2] (Princeton, 1955), pp. 25–29.
14 These distinctions between ecstasy and enthusiasm, useful for biblical studies, were suggested to me by Prof. R.J. Zwi Werblowsky of Jerusalem. A somewhat different terminology was proposed by R.R. Wilson, "Prophecy and Ecstasy: A Reexamination," *JBL* 98 (1979), pp. 321–337.
15 The beginnings of such an interpretation of the Micaiah story, without appropriate terminology, is presented by E. Würthwein, "Zur Komposition von I Reg-22[1-38]," *Festschrift Leonhard Rost* [BZAW 105] (Berlin, 1967), pp. 245–254. See also R. Hallevy, "Micaiah ben Imlah, The Ideal Prophet" (Heb.), *Beth Mikra* 12/3 (31) (1967), pp. 102–106, who believes, however, that the main purpose of this story is to portray the proper conduct suitable to a prophet.
16 See P. Volz, *Der Geist Gottes* (Tübingen, 1910), pp. 62–69; A Jepsen, *Nabi*

This distinguishes them from the early prophets, such as those mentioned in the Book of Samuel, and possibly Elijah and Elisha (2Kgs 2:9, 17),[17] as well as from the later prophets, Ezekiel, Zechariah 1–8, Joel, and Trito-Isaiah. Deutero-Zechariah (9–14), an anonymous prophet of unknown date, presents a sharp denunciation of the prophets (chap. 13), among whose characterististics he lists wearing hairy mantles (v 4) and wounding themselves (v 6). This is reminiscent of the self-inflicted wounds of the prophets of Baal on Mount Carmel. Deutero-Zechariah mentions these prophets and the "spirit of impurity" in the same breath (13:2). The meaning of this expression is, in my opinion, "the spirit, which is impurity,"[18] Deutero-Zechariah speaks of no other "pure" spirit. The silence of most of the classical prophets regarding the Spirit of the Lord, together with Deutero-Zechariah's comments, attest to their reservations about enthusiasm as a source of prophetic inspiration. Other qualities are preferred: prophetic vision, "This is what my Lord God showed me," or the Word, "Listen to the Word of the Lord," "The Word of the Lord came to me, saying" as in the case of Micaiah.

The story of Micaiah thus expresses a prophetic theology characteristic of the classical prophets of the late Monarchy period.

(München, 1934), pp. 24–40; S. Mowinckel, "The 'Spirit' and the 'Word' in the Pre-Exilic Reforming Prophets," *JBL* 53 (1934), pp. 199–227; and recently: M. Haran, "From Early to Classical Prophecy: Continuity and Change," *VT* 27 (1977), pp. 385–397.

17 Y. Kaufmann firmly maintained that throughout Israelite prophecy, even at its very beginning, "the spirit" was never the source, but only incidental to it. See תולדות האמונה הישראלית (Tel Aviv, 1952), I:511–532, II:244–246; in abridged form, *The Religion of Israel,* trans. M. Greenberg (Chicago, 1960), pp. 87–101. I cannot accept this position. The "spirit" of Elijah which settled upon Elisha (2Kgs 2:1–18) prepared him for the miracles he would perform, including clairvoyance. The "utterance of David" in 2Sam 23:1–7 is couched in language characteristic of early prophecy (cf. v 1 with Num 24:3–4, 15–16), and presents a unique portrait of David as a prophet (v 3). This speech opens with the prophet's statement: "The spirit of the Lord has spoken through me, and His message is on my tongue" (v 2). The prophets in 1Sam 10:6–19 do not speak the Word of the Lord, only behave in a frenzied manner, yet they are still called prophets! This can only be understood if their spirit-induced actions were usually held to be characteristic of other kinds of prophets as well.

18 This is a case of *genitivus epexegeticus,* such as בתולת ישראל in Amos 5:2 which means "the virgin, i.e., Israel" as opposed to Deut 22:19, a regular construct, in which it means "an Israelite virgin." Similarly Judg 19:24 דבר הנבלה הזאת means "this outrageous thing," and Jer 44:4 means "this abominable thing."

The correspondence between their outlooks serves to confirm our interpretation of their teachings. At the same time, it indicates that the period of classical prophecy was the most probable one for the composition of this story.

This story therefore does not reflect the religious realities of the Israelite monarchy in the ninth century, which were characterised by the struggle with Baal, as attested to by the Elijah epopee (1Kgs 16:29–19:18) and the account of Jehu's rebellion (2Kgs 9:1–10:28). Jeremiah as well notes that unlike the situation at his time in Judah, in former days Samaria and the Northern Kingdom had strayed after Baal (Jer 23:13: "In the prophets of Samaria I saw a repulsive thing: they prophesied by Baal and led My people Israel astray"; v 27: "just as their fathers forgot My name because of Baal"). No hint of this situation is reflected in the Micaiah story, which concentrates on the problem of conflicting prophets of the Lord: true versus false prophets. This problem existed only in the period of the classical prophets: Isaiah was the first to raise the issue of "prophets who give false instruction" (9:14) and priests and prophets who "are muddled by liquor, confused by wine ... muddled in their visions, they stumble in judgment" (28:7). Micah describes: "The prophets who lead My people astray, who cry ' Peace!' when they have something to chew, but launch a war on him who fails to fill their mouths" (3:5).

This problem is presented in an especially harsh manner by Jeremiah who charges the prophets with the most extreme wrong-doing (23:13ff; 29:23), accusing them of adultery and conspiracy with evil-doers. He also raises the question of distinguishing between true and false prophets (23:16–22; 27:14–18; 28) and the issue of true inspiration. Jeremiah rejects the value of dreams as a source of veridical prophecy (23:23–32). Above all, he negated the other prophets' oracles because in his view they have not "stood in the council of the Lord" (23:18, 22), that is God's assembly, exactly as was claimed by Micaiah son of Imlah.

The confrontation between true and false prophets is one of the main themes in the Book of Jeremiah. It has already been noted that similarities exist between Jeremiah and Micaiah.[19] Both stand alone

---

19 M. Duvshani, "Micaiah ben Imlah: The Link between Early and Later Prophets" (Heb.), *Beth Mikra* 36 (1969), pp. 80–87. There seems to be, however, no justification for his claim that the story of Micaiah as presented here is historical.

when prophesying impending doom, confronting a multitude of other prophets who predict deliverance and victory. Both are ignored. Both are beaten and imprisoned, but refuse to recant. Both clash with false prophets who perform magical-symbolic acts (Zedekiah son of Chenaanah, Hananiah son of Azzur). Both are assaulted by the false prophets (smiting Micaiah on the cheek, breaking Jeremiah's yoke) but adamantly stand firm and castigate their assailants. It is difficult to view these similarities as accidental. On the contrary, the story of Micaiah should apparently be understood as a peripatetic paradigm from the age of classical prophecy, which was composed through the influence of the person and sermons of the prophet Jeremiah, possibly by one of his disciples, some time at the beginning of the sixth century BCE.

This conclusion, which may seem somewhat surprising at first glance, nevertheless, conforms with what we shall later observe regarding the date of composition of similar stories. The parable about the Man of God at Bethel (1 Kgs 12:33–13:32) does not predate the sixth century, and the Book of Jonah is later still. Furthermore, the paradigm of Rebekah's bethrothal (Gen 24) is directed to the group which returned to Jerusalem in the Persian period.[20] Though it is hazardous to assign dates to the emergence of the various *gattungen,* here the form critical argument in combination with other considerations appears to indicate that the Micaiah story should be attributed to the end of the period of the Monarchy.

This conclusion does not preclude the possibility that the author of this story made use of older historical sources. Indeed, not all the political details included here are an accurate reflection of Ahab's time. Some are anachronistic, such as the titles of "son of the king" and "city governor," which biblical and archeological considerations ascribe to the end of the Judean Monarchy.[21] But, on the other hand,

---

This objection also applies to E. Haller, *Charisma und Ekstasis – Die Erzählung von dem Propheten Micha ben Jimla, 1 Kön 22, 1–28a* (Theologische Existenz heute; N.F. 82, 1960).

20　See above, n. 1.

21　Regarding בן המלך "the prince," see G. Brin, "On the Title בן המלך" (Heb.), לשוננו 31 (1967), pp. 5–20, 85–96, and the earlier literature cited there; N. Avigad, "A Group of Hebrew Seals" (Heb.), *Eretz Yisrael* 9 [*W.F. Albright Volume*] (Jerusalem, 1969), pp. 1–9, esp. p. 9. Regarding the city governor, see N. Avigad, 'The Governor'(*Sar Ha-'ir*) (Heb.), *Qadmoniot* 10 (1977), pp. 68–69; G. Barkay,

there is no doubt regarding the historical framework of the story: the alliance between Ahab and Jehoshaphat, which was strengthened by marriage, and the battle for the conquest of Ramoth-gilead.[22] Since such historical details are confirmed by other, more reliable sources of information, there is no doubt that their historical sources were available to the author of the tale.

If our interpretation of the Micaiah story is correct, it should not be considered an accurate historical source for the times of Ahab. It cannot provide information about the Northern Kingdom's administrative system, nor about Israelite religion in the ninth century, and certainly not about the history of prophecy. It can only reflect the realities of its author's era – the civil procedure (prison), the administration, and the views of prophecy current in the Judean Monarchy in its last days. Nevertheless, since the author employed historical sources in the composition of this work, and did not invent the entire account, this story is to be considered an *exemplum* and not a parable, by the criteria presented above. The early prophet, Micaiah son of Imlah, is portrayed as an example of a true prophet on all counts:

"A Second Bulla of a *Sar Ha-'ir*" (Heb.), *ibid.,* pp. 69–73. Both these seals are dated by the above authorities to the Assyrian period. See also R. Hestrin and M. Dayagi-Mendels, *Seals From the First Temple Period* (Jerusalem, 1978), pp. 10–21, and the most recent discussion with literature in N. Avigad, *Hebrew Bullae from the Time of Jeremiah* (Heb.) (Jerusalem, 1986), pp. 26–27, 29–32. The extra-biblical materials demonstrate that these titles were not introduced at the end of the Monarchy period in Judah, but the fact remains that prior to the seventh century BCE no historical personages from either Judah or Israel bear either of these two titles (Maaseiah בן המלך in 2Chr 28:7 may have been the king's actual son, like Jotham the king's son in 2Kgs 15:5). The evidence may, of course, be altered as a result of future discoveries, such as that of the inscription לשרער published by Z. Meshel, "Kuntilat 'Ajrud – An Israelite Site on the Sinai Border" (Heb.), *Qadmoniot* 9 (1976), pp. 119–124, ad p. 122.

22   During the reign of Joram son of Ahab, Ramoth-gilead was under the rule of Israel (2Kgs 9:1–15). Therefore, the view of E. Lipinski, "Le Ben Hadad II de la Bible et l'histoire," *Proceedings of the Fifth World Congress of Jewish Studies* (Jerusalem, n.d.), pp. 157–173, that 1Kgs 22 originally described the death of Joram son of Ahab in battle at Ramoth-gilead, is untenable. The view of A. Jepsen, "Israel und Damaskus," *AOF* 14 (1942), pp. 153–172, that this chapter originally described a victory by Joash in Ramoth-gilead, and that of J.M. Miller, "The Elisha Cycle and the Account of the Omride Wars," *JBL* 85 (1966), pp. 441–454; idem, "The Rest of the Acts of Jehoahaz etc." *ZAW* 80 (1968), pp. 337–343, that the battle was fought by Jehoahaz, cannot be accepted, because the Israelite *reconquista* led by him began with the battle of Aphek in the south-west Golan.

knowledgeable, forthright, and courageous. Using his example, the author strives to teach later generations the proper manner of prophetic inspiration: presence at the "council of the Lord."

3. The Book of Jonah

There is almost complete agreement among biblical scholars that the Book of Jonah was composed in post-exilic times. Testifying to the lateness of the work are numerous linguistic criteria: vocabulary idioms, and syntax. In all these respects Jonah resembles literary works of the Persian period and later – the late biblical books, documents and inscriptions in Imperial or Jewish Aramaic, post-exilic sources, or rabbinic writings. The following list of terms and expressions from the Book of Jonah are found elsewhere only in exilic and post-exilic sources.[23]

גורלות "lots" (1:7–2x) – In plural, especially in Second Temple literature: Neh 10:35, 11:1; 1 Chr 24:5, 31; 25:8; 26:14; 1 QM 1:13; 1QS 4:26; t Yoma 2:2 (2x); m Sota 1:7; m Bbat 3:7; b Sanh 11a; 43b–(3x); also Lev 16:8 (P). Early sources use the singular, cf. Josh 18:6, 8, 10; Nah 3:10; Obad 11; and in later sources Isa 34:17; Joel 4:3. In general, plural forms are often used in later sources instead of the singular of early usage, as in עתים, בקרים, פסחים and in construct שרי החילים, עמי הארצות[24]. The verb used in this verse, (להפיל גורלות) is also characteristic of late sources (נפ"ל) in hiph'il; early sources use ידה (qal), של"ך (hiph'il). נד"ה (hiph'il), but never נפ"ל.

דרך "walk" (3:3–4) – Ezek 42:4;[25] Neh 2:6; Sir 11:12(7);[26] often in Mishnah, Tosefta, Sifrei, and Mekhilta: should be construed as a unit

---

23 In preparing this list I consulted, aside from the main encyclopaedia entries and critical commentaries on the Book of Jonah, the following works: A Bendavid, *Biblical Hebrew and Mishnaic Hebrew*[2] (Heb.), Vol. I (Tel Aviv, 1967), especially pp. 60–63; R. Polzin, *Late Biblical Hebrew – Toward an Historical Typology of Biblical Prose* (HSM 12; Missoula, MO, 1976); A. Brenner, "The Language of the Book of Jonah as a Criterion for Dating its Authorship" (Heb.), *Beth Mikra* 24 (1979), pp. 396–405; E. Qimron, "The Language of the Book of Jonah" (Heb.), *Beth Mikra* 25 (1980), pp. 181–182. For general remarks on this question, see A. Hurvitz, *The Transition Period in Biblical Hebrew* (Heb.), (Jerusalem, 1972).
24 Polzin (n. 23), pp. 42–43.
25 The date of Ezek 40–48 has not yet been established.
26 His grandson translated 'αντίλημψις; did he read here מלך = "advice"?

of distance which can be travelled in a certain amount of time,[27] which is the meaning often denoted by the *derek* in classical biblical Hebrew. And in fact it is occasionally used in the Aramaic Targums as a translation of דרך in this meaning, as in Onqelos Gen 30:36; 31:23; Exod 3:18; Num 10:33; 33:8; Jonathan 2Kgs 3:9. Equally instructive is the rabbinic usage of מהלך to explain the biblical דרך appearing in the words of R. Jose the Galilean, tPesah 8:3.

זעף "*storm*" (1:15) – Nowhere else in the Bible does the word appear with this meaning.[28] It is found in this sense at Qumran (1 QH 6:22–23; 7:5), and in rabbinic Hebrew: Sifrei Dt 42; m Taʻan 3:8; m Ohol 18:6; b Yoma 31a; y Ber 9:2. The word זלעפות in the sense of storm appears in Ps 11:6; Sir 43:17 (Ms. B). זעף in Aramaic is equivalent to the Hebrew רוח (Job 1:19); cf. b Ber 59a: "What are רוחות Abaye said: זעפא".

טעם "*decree*" (3:7) – not used in this sense elsewhere in the Bible. Here we see a semantic calque[29] of the Aramaic usage of טעם[30] which appears in both imperial and biblical Aramaic (cf. Dan 3:10, Ezra 4:19, and elsewhere). This meaning does not seem to have become widespread in later Hebrew, as it is nowhere attested at Qumran or in rabbinic writings.[31]

למחרת "*the next day*" (4:7)[32] – found only in 1 Chr 29:27. למחרתם in 1 Sam 30:17 is considered by commentators to be a corruption of ויחרימם or להחרימם. Classical biblical Hebrew uses ממחרת exclusively, but rabbinic Hebrew consistently prefers למחרת; cf. m Sukk 3:13; m Sanh 5:5; t Zebah 2:17; t Nazir 6:1; b ʻErub 51b. ממחרת is often found in halakhic Midrashim, but mostly in the context of scriptural exposition.

מנה "*appoint*" (2:1; 4:6, 7, 8) – In the early biblical books, only in qal and niphʻal. The piʻel form is found only in the later books: Job 7:3; Dan 1:5, 10, 11; it is also common in the Mishnah and Tosefta,

---

27   Brenner (above, n. 23), p. 400.

28   Brenner (above, n. 23), p. 399.

29   Y. Kutscher, "Aramaic Calque in Hebrew" (Heb.), *Tarbiz* 33 (1964), pp. 118–130, esp. pp. 121–122 =*Hebrew and Aramaic Studies* (Jerusalem, 1977), pp. שצז–ח.

30   *DISO* p. 102.

31   Similarly, even words and forms present in late biblical Hebrew, also used in Aramaic, were sometimes rejected by rabbinic Hebrew; see Bendavid (above, n. 23), pp. 132–134.

32   Bendavid (above, n. 23), p. 61; Brenner (above, n. 23), p. 402.

in the sense of "ordain, command." מנ"י (pa'el) has the same meaning in Imperial Aramaic;[33] it is used by Onqelos as a translation of פק"ד (hip'il) in Gen 39:4, 5; 41:34; Num 1:50. In 11Q tgJob it appears as a translation of צוית in 38:12; and 1QapGen 20:32 represents Gen 12:20: ויצו עליו פרעה אנשים as ויצו עמי אנוש די.[34] ממונה in rabbinic Hebrew is thus equivalent to the biblical פקיד (cf. 1 Chr 9:29). Here too וימן means "to command," "to appoint"; in contrast to the rebellious prophet God has many faithful servants: fish, plants, insects, and storms – the entire world.

ספינה "vessel" (1:5) – a biblical *hapax legomenon*. In rabbinic Hebrew this completely replaced the biblical אניה. Cf. m Sabb 9:2: "Whence do we learn of a ship (ספינה) that it is not susceptible to uncleanness? Because it is written: 'The way of a ship (אניה) in the midst of the sea' (Prov 30:19)." As in the case of דרך = מהלך, this is another good example of biblical words explained by their rabbinic equivalents. At Qumran, in contrast, we find only אוניה – which clearly illustrates the archaising tendencies of that sect's writings.[35]

ספינה is attested in both Imperial[36] and Targumic Aramaic. In light of the increasing evidence, there seems no justification for explaining ספינה in any other way (e.g., as deck, or the like).

עש"ת "think" (1:6) – This root is the Aramaic equivalent of the Hebrew חש"ב. It is found in Ancient Aramaic (Sefire II:B:5) and is common in Imperial Aramaic,[37] from which it entered Dan 6:4. It was from Aramaic that late biblical Hebrew derived the nouns עשתות, עשתון (Ps 146:4; Job 12:5; Sir 3:24). This borrowing seems not to have taken hold in later Hebrew, however, since the root is not found at Qumran, in the Mishnah, Tosefta, or the halakhic Midrashim.[38]

רבו "ten thousand" (4:11) – appears mainly in late biblical books (Dan 11:12; Ezra 2:64, 69; Neh 7:66, 71, 72; 1 Chr 29:7) and in post-biblical literature (Mishnah, Tosefta, Midrashim). The classical term is רבבה; רבתים in Ps 68:18 is a dual form, as in Ugaritic (sing.:

33 *DISO*, p. 159.

34 J.A. Fitzmyer, *The Genesis Apocryphon of Qumran Cave I–A Commentary²* (Bib et Or 18A) (Rome, 1971).

35 Though these archaising writers are easily detected through their semantic slips; see above regarding זעף.

36 *DISO*, p. 196.

37 *DISO*, pp. 223–224.

38 See above regarding טעם.

rbt; pl.: *rbbt*).[39] In the halakhic Midrashim רבבה is found only in biblical citations.

שת"ק *"calm down"* (1:11–12) – elsewhere in the Bible in Ps 107:30 (late),[40] and Prov 26:20 (not dated). It is well documented in Ancient and Imperial Aramaic and probably derived from it; became very common in rabbinic Hebrew. Its classical biblical Hebrew equivalent was החרש, which rarely appears in rabbinic Hebrew (with the exception of Sifrei Num 103; Sifrei Num 153–56, where both the verb החריש and the noun חרישה occur in an exposition of Num 30, which uses החריש extensively :vv 5, 8, 12, 15 [3x]). Though it was possibly borrowed from Aramaic in the pre-exilic period, the evidence in general indicates that it too reflects a later development.

ה' אלהי השמים *"The Lord, God of Heaven"* (1:9) – As shown elsewhere[41] this title, as well as other similar ones ("the Lord of Heaven," "the King of Heaven") are characteristic of documents and literary sources from the Persian period onwards. To the previously mentioned references one should add 1QAp Gen 2:14: מלך ש[מיא] 7:7; 12:17: מרה שמיא. In 22:16, 21, מרה שמיא וארעא is used for קנה שמים וארץ of Gen 14:10, 22.

בן לילה *"overnight"* (4:10) – As has been noted,[42] this construction lacks parallel in the Bible. Aramaic and rabbinic Hebrew, however, contain phrases such as בן יומן *"on that day."*

בשלי, באשר למי, בשל מי *"on whose/my account"* (1:7, 8, 12) – These are all calque translations of common Aramaic phrases, as was pointed out by Kutscher.[43] For additional evidence see now also 11Q tgJob 29:7; 38:3; 1QApGen 19:10; 20:10, 25–26.

---

39   C.H. Gordon, *Ugaritic Manual* [AnOr 35] (Rome, 1955), p. 322.

40   Cf. vv 2–3: "Thus let the redeemed of the Lord say, those He redeemed from adversity, whom He gathered in from the lands, from east and west, from the north and from the sea." These verses seem to be an integral part of the Psalm; they apparently do not describe a deliverance from an enemy and ingathering of exiles, but, in accordance with the context, pilgrims delivered from various perils who gather in Jerusalem in order to praise the Lord. See the commentaries of Abraham Ibn Ezra (in מקראות גדולות) David Kimhi (his complete commentary on Psalms ed. A. Darom [Jerusalem, 1974³]) and more recent H. Gunkel, *Die Psalmen, übersetzt und erklärt* (GHAT; Göttingen, 1929).

41   See my "Betrothal of Rebekah" (above, n. 1), pp. 49–50, and earlier literature there.

42   Qimron (above, n. 23), p. 181, following Yalon (cited there).

43   Kutscher (above, n. 29), *ibid.*

מגדולם ועד קטנם "great and small alike" (3:5) – It has already been noted[44] that this order, "great and small," is characteristic of the late biblical books, while the opposite order is found in the early writings. Interestingly enough rabbinic Hebrew preserves both terms: "great and small" in mTer 8:6; mBM 8:4; mKel 17:8; "small and great" in mMa'as 1:1, mKelim 17:5.

הרבה מ־ "more than" (4:11) – This construction as well is found only in the later biblical books (2 Chr 25:9) and in rabbinic literature (tPesah 4:1).[45]

חנון ורחום (4:2) – Here too, the order of these terms conforms with later usage, while the early books contain the opposite: רחום וחנון.[46]

וירע אל (4:1) – Classical biblical Hebrew employed the construction רע בעיני "bad in the eyes of" to denote something abhorrent or hated. The construction רע ל ע"ל had a different meaning: to cause damage. Thus 2 Sam 19:8: "And that would be a greater disaster for you than any disaster that has befallen you" (ורעה לך זאת מכל הרעה); 20:6: "Sheba son of Bichri will cause us more trouble"(ירע לנו).Only in late biblical Hebrew did the combination רע ל־ receive the meaning of repulsion or condemnation,[47] as in Neh 2:10: "It displeased them greatly"(וירע להם רעה גדולה); 13:8: "I was greatly displeased" (וירע לי מאד). This change of meaning can be noted in the description of Israel's sins during the period of the Judges. Whereas the Book of Judges repeatedly speaks of הרע בעיני ה', Neh 9:28 speaks of their having ישובו לעשות הרע לפניך. In its context in Jonah 4:1 the expression can mean only that it was displeasing to Jonah and he became angry, an explanation that is possible only if we assume the language there dated from the Second Temple period.

Relevant syntactic patterns include:

מה לך נרדם (1:6) – In classical Hebrew such a question would have been phrased in the following manner: ל+מה+ל + pronoun/noun + כי + a finite verb. For example: מה לך כי נזעקת (Judg 18:23); מה לעם כי יבכו (1 Sam 11:5); see also Isa 3:15; 22:1; Ps 114:5.[48]

---

44 A. Hurvitz, "Diachronic Chiasm in Biblical Hebrew" (Heb.), *Bible and Jewish History Studies . . . Jacob Liver* (Tel Aviv, 1972), pp. 248–255, ad pp. 251–253.

45 Qimron (above, n. 23), p. 181.

46 Hurvitz (above, n. 23), pp. 104–106.

47 As was noted by Brenner (above, n. 23); I have here restated her arguments.

48 Bendavid (above, n. 23), p. 61.

The structure מה+ל+ pronoun + participle first appears in Ezek 18:2 and is characteristic of rabbinic Hebrew: מה לך יוצא ליהרג וכו' מה (mMid 2:2); מה לך מקיף לשמאל (Mekhilta Bachodesh 6); לך לוקה מאפרגל עקיבא, מה לך אתה מכניס ראשך בין המחלוק(ו)ת (tBer 5:9; tBez 2:12).

כי אתה אל חנון ורחום (4:2) – In classical biblical Hebrew the nominative predicate precedes the subject in such explanatory clauses.[49] Compare כי עפר אתה (Gen 3:19); אתה (Gen כי ירא אלהים אתה 22:12); כי חתן דמים אתה לי (Exod 4:25); כי עם קשה ערף אתה (Exod 33:3; Deut 9:6), and also Deut 7:6; 14:2, 21; Judg 11:2. But in explanatory clauses in later writings, the subject comes first, followed by the nominative predicate. Cf. כי אתה בחן לבב (Ps 25:5); כי אתה אלהי ישעי אתה (1 Chr 29:17); וידעו כל אפסי ארץ כי אתה אל [עו]ל[ם] (Sir 36:22); כי צדיק ואמת כל בחיריך (1 QH 14:15). The dates of composition of Ps 42–43 (see 43:2) and 71 (see v 5) are still open to investigation.

And finally, a word on the manner in which verbs are emphasized. In classical biblical Hebrew emphasis is achieved by the combination of the finitive absolute with the finite verb of the same root, as in Gen 31:15: ויאכל גם אבול את כספנו or 31:30. In Jonah, on the other hand, as in late biblical and rabbinic Hebrew, the infinitive is not employed in this manner.[50] Instead, we find the use of an internal object, i.e., an object in the form or a noun derived from the same root as the verb:[51] וקרא אליה את הקריאה (3:2); וייראו האנשים יראה גדולה (1:10, 16); וישמח יונה על הקיקיון (4:1; cf.Neh 2:10) וירע אל יונה רעה גדולה שמחה גדולה (4:7).

The list presented above constitutes, in my opinion, sound linguistic evidence for the late dating of the Book of Jonah. I have not included here matters of orthography, such as the *scriptio plena* of נקיא (1:14),[52] which may possibly be the work of later scribes, or loan words rare in standard biblical Hebrew, such as מלח, "sailor."[53] Nor have I

---

49   *Ibid.*
50   M.H. Segal, *A Grammar of Mishnaic Hebrew* (Oxford, 1927), p. 155–156.
51   Gesenius-Kautzsch-Cowley, *Hebrew Grammar*[2] (Oxford, 1910), par 117q (p. 367): "Such a substantive ... is like the infinitive absolute, never altogether without force but rather serves like it to strengthen the verbal idea."
52   Qimron (above, n. 23), p. 181.
53   Thus Brenner (above, n. 23), p. 398. The word is attested in a late Phoenician inscription (*DISO*, p. 152; *KAI* 49:2). The rarity of this term in biblical Hebrew (elsewhere only in Ezek 27:9, 27, 29) may be the result of the ancient Israelites'

taken into account forms found only rarely in early writings, such as: חו״ס when the subject is not the eye but the person (also found in Jer 13:14; 21:7; Ezek 24:14; Ps 72:13); הטיל instead of השליך (also in 1 Sam 18:11; 20:33; Jer 16:13; 22:26, 28); ויעבר אדרתו instead of ויסר (2 Sam 3:10; 24:10; 1 Kgs 15:12; Zech 3:4); עמ״ל in the sense of ordinary work (also in Judg 5:26); ויקרב instead of ויגש (also in Deut 5:24 and elsewhere).[54] Even without these additional points, there is still sufficient evidence to prove conclusively and with no reservations that the Book of Jonah was composed in the post-exilic age.[55] If we also take into consideration the fact that the author attempted to write in proper classical biblical Hebrew, using, for example, the narrative imperfect with waw consecutive and occasionally choosing archaic words (אניה three times and the contemporary ספינה only once), the numerous late forms compel us to date the work not at the beginning of the Second Temple period but several generations later – probably some time in the middle of the fifth century BCE.

The examination of the historical background of the story leads us to a similar conclusion. There is no trace of the historical Nineveh here – the Nineveh which Sennacherib made his capital and which continued in that role for over one hundred years, ruling a world empire which exiled Israel and dominated Judah.[56] That reality is reflected in Nahum (1:11–3:19) and Zephaniah (2:13–15), but nowhere in Jonah is there a hint of it. The Nineveh of Jonah has no connection whatsoever with the history of Israel. It is ruled by the "king of Nineveh" (3:6), not the "king of Assyria" (as in Isa 7:17; 8:7; 10:12; 36:4, etc.). Jonah's Nineveh is any great city far away in place

---

lack of maritime pursuits; see Y. Kutscher, *Words and their History* (Heb.), (Jerusalem, 1965), pp. 58–59.

54 Contra Bendavid and Brenner (above, n. 23), who consider these forms as proof of a late date.

55 For a rejection of the view that the language of Jonah reflects a northern Israelite dialect, rather than late Hebrew, see E. König, "Jonah," *Dictionary of the Bible*, Vol. II (Edinburgh, 1899), pp. 744–753, ad pp. 747–748.

56 Sh. Abramsky, "Jonah ben Amittai (A Literary-historial Study)" (Heb.), *Gazit* 17 (1959), No. 3–4, pp. 5–10. From this "unawareness" of Nineveh's role as capital of Assyria, Kaufmann attempted to deduce that Jonah was composed before Sennacherib's reign; see his תולדות האמונה הישראלית Vol. 2 (Tel Aviv, 1947²), pp. 279–287; translated and abridged by M. Greenberg in *The Religion of Israel* (Chicago, 1960), pp. 282–286. But the above-mentioned linguistic considerations make this impossible.

and time. It is a symbolic city, like the Land of Uz[57] in the Book of Job or India in medieval Jewish philosophy.[58] To the extent that the story contains historical allusions, they relate to the Persian period. The royal edict of Nineveh is issued in the name of the king and his "nobles" (3:7), which was the accepted practice in the Persian empire.[59] The attribution of the Book of Jonah to the Persian period, supported as it is by both linguistic and historical criteria, is crucial for the understanding of this work, as we shall attempt to show in what follows.

Nearly unanimous agreement exists among scholars as to the literary genre of Jonah. It is clear that the book is neither historical nor biographical. It exhibits no interest in the life of Jonah son of Amittai before the Nineveh incident or after it. Neither is it concerned with what happened to Nineveh subsequent to its miraculous deliverance. The city is not portrayed realistically – no persons are identified, nor are any specific dates mentioned. Nineveh is merely a far-off city over which hangs a decree that it will be "overthrown" like Sodom and Gomorrah of biblical legend. The story's fantastic nature (Jonah swallowed by the fish later to be cast forth upon the shore; the plant growing overnight), somewhat resembles the *legenda,* though it lacks the most essential features of this genre: the prophet performs no miracles – miracles rather, happen to him; he is not venerated by a circle of admirers, but is castigated by God for his behavior, nor is he spared God's mocking derision (4:4, 9). Moreover, there is no doubt as to whose side the author – and his audience is on.

These features of the Book of Jonah point to the literary genre to which it belongs. The theoretical debate between God and Jonah, which finds expression in their actions as well, leaves no doubt that the Book of Jonah is a parable.[60] Because of its legendary character,

---

57 Still, the choice of city or country is not without significance; see M. Weiss, *The Story of Job's Beginnings* (Jerusalem, 1983), pp. 21–24.

58 E.g., Judah Halevi, *Kitab al Khazari,* I, 19–24, trans. H. Hirschfeld (London, 1931), p. 40, preceded by rabbinic stories about Alexander in Kazia: Bereshit Rabba 33:1, yBMes 2:5.

59 Cf. Ezra 7:14: "For you are commissioned by the king and his seven advisers to regulate Judah and Jerusalem . . ."

60 Thus F. Hitzig, *Die zwölf kleinen Propheten* [KEHAT] (Leipzig, 1838), and

it is not an *exemplum,* based on historical fact, but an imaginary parable.[61] Yet this conclusion alone cannot resolve the question which has intrigued biblical scholarship for so many years: what was the message of the story, what was Jonah's viewpoint which the book intended to negate, and what was the moral principle conveyed by God in response to Jonah?[62]

One opinion, widespread especially among Christian scholars, is that the book was a polemic against the trend towards Jewish particularism in the fifth century BCE. Jonah son of Amittai represents Ezra, Nehemiah, and their followers, who expelled the foreign wives and built the walls of Jerusalem as a barrier against the impurity of foreigners. These people anticipated that the pagan nations would face destruction because of their sins, in fulfillment of the ancient oracles against the nations. The Book of Jonah preaches the direct opposite of this doctrine – namely, that the nations, symbolized by Nineveh, are also creatures of God, equally precious in His eyes, equally deserving of His mercy and as such should also be allowed the opportunity to repent and return unto Him. This interpretation considers the book a propagandist tract of the universalistic movement propagated by the followers of Deutero-Isaiah, which protested against the particularistic trend that came to dominate Second Temple Judaism.[63]

recently at greater length: G.M. Landes, "Jonah: A Māšāl?" *Israelite Wisdom – S. Terrien Festschrift* (Missoula, MO 1978), pp. 137–158.

61 On the legendary sources of the story see M.Y. Bin Gorion, "The First Chapter of Jonah – A Critical Study" (Heb.), הגרן 10 (1928), pp. 5–10. Earlier, a more folkloristic approach was taken by H. Schmidt, *Jona – Eine Untersuchung zur vergleichenden Religionsgeschichte* [FRLANT 9] (Göttingen, 1907).

62 Literary criticism indeed contributes towards elucidating additional strata of meaning in the text. But a conflict of opinions between the main characters demands our primary attention. Examining this conflict, we first analyze the explicit meaning of the story. *Pace* J. Magonet, *Form and Meaning: Studies in Literary Techniques in the Book of Jonah* (Bern-Frankfurt/M., 1976).

63 Aside from the references listed in my article "Classes in the Prophetical Stories: Didactic Legenda and Parable," *SVT* 26 (1974), pp. 143–164 ad p. 155, n. 2, see: G.M. Landes, "The Kerygma of the Book of Jonah," *Interpretation* 21 (1967), pp. 3–31; B.S. Childs, "The Canonical Shape of Jonah," *W. La Sor Festschrift* (Grand Rapids, MI, 1978), pp. 122–128; idem, *Introduction to the Old Testament as Scripture* (London, 1979), pp. 417–427. Following Landes, Childs now differentiates between the story's original meaning, before the addition of the psalm (2:3–10), and its present message. The addition of the prayer portrays Jonah as a person with double standards. Toward himself, the loyal Israelite, he expects

There is, however, no actual textual evidence for this interpretation. The Book of Jonah nowhere draws sharp distinctions between Jews and non-Jews. On board the ship, Jonah presents himself as a Hebrew who fears the God of Heaven, who has created land and sea, but nowhere does he express disapproval of the gods of the other nations, or of the sailors who called on them in prayer. The pagan sailors readily affirm their fear of the Lord; they recognize His power, offer sacrifices and make vows to Him. Their righteousness is demonstrated by their determination to row back to the shore in the teeth of the storm, rather than sacrifice Jonah. Jonah, for his part, does not want them to perish because of his iniquity; he straightway reveals his offence and advises them to cast him overboard without delay. There is definitely a universalistic atmosphere pervading the narrative, but without display of any anti-particularistic polemical intent.

The same is true of the Nineveh incident. Nineveh is portrayed merely as a large city – not the capital of the Assyrian empire which was the perpetrator of Israel's subjugation, destruction and exile, not even simply as the capital of an anonymous pagan empire (a model for Persia). Its sin is neither politico-historical, nor religious (idolatry, impurity, sorcery, etc.), the city is indicted for ethical crimes – "the injustice of which he is guilty" (3:8), namely sins against fellow men, as at Sodom, whose outcry came before God (Gen 18:21). Like Sodom, Nineveh is in danger of being overthrown (3:4).[64] The repentance of the people of Nineveh comes not as a result of their recognition of God and acceptance of His commandments, in the spirit of Deutero-Isaiah (45:14–15, 22–23) and the putative universalistic movement, but as repentance of their "evil ways" and commitment to the observance of those "natural laws" which are described in the Bible in most general terms as יראת אלהים "fear of God" (Gen 20:11; 42:18; Exod 1:17; Job 1:1). Nowhere in his tirade

God to have mercy and save him, while he expects the pagan city of Nineveh to be destroyed. In my opinion, the addition of the psalm to the Book of Jonah must be viewed together with the same phenomenon occurring in 1Sam 2:1–10; Isa 38:9–20; in all these cases, there is no attempt to recast the protagonist's character, only to enhance it, or to stress its piety.

64 The overthrowing of cities in the Bible invariably refers to Sodom and Gomorrah; cf. Gen 19:21, 25, 29 (2x); Deut. 29:22; Isa 13:19; Jer 20:16; 49:18; 50:40; Amos 4:11; Lam 4:6. The allusion to Sodom was noted by Kaufmann (above, n. 56).

does Jonah complain that God is too merciful with gentiles. Neither does he express any particular objection to God's behavior towards Nineveh; it is God's attributes themselves, irrespective of their application to one nation or another, which are the prophet's problem. It is difficult to find evidence for, or even a hint of, a polemic against Jewish particularism in the Book of Jonah.[65] The popularity of this view can only be a survival of the typological exegesis: the Book of Jonah seen as a precursor of the dispute between the increasingly insular Judaism and the more widespread Christianity of the early centuries of the common era.

Another interpretation, advocated primarily by Jewish scholars,[66] is that the aim of the book is to teach the greatness of repentance. Even sinful Nineveh was able to escape its terrible fate when each inhabitant "turn back from his evil ways and from the injustice of which he is guilty" (3:8). How much more so can repentance save Israel, the remnant of God's inheritance (cf. Mic 7:18), and bring it forgiveness and mercy. It is indeed possible to learn about true repentance from the Book of Jonah, as did the Rabbis,[67] and of its power to annul punishment. Still, it is not clear whether repentance is the central idea of the book, or only a secondary theme, for to teach the value of repentance the first three chapters of the book would have sufficed. What should be more convincing than to conclude with 3:10: "God saw what they did, how they were turning back from their evil ways. And God renounced the punishment He had planned to bring upon them, and did not carry it out." What can the argument between God and Jonah in Chapter Four add to this theme? Yet there is no

65 A particularistic tendency is ascribed to Jonah only in the Midrash; see ySanh 11:5: " . . . Jonah said: 'I know that the nations are prone to repent. If I go to prophesy to them and they repent, the Holy One, Blessed be He, will exact punishment from Israel (literally: the enemies of Israel – a euphemism)! What shall I do? Flee!' . . . "

66 In addition to Kaufmann and Abramsky (above, n. 56), see also U. Cassuto, "Jona," *Encyclopaedia Judaica,* Vol. 9 (1932), pp. 268–272; H.L. Ginsberg, *The Five Megiloth and Jonah – A New Translation* (Philadelphia, PA, 1969), pp. 114–116; A. Segré, "Joná, il libro del pentimento," *RMI* 41 (1975), pp. 389–407; R.E. Clements, "The Purpose of the Book of Jonah," *SVT* 28 (1975), pp. 16–28.

67 mTa'an 2:1: "The eldest among them uttered before them words of admonition: Brethren, it is not written of the men of Nineveh that 'God saw their sack cloth and fasting,' but 'and God saw their works that they turned from their evil way' and in [his] protest [the Prophet Joel] says: 'Rend your heart and not your garments' " (trans. H. Danby [Oxford, 1950], p. 195).

doubt that the last chapter is an integral part of the book, and necessary for its understanding, for only there does Jonah reveal the reason of his initial flight to Tarshish. However, the argument in this chapter has no connection with penitence. Jonah casts no doubt on its worth, and God, for His part, says nothing in its defense. The argument concerns God's attributes, Jonah being unwilling that He act as "a compassionate and gracious God, slow to anger, abounding in kindness, renouncing punishment" (4:2), and God teaching him, by the example of the plant, that Nineveh is worthy of His care and compassion (4:10–11).

We thus have here a different explanation of the book's meaning.[68] According to this interpretation, the Book of Jonah is a defense of God's attributes of mercy and compassion which extend to all His creatures (cf. Ps 145:9). For this reason He spared Nineveh, while Jonah protested against His leniency and demanded that He practise strict justice. The incident of the plant demonstrates his error to Jonah, by pointing out his inconsistency: is Nineveh to be shown no mercy, while he and his plant are spared! Without God's mercy, Jonah himself would not have been able to survive; indeed, he would have long ago found himself at the bottom of the sea.

This interpretation correctly indicates that the main focus is on God's qualities. These were the object of Jonah's contentions and the reason for his original flight to Tarshish. But this still does not provide a convincing explanation of the concluding dialogue between Jonah and God. God's mercy towards Jonah is not mentioned in this exchange. אתה חסת על הקיקיון "You cared about the plant" (4:10), says God to Jonah, and not "You asked me to spare you and your plant." Despite the usual interpretation of the word חו"ס, mercy and compassion are not the point of God's final rejoinder to Jonah.[69] In the same manner, it is clear that the words אתה חסת על הקיקיון do not

---

68 L. Frankel, "And His Mercies Extend to All His Works," מעינות 9 (1968) [The Days of Awe/1], pp. 193–207; G.H. Cohn, *Das Buch Jona im Lichte der biblischen Erzählkunst* (Assen, 1969), pp. 99–101; U. Simon, "The Book of Jonah – Structure and Meaning" (Heb.), *I.L. Seeligmann Volume*, Vol. II, (Jerusalem, 1983), pp. 291–318.

69 A. B. Ehrlich, מקרא כפשוטו, Vol. III (Berlin, 1901), on Jonah 4; A.S. van der Woude, "Nachholende Erzählung im Buche Jona," *I.L. Seeligmann Volume*, Vol. III (Jerusalem, 1983), pp. 263–272.

mean that Jonah was concerned for the welfare of the plant – it was for himself that he was concerned! The word חו"ס is not used here in the sense of compassion, but as concern for the loss of waste or property,[70] as in rabbinic Hebrew, whose strong affinity with Jonah's language we have already noted, where the root חו"ס generally has this meaning:[71] "If one extinguishes a lamp because he fears ... he is exempt; when [he does so] to spare (כחס) the lamp, to spare the wick, or to spare the oil, he is liable" (m. Sabb 2:5). We can thus conclude that in God's final response to Jonah, He does not stress the importance of mercy, but His concern lest His world and His creatures be destroyed.

This explanation of the significance of the dialogue between God and Jonah contributes to the understanding of the message of the entire book. As we have noted, it is God's qualities which are the focal point of Jonah's ire; his prior knowledge of God's response to the people of Nineveh, he claimed, had led him to flee in the first place, in an attempt to escape his prophetic responsibilities. Among the attributes of God mentioned here is one which also appears in Joel 2:13, but is not found elsewhere in similar catalogues.[72] This is God's quality of "renouncing punishment." As this was a "new" attribute, it is possible that Jonah's criticism was directed specifically against it. For it, without doubt, was the cause of his refusal to assume his prophetic task, lest he be denounced as an imposter,[73] when his prediction of doom (1:2) did not come to pass.[74] Moreover, this attribute is revealed when God decides to forgive Nineveh and so aroused Jonah's anger. The people of Nineveh say: "Who knows but that God may turn and relent (ונחם)" (3:9), and the author directly follows this with the statement: "And God renounced the punishment (וינחם על הרעה ...)". Jonah's objections were thus directed against

---

70   The exception is Gen 45:20 ועינכם אל תחס על כליכם.

71   Because of the importance of this point, I have included here a complete list of references: mHag 2:1; mErechin 8:4; mKil 6:8 ; mNeg 12:5; tErechin 4:25 (2x); tDem 1:1; t'Erub 11:21; tSebu 1:2.

72   Cf. Exod 20:5–6 = Deut 5:9–10; Exod 34:6–7; Num 14:17–18; Deut 7:9–10; Nah 1:2–3; Ps 86:5, 15; 103:8; 111:4; 145:8; Neh 9:17, 31; 2Chr 30–9.

73   Pirke de Rabbi Eliezer, chap. 33.

74   For this explanation, see S.D. Goitein, *Bible Studies*[2] (Heb.), (Tel Aviv, 1967), pp. 80–87, esp. p. 84, and earlier, idem, "Some Observations on Jonah," *JPOS* 17 (1937), pp. 63–77, ad p. 77.

God's attribute of renouncing punishment, especially since the punishment had been proclaimed by a prophet.[75] God responds with the example of the plant. Does Jonah regret the plant's death – the plant which grew overnight and for which he toiled not? How much more should God regret the destruction of Nineveh, its inhabitants and animals! There are many things in this world which are dear to God, and which are far more important than the empty satisfaction of fulfilling something which "He had spoken to bring" (3:10, cf. NJPS). The fulfillment of a prophecy already decreed is only one small detail in God's world order, and God may relent when it is a question of the existence of His great city[76] "in which there are more than a hundred and twenty thousand persons . . . and many beasts as well" (4:11).

Prophecies, primarily those of imminent destruction decreed by God's prophets, do not always necessarily come to pass because God often has other priorities.[77] This interpretation of the teaching of the

75 So the Midrash in *Pirke de Rabbi Eliezer,* trans. G. Friedlander (London, 1916; reprinted N.Y., 1975), chap. 10, pp. 65–66:
> On the fifth day Jonah fled before his God. Why did he flee? Because on the first occasion when (God) sent him to restore the border of Israel, his words were fulfilled, as it is said, "And he restored the border of Israel from the entering in of Hamath" (2 Kings xiv 25). On the second occasion (God) sent him to Jerusalem to (prophesy that He would) destroy it. But the Holy One, blessed be He, did according to the abundance of His tender mercy and repented of the evil (decree), and He did not destroy it; thereupon they called him a lying prophet. On the third occasion (God) sent him against Nineveh to destroy it. Jonah argued with himself, saying, I know that the nations are nigh to repentance, now they will repent [and the Holy One, blessed by He, will direct His anger against Israel.] And is it not enough for me that Israel should call me a lying prophet; but shall also the nations of the world (do likewise)? Therefore, behold, I will escape from His presence to a place where His glory is not declared.

In my opinion, the bracketed words, "And the Holy One, blessed be He, will direct his anger against Israel," are not an integral part of the text. If not an interpolation, they were taken from the earlier source ySanh 11:5 (above, n. 65), even though the latter had explained Jonah's motives for his flight in quite a different way.

76 On ל-genetivus, see the dictionaries, e.g., *KB,* p. 464; *BDB,* p. 513, see also above, n. 9.

77 This explanation was favored by Goitein (above, n. 74); E. Bickerman, *Four Strange Books of the Bible* (New York, 1967), pp. 1–49: "Jonah, or the Unfulfilled Prophecy"; Rofé (above, n. 63); G.I. Emmerson, "Another Look at the Book of Jonah," *ExT* 88 (1976), pp. 86–88; A.S. van der Woude (above, n. 69); Z. Shazar, "The Book of Jonah" (Heb.), in B.Z. Luria, ed. ירמידו בספר עיונים (n.p., n.d.), Vol. 2, pp. 229–237.

Book of Jonah enables it to be understood against the background of the discussions and doubts regarding the fulfillment of the Divine Word which reached their peak in the sixth and fifth centuries BCE, i.e., the period immediately preceding the composition of the Book of Jonah. This question, however, was not an innovation of the Exilic era, its traces can be noted in earlier biblical literature.

We have noted [78] that the belief that the Word of God as proclaimed by His prophets always came to pass took root in Israelite historiography as early as the ninth century BCE. This belief was based on the primitive, mantic character of prophecy and enjoyed wide acceptance, often being taken for granted by the people. Saul's servant, for example, when suggesting to his master that they go to Samuel to find the lost asses, describes the "Man of God" as highly esteemed: "everything that he says comes true" (1 Sam 9:6). On the other hand, when David's men see Saul fall into their power in the cave, they say to David: "This is the day of which the Lord said to you: 'I will deliver your enemy into your hands; you can do with him as you please' " (1 Sam 24:4). Just as all the predictions of God's prophet are fulfilled, so everything that happens in the sphere of human affairs must have been foreseen: "The day of which the Lord said to you." In prophecy this principle is brought to its logical conclusion by insisting that God, unlike mortals, never goes back on His word. Thus Balaam says: "God is not man to be capricious, or mortal to change His mind. Would He speak and not act, promise and not fulfill?" (Num 23:19); and so Samuel: "The Glory of Israel does not deceive or change His mind, for He is not human that He should change His mind" (1 Sam 15:29). In both these statements remorse or reconsidering an affirmed decision is considered lying or trickery: the Lord, as the God of Truth, *must* fulfill His Word!

This idea was also expressed, in a more abstract form, by the writers themselves. The author of the story of Samuel's prophetic call (1 Sam 3:1–4:1a) states: "Samuel grew up and the Lord was with him: He did not leave any of Samuel's predictions unfulfilled" (3:19); [79] this was

---

78   See above, Chapter 5; A. Rofé, "Isaiah 55:6–11: The Problem of the Fulfillment of Prophecies and Trito-Isaiah" (Heb.), *Proceedings of the Sixth World Congress of Jewish Studies* (Jerusalem, 1977), Vol. 1, Hebrew Section, pp. 213–221.

79   The idiom in this form – probably its original – appears also in 2Kgs 10:10. Without the word ארצה it is also found in Josh 21:23; 23:14; 1Kgs 8:56. A fulfilled

intended to apply to Samuel's entire prophetic career.[80] This principle
also underlies the story of Jehu's revolt (2 Kgs 9:1–10, 28) in which
it is a refrain in Jehu's justification of his actions. In the first account
of Sennacherib's campaign (2 Kgs 18:17–19, 9a, 36–37), prophecy
and fulfillment are juxtaposed. We have already seen how this principle was employed by the two editors of the Book of Kings – one from
the Northern Kingdom, and a later editor who wrote in Judah shortly
after the fall of Jerusalem. This was the prevalent view among the
Deuteronomists, and is therefore also found in the Deuteronomistic
edition of the Book of Joshua. The conquest of the Land represents
the fulfillment of the Word of God as expressed in His promises to
the Patriarchs: "The Lord gave to Israel the whole country which He
had sworn to their fathers . . . Not one of the good things which the
Lord had promised to the House of Israel was lacking. Everything was
fulfilled" (Josh 21:41–43; cf. 23:14–15).[81] In Deuteronomy itself we
find the unequivocal statement that the truth of a prophecy is proved
through its fulfillment (Deut 18:21–22).

Deutero-Isaiah, the prophet of consolation of the Babylonian
exiles, in the mid-sixth century BCE, was an outspoken advocate of
the school which taught that "the Word of our God is always fulfilled!"
(Isa 40:8). In his opinion this quality represents the main difference
between God and man. God's pronouncements are similar to acts of
creation – the things predicted already exist, the only question being
when God will reveal them to man: "I have spoken, so I will bring it
to pass; I have designed it, so I will complete it" (Isa 46:11). This
quality also differentiates God from the idols of the pagan nations,
who are powerless: "Their works are nullity" (Isa 41:29), and there is
no doubt that they are incapable of revealing the course of future
events (41:22). Just as this quality enables God to be distinguished

prophecy is likened to a living person standing upright, an unfulfilled prophecy
to a dead man lying on the ground (Judg 3:25; 1Sam 17:49) or to one fainting
(1Sam 28:20).

80   There is no doubt that 1Sam 3:19–20 does not refer only to Samuel's prophecy
regarding the house of Eli, but, like the whole of chapter 3, to Samuel's prophetic
dedication. This is also true of vv 3:21–4:1a. The succeeding (4:1b–7:2) is not a
continuation of chap. 3, but derives from a different source, and deals with the
history of the Ark, neither mentioning nor alluding to Samuel.
81   Cf. I.L. Seeligmann, "From Historic Reality to Historiosophic Conception in the
Bible" (Heb.), *Peraqim* 2 (Jerusalem, 1969–1974), pp. 273–313.

from the false pagan gods, it also proves the truthfulness of His prophets, as opposed to the pagan sorcerers. God "annuls the omens of diviners and makes fools of the augurs, turns sages back and makes nonsense of their knowledge but confirms the word of His servants (read: עבדיו) and fulfills the prediction of His messengers" (44:25-26). Fully in keeping with this idea is the opinion of Deutero-Isaiah that Israel's repentance has little effect on the question of its redemption. It is God who for His own sake "wipes their transgressions away" (43:25, 44:22), redeems Israel and simultaneously calls upon them to repent: "Come back to Me, for I redeem you" (44:22).

Towards the end of the First Temple period, however, a change occurred in the perception of the nature of prophecy. Through the influence of the classical prophets – Hosea, Amos, Isaiah, and Micah – the ethical-admonitory aspect of prophecy became predominant. This view of prophecy may also be discerned in the prophetic elements in Psalms, such as Ps 81, in the Song of Moses (Deut 32), as well as in the speeches contained in the historical books: Josh 24:1-28, Judg 6:7-10, 1 Sam 12. In these passages the prophets are portrayed as reprovers and admonishers, not as predicters. This is also true, as we have seen, of the addition to the historical narrative in 2Kgs 17:13-15. There is no reason for the preaching role to exclude that of prediction, but one or the other must have the predominant function. In Jeremiah, for example, the admonitory aspect of prophecy is explicitly stressed. There it is emphasized that any predictions made by the prophet are subject to change in accordance with the behavior of the people to whom the prophecy is addressed:

> At one moment I may decree that a nation or a kingdom shall be uprooted and pulled down and destroyed; but if that nation against which I made the decree turns back from its wickedness, I change My mind concerning the punishment I planned to bring on it. At another moment I may decree that a nation or a kingdom shall be built and planted; but if it does what is displeasing to Me and does not obey Me, then I change My mind concerning the good I planned to bestow upon it (Jer 18:7-10).

In complete conformity with the above principle, most of the prose speeches in Jeremiah stress the fact that the people possess free choice, especially with regard to their capacity for repentance (Jer 7:1-15;

11:1-8; 17:19-27; 22:1-5; 25:1-14; 26:1-19; 35; 44).[82] Both the principle and its manner of expression in the speeches were apparently the work of the Deuteronomistic editor of Jeremiah, who responded in this fashion to the prophetic viewpoint adhered to by the editors of the Book of Kings.[83]

A similar view of the function of the Word of God and of the role of the prophet who serves as His messenger is formulated in personal terms in Ezek 33:12-20, where it is stressed that the Word of God – whether predicting life or death – is completely dependent upon the behavior of its addressee after its pronouncement. This led the people to claim that:"The way of the Lord is imponderable!" (33:17, 20; לא יתכן cf. NJPS), in that it cannot be surmised in advance,[84] as it is not absolute, being dependent upon man's reactions. Ezekiel responds that this is indeed the case: the way of the Lord cannot be predicted – because man's behavior cannot be predicted: "It is their way that is imponderable!" (v 17), and God judges them in accordance with their behavior: "I will judge each one of you according to his ways, O House of Israel!" (v 20).

This controversy regarding the nature of the Word of God – whether it is absolute and destined to be fulfilled, or conditional and realized only *rebus stantibus* – was widely debated in the periods of the Exile and the Restoration. Against the background of this dispute we can understand the theological standpoint of the Book of Jonah which maintained that prophecies (at least those of destruction and doom) are invariably conditional, because in the Divine order they amount to less than the least of God's creatures.

A different, no less daring solution to this problem is provided by the anonymous prophet whose words have been preserved in Isaiah 54-66.[85] Probably a disciple of Deutero-Isaiah, Trito-Isaiah (as he is designated in biblical studies) was active, according to several

---

82   A. Feuillet, "Les sources du livre de Jonas," *RB* 54 (1947), pp 161-186, ad pp. 170-171, who pointed out the strong dependence of the Book of Jonah on the Book of Jeremiah, correctly noted that the idea that human repentance causes God to repent of the evil He had planned is similarly expressed in both books.

83   Cf. A. Rofé, "Studies on the Composition of the Book of Jeremiah" (Heb.), *Tarbiz* 44 (1975), pp. 1-29.

84   N.H. Tur-Sinai (Torczyner), "Mistaken Expressions" (Heb.), in הלשון והספר Vol. 1, (Jerusalem, 1954), p. 392.

85   See my article, above, n. 78.

indications, during the first half of the fifth century BCE, some time before Nehemiah's arrival in Jerusalem. In Isa 55:6–11 he compares the Word of God with rain and snow which descend from heaven and return not, rather soak the earth, making it fertile to bring forth seed and bread; so the Word of God, whose importance lies not in its fulfillment in a vacuum, but in the chain of events which it sets into motion: the responses of the people who hear the Word and obey it. Rather than the Word being fulfilled, it *fulfills*. Therefore, the prophet produces his parable with a call to repentance, addressed to the people in general and to the wicked in particular (55:6–7), as no verdict is final. The true purpose of the Word of God can never be known, as His thoughts are beyond human comprehension, just as the heavens are beyond the earth.

These, in my opinion, were the issues and conclusions which were generated by the discussion of the Word of God in the late biblical period, a discussion which only reflects in prophetic terms the larger theological problem: man's freedom *vis-à-vis* God's omnipotence.

4. The Man of God at Bethel [86]

There is a prophetic story in the Book of Kings which exhibits a striking similarity to the story of Jonah. This is the tale of the Man of God from Judah who prophesied at Bethel (1 Kgs 13).

The beginning and end of this story have become somewhat obscured by the late division of the Bible into chapters. The story actually begins in 1 Kgs 12:33, with a description of the dedication of the altar at Bethel by Jeroboam, King of Israel, during the feast (i.e., Sukkot) on the fifteenth day of the eighth month. As Jeroboam ascended the altar to present the first offering, the Man of God from Judah appeared. The verses preceding this particular episode do not deal with it, being concerned rather with Jeroboam's general reforms: the placing of golden calves at Bethel and Dan (12:26–30), the erection of cultic places (31a), the appointment of priests not of Levite descent from among the ranks of the people (31b), the institution of a new festival on the fifteenth day of the eighth month, the participation of the king in the cult, and the placing of priests at the

---

86 This section is an expansion and revision of the subject as discussed in my book, *Israelite Belief in Angels* (Heb.), (Jerusalem, 1979), pp. 313–329.

shrines at Bethel (32). Verse 33 is appended to the general list of innovations (26–32) and quotes from it, but focuses on this one particular incident before proceeding to describe it in detail.[87] The story ends in 13:32 with the conclusion of the story of the Man of God and the old prophet, after which the story resumes the discussion of Jeroboam's innovations: "Even after this incident, Jeroboam did not turn back from his evil way, but kept on appointing priests for the shrines from the ranks of the people . . ." (v 33). This verse employs the stylistic device of resumptive repetition[88] i.e., it repeats the last part of 12:32 in order to establish a connection between the two sections.

An appendix to this story is found in 2 Kgs 23:16–18, whose original formulation is preserved in the Septuagint.[89] It describes how the prophecy of the Man of God was fulfilled by Josiah and how the bones of the "prophet who came from Samaria" were spared desecration along with the bones of the "Man of God who came from Judah" when Josiah defiled the graves of Bethel.

The main similarities between this story and the story of Jonah are as follows: in both stories a prophet is sent to proclaim the Word of God in a foreign place, and the people in each place believe him; in both the prophet disobeys God's command, and one party (either God or the prophet) upbraids the other for his behavior (Jonah 4:2; 1 Kgs 13:20–22); in both God punishes the prophet with death, or near death and a last-minute rescue; in both God deals with the prophet through an animal (fish, lion), the animal proving to be a more faithful agent than the man, in that it obeys God's orders, even against its nature. These similarities, which show no trace of imitation on either side, suggest that these two tales are closely related in date and provenance, or even that they originated in the same circle.[90]

---

87 On the technique of related expansion, see A. Rofé, *The Book of Balaam* (Heb.), (Jerusalem, 1980), p. 86 and n. 108; a review of the preceding by Y. Zakovitch, *Kiryat Sefer* 54 (1979) (published in 1980), pp. 785–789, esp. p. 788.

88 See Rofé (n. 87), p. 55, and literature cited there.

89 The Septuagint to 2Kgs 23:16 reflects the following Hebrew text: וישלח ... ויקח את העצמות מן הקברים, וישרף על המזבח ויטמאהו כדבר ה', אשר קרא איש האלהים/בעמד ירבעם בחג על המזבח. ויפן וישא את עיניו אל קבר איש האלהים/אשר קרא את הדברים האלה. There is no doubt that this was the original text which was corrupted through homoeoteleuton.

90 A third story, bearing points of similarity to the above two, is the tale of "Balaam, the Ass, and the Angel" (Num 22:22–35); see Rofé (above, n. 87), pp. 52–54.

At any rate, the stories of Jonah and of the Man of God seem to be nearly contemporary. The latter story cannot have been composed prior to the end of the monarchy. It speaks of Samaria as the name of a region (1 Kgs 13:32; 2 Kgs 23:18), a title it received only during the Assyrian period, after 722 BCE.[91] It makes no mention of the calves at Bethel, "the sin which Jeroboam son of Nebat caused Israel to commit"; moreover, it was only inserted as an addition to the account of "the sins of Jeroboam," i.e., his cultic innovations, as is demonstrated by the stylistic features of attached expansion and resumptive repetition (as shown above). All this points to a very late date of composition for the story, and indicates that it was completely unrelated to the first edition of the Book of Kings written in Northern Israel, which stressed Jeroboam's cultic sins.[92] Our story mentions Josiah by name and details his acts in Bethel (1 Kings 13:2; 2 Kgs 23:16–18); it must therefore have been composed after the reform of 622 BCE. The linguistic criteria, however, point to a much later date.

One late feature is the use of the term סע"ד (by itself) in the sense of eating (13:7).[93] Classical biblical Hebrew employs the term סע"ד לב (Gen 18:5; Judg 19:5, 8; Ps 104:15). The verb סע"ד appears alone elsewhere only in rabbinic literature (b, Erub 53b; Deut Rab 9:1). The same is true of the term מתת which appears in late biblical sources only (Ezek 46:5, 11; Ps 25:14; Eccl 3:13; 5:18). Classical biblical Hebrew employs a special term to designate a gift given by a king to a departing subject: משאת (Gen 43:34; 2 Sam 11:8; Jer 40:5; Sir 38:2).

Another late usage is the verb לדבר where classical Hebrew would have used לאמר (as in 13:7, 12, 22, and possibly in v 17, if we read כי דבר אלי בדבר ה' etc. – cf. v 18).[94] This usage is characteristic of the late chapters of the Book of Kings (1 Kgs 20:11; 21:5–6; 2 Kgs 1:3–16).[95] It seems to derive from the discontinuance, in Second Temple Hebrew, of such constructions as וידבר . . . לאמר or וידבר . . .

91 C.F. Burney, *Notes on the Hebrew Text of the Book of Kings* (Oxford, 1903, reprint N.Y., 1970), *ad loc.*

92 See above, chap. 5, sect. 5. In the view of A. Jepsen, "Gottesmann und Prophet: Anmerkungen zur Kapitel I. Könige 13," *Fs. G. von Rad* (Munich, 1971), pp. 171–182, this story was intended as a protest against the reconstruction of the altar in Bethel; the city itself still flourished in the sixth century BCE.

93 A. Šanda, *Die Bücher der Könige* [EHAT] (Münster in Westf., 1911–12), *ad loc.*

94 O. Thenius, *Die Bücher der Könige erklärt²* [KEHAT] (Leipzig 1873), p. 189.

95 For additional references see above, chap. 2, n. 24.

ויאמר in which וידבר appears before a direct address. This would have led a later writer attempting to imitate classical style to err and use וידבר omitting the following ויאמר.

Other examples of late authorship are phrases such as כי כן צוה אתי בדבר ה' (13:9), כי דבר אלי בדבר ה' (13:17), instead of the classical usage of כי כן צוני ה' ; כי ה' דבר אלי respectively. The former constructions are apparently an attempt to avoid anthropomorphism, as in the Aramaic Targum's מימרא דה'.[96]

It thus appears that the account of the Man of God was composed at the beginning of the Second Temple period, about the same time as the Book of Jonah. The fact that only a few instances of late linguistic forms occur here, as compared with Jonah, indicates that its author was more successful than the author of Jonah in imitating archaic Hebrew, and betrayed himself only through semantic errors, rather than in vocabulary or syntax.

Its thematic similarity with the Book of Jonah naturally raises the question of the *gattung* of the story of the Man of God. It is neither biography nor history, as its characters are anonymous and its narrative is studded with miracles; neither is it a *legenda* because veneration of an anonymous holy man makes no sense at all. Moreover, the Man of God here is not praised but castigated because of his sin, and he himself is the object of more miracles than he performs (13:24).[97] This leads us to assume that it was intended as a parable: the dynamics of the story are between the prophet and his God; in consequence the human protagonist is humbled, and he is transformed into a passive object of God's action.

Yet if this story is a parable, it is a moot point whether it intended to convey a moral. The opposite seems true; the story seems to express a doubtful moral level. The Man of God falls victim to an act of premeditated trickery: returning home from Bethel he is ensnared by

---

96   Thenius (above, n. 94), p. 188.
97   Though the suggestion has sometimes been made that a *legenda* about a Man of God who performed miracles at the altar of Bethel is submerged in this story and can still be distinguished in its first few verses. See I. Plein, "Erwägungen zur Ueberlieferung von I Reg 11^{38} – 14^{20}," *ZAW* 78 (1966), pp. 8–24; E. Würthwein, "Die Erzählung von Gottesmann aus Juda in Bethel – Zur Composition von 1 Kön 13," *Wort und Geschichte – Fs K. Elliger* (Neukirchen-Vluyn, 1973), pp. 181–189. In any event, we are concerned here not with the sources of the story but with its final form.

an old local prophet; he returns, eats and drinks at Bethel despite God's prohibition, and pays for his disobedience with his life. The prophet who lied to him, on the other hand, was immediately granted a prophetic revelation (13:20–22) and was later rewarded with the opportunity to save his remains on the day of retribution. Can this story teach a moral lesson, or does it merely reflect the low moral standards of its authors?[98]

To understand this story, we must begin with the significance of the prohibitions laid upon the Man of God. They are mentioned so many times both in command and breach – vv 9, 16, 17, 18, 19, 22 – that there is no doubt of their primary role in the story. The Man of God was forbidden to eat bread and to drink water while at Bethel; this seems to include all food and drink. Furthermore, he was forbidden "to return." Verses 9–10 and 17 seem to indicate that the prohibition was against returning to Judah along the same road he had taken to Bethel. But other verses indicate otherwise: "I may not go back with you . . . and may not eat bread or drink water" (v 16); "Bring him back with you to your house, that he may eat bread and drink water" (v 18); "So he went back with him, and he ate bread and drank water in his house" (v 19); "but have gone back and eaten bread and drunk water" (v 22). The Septuagint codices Alexandrinus and Vaticanus and the Syro-Hexaplaric version of verse 17 read as follows: "You shall not eat bread or drink water here, nor shall you *return there* by the road on which you came." According to these the primary prohibition concerned the return to Bethel after his departure, which contradicts the version presented in vv 9b–10.[99] If we want to include these two verses, we must assume that the Man of God was forbidden to return to any place where he had already been, and that this applied to Bethel as well as to the road leading to that city.

What was the reason for these prohibitions? We may consider them as relating either to the messenger, the Man of God, or to the mission, the prediction of the destruction of Bethel. Most scholars have preferred the second alternative: the prohibitions refer to the unequivocal rejection of Bethel from the moment that God spoke

---

98   J. Gray, *I and II Kings* [OTL] (London, 1963); M. Noth, *Könige,* 1 Teilband [BK] (Neukirchen, 1968).

99   See A.B. Ehrlich, מקרא כפשוטו, Vol. II (Berlin, 1900), *ad loc.*

against it.[100] They represent a kind of sign.[101] With it the process of Bethel's ultimate destruction is started. The difficulty with this interpretation is that the Man of God has no objection to praying for Jeroboam, who is the symbol par excellence of the sin of Bethel and its disaster. The Man of God, moreover, converses freely with him and with the old prophet. In contrast, the prohibition against eating and drinking is total. It is phrased in such a way that the Man of God is specifically forbidden to partake of any food or drink – even his own, and not only food provided for him. This fact seems to argue in favor of the first interpretation: that the prohibitions are related to the Man of God's role as messenger, rather than to the message.[102]

A close analogy to the messenger who neither eats nor drinks is found in both biblical and post-biblical literature – that of the angel. Manoah says to the angel of God: "Let us detain you and prepare a kid for you. But the angel of the Lord said to Manoah: 'If you detain me, I shall not eat your food; and if you prepare it – present it as a burnt offering to the Lord.' "[103] Rather than partrake of Manoah's kid, the angel leaped skyward in the flames of the holocaust (Judg 13:15–20). Though the angel who appeared before Gideon did not explicitly refuse to partake of his offering, he did not in fact eat anything, but instead set the offering on fire with the tip of his staff (Judg 6:17–27). This view of angelic behavior is also found in Tobit, whose date of composition was apparently close to that of the parable of the Man of God, no less than the accounts in Judg 6:11–24 and 13.[104] When the angel Raphael is about to take leave of Tobit and

---

100 See my book (above, n. 86), p. 319, for a summary and literature, and also M.A. Klopfenstein, "I Könige 13," *Parrhesia, K. Barth zur 80 Geburtstag,* (Zurich, 1966), pp. 639–672.

101 This position has recently been defended at length by U. Simon, "I Kings 13: A Prophetic Sign – Denial and Persistence," *HUCA* 47 (1976), pp. 81–117. Simon, however, has conveniently disregarded the uncomfortable fact that the *sign,* אות, such a central idea in prophetic literature, is not once mentioned in 1Kgs 13. Vv 3 and 5, which mention a portent (מופת), are regarded, by Simon as well, as additions.

102 Thenius (above, n. 94), p. 191.

103 I prefer to punctuate the verse thus; cf. *NJPS.*

104 The story of the Man of God, like the Book of Jonah, can be attributed to the beginning of the fifth century BCE (see above regarding the similarity between the two stories). The Book of Tobit has been variously dated from the fourth to the second centuries BCE. See M.M. Schumpp, *Das Buch Tobias* [EHAT] (Münster i. Westf., 1933); D. Hilier, "The Book of Toviah," (Heb.), in הספרים החיצוניים, ed.

Tobias he says to them: "All these days did I appear unto you; and I did neither eat nor drink, but it was a vision ye yourselves saw" (Tob 12:19).[105] This belief that angels neither ate nor drank was so widespread during the Second Temple period that in homiletic expositions of the old, semi-mythical[106] story of the angels visiting Abraham at the terebinths of Mamre, they are portrayed as not actually eating at all. This view is also expressed in *The Testament of Abraham,*[107] in Josephus' work,[108] and in a dispute between sages preserved in bBMes 86b: "R. Tanhum b. Hanilai said: One should never depart from custom, as when Moses ascended to the heavens he ate not, and when the ministering angels descended to earth they ate. But did they indeed eat? Rather say that they seemed to eat."[109] This analogy with stories about angels dating from First and especially from Second Temple times (at the beginning of which the story about the Man of God was composed) provides us with the reason for the prohibition against eating and drinking: the desire to equate the Man of God to the heavenly angels of popular legend.

The above-mentioned stories in Judges 6 and 13 and Tobit 12 provide a further analogy with the story of the Man of God. It is the characteristic of angels to disappear suddenly and it was this trait of

A. Kahana, Vol. 2 (Tel Aviv, 1937). Both present convincing reasons for preferring an earlier date. This view is also supported by D.C. Simpson, "The Book of Tobit," in *The Apocrypha and Pseudepigrapha of the Old Testament,* ed. R.H. Charles, Vol. 1 (London, 1913), who relies, *inter alia,* on arguments from the study of Persian religion which I am unable to check.

105 I prefer this reading, found in mss. A and B, to the reading of ms. S: "And ye behold me that I have eaten nothing but a vision hath appeared to you," since the statement seems to emphasize that although Tobit and his wife saw the angel eat, it was only an illusion, and he in fact ate nothing.
106 See H. Gunkel, *Genesis übersetzt und erklärt²* [GHAT] (Göttingen, 1902); J. Skinner, *Commentary on Genesis²* [ICC] (Edinburgh, 1930).
107 See the edition of M.R. James, *The Testament of Abraham* (Cambridge, 1892). Here the angel Michael eats with Abraham, but the Lord sends a spirit which devours everything. For views on the eating habits of angels see L. Ginzberg, "Abraham, Testament of," *Jewish Encyclopaedia,* Vol. 1 (1907), cols. 93–96, ad col. 94a. The Book of Jubilees (16:1–4) tells of the angels' appearance at the Terebinths of Mamre, but omits all details of the feast prepared for them by Abraham.
108 Ant. Jud. 1:197.
109 So Gen. Rab. 45; Lev Rab. 34:8; Ec. Rab. 3:14; Pseudo-Jonathan to Gen 18:8 (ודמי ליה כאילו אכלין). On the entire question see also L. Ginzberg, *Legends of the Jews,* Vol. 5 (Philadelphia, PA 1942–6), p. 236.

the angel in Judges 6 which indicated to Gideon that he had in fact been in the presence of an angel: "And the angel of the Lord vanished from his sight. Then Gideon realized that it was an angel of the Lord . . ." (6:21–22). So too with Manoah and his wife: "As the flames leapt up from the altar toward the sky, the angel of the Lord ascended in the flames of the altar, while Manoah and his wife looked on; and they flung themselves on their faces to the ground. The angel of the Lord was not seen again by Manoah and his wife [cf. NJPS]. Manoah then realized that it had been an angel of the Lord." The positive identification of the mysterious party as an angel is reached not through his performance of miraculous acts – for there are many agents of miracles – but by his marvelous and swift departure. An abrupt departure is also made by Raphael, the angel of Tob 12:21: "And they rose up and saw him no more."[110] The injunction against the Man of God returning to places he had already visited is thus aimed at equating his behavior with that of the celestial angels of folk legends.

In light of these analogies, the Man of God in this story is in fact a (human) *angel of the Lord.* This role is also reflected in the precise nature of the story's terminology. The prophet from Bethel is consistently called "prophet," while the visitor from Judah is always called "Man of God." These titles are not interchangeable here, as they are in the stories of Elijah and Elisha.[111] By the use of these terms the author apparently wished to underline his conviction that the man *belongs* to God, much as an angel belongs to his Sender. The Man of God is an *angel,* but a mortal one.[112]

---

110 In Ms.S: "And they rose up and could no longer see him."

111 The text of 13:23 is corrupt and the Septuagint version should be followed in reading ויחבש לו החמור. וישב וילך וימצאהו אריה.

112 There are a significant number of elements in the appearance of the Man of God which seem to be borrowed from angelological legends: (A) The Man of God proclaims: "A son shall be born to the House of David, Josiah by name." There is nothing analogous to this in prophecy or apocalypse (in Isa 7 the name is a sign), but similar language is used in foretelling names by God and His angels (Gen 16:11; 17:19). See Mekilta d'R Ishmael, Piska 16; Gen. Rab. 45:8. (B) Other expressions employed here are also strikingly similar to those of angelological descriptions; cf. v 14 with similar wording in Judg 13:11. (C) The old man finds the Man of God sitting under a terebinth, similar to the angel who appeared to Gideon in Judg 6:11. This is not merely a figure of speech. One of the common sites of divine revelation, and later angelophanies, is the shade of a tree; see R. de Vaux,

Thus, we can also attempt an explanation of the second difficulty in this story – the sin committed by the Man of God.[113] It now becomes clear that in returning to Bethel, and in eating and drinking there, the Man of God is not only disobeying a mere order (the counter-order given him by the prophet of Bethel could have cancelled his earlier instructions), but is completely undermining his role as a messenger. By divesting himself of his angelic stature, he in effect altogether denies his dispatcher. The Divine protection which had preserved the human messenger in his previous confrontation is removed, he is killed by a lion, who proves to be a more loyal messenger. In any case, because of its content alone, the message of the prophet from Bethel should not have been believed. To use an analogy, it is as if a priest or king were commanded to divest themselves of the trappings of their office in the process of establishing their legitimacy – a self-contradictory action. The old prophet himself, by inviting the Man of God to eat with him, shows that he cannot possibly be, as he claims, "a prophet like you"; the Man of God, being an angel, could never have eaten with him in Bethel.

This conclusion is confirmed by a study of the prophetic writings themselves. The familiar forms of prophetic speech – "thus said the Lord," "declares the Lord" – which have been recognized as reflecting a messenger formula, indicate how the prophets perceived their role.[114] This concept is explicitly applied to themselves by Isaiah, Jeremiah, and Ezekiel, who in their inaugural visions use the verb של״ח "to send" to describe their status *vis-à-vis* God (Isa 6:8; Jer 1:7; Ezek 2:3;3:5–6). This verb was also popular among the editors of

Les institutions de l'Ancien Testament, ii (Paris, 1960), pp. 97–100. This then is an additional characteristic of angelology which was deliberately transferred to the Man of God.

113 Most commentators agree that the Man of God should not have trusted the prophet from Bethel, but only the prophecy which he himself received. But this would be a strange message; was it ever really forbidden for prophets to believe their colleagues? Others have claimed that angelic revelation is inferior to direct revelation. But such a rationalistic claim would not have been made by the author of this story had he believed in the existence and sanctity of angels. Gersonides correctly compares our story with the announcements made to Abraham in Gen 22, in which an angel commands Abraham to disregard an order previously given to him directly by God.

114 See C. Westermann, *Basic Forms of Prophetic Speech* [Engl. transl.] (Philadelphia, PA, 1967), esp. pp. 90–128.

Jeremiah's prose sermons (7:25; 14:14–15; 23:21, 32; 25:4, 15; 26:5; 27:15; 29:19; 35:15; 44:4). In addition, in the exilic and post exilic periods the prophets are called מלאכים (angels, messengers) by themselves (Isa 44:26), by their editors (Hag 1:13; Mal 1:1), and by the later historiographers and authors (2 Chr 36:16; Ps 151:4 LXX).[115]

A further point requires consideration. Once we have determined that in accordance with the concepts popular among the classical prophets and their disciples, the Man of God was perceived as a messenger of God, we must inquire whether this mortal angel *supplemented* or *replaced* the heavenly angels. This question may be answered deductively by examining the attitude towards the belief in angels in several sections of biblical literature. Such an examination indicates that in all of classical prophetical literature, with the exception of Zechariah 1–6, angels are nowhere mentioned as intermediaries between God and man. The only exception, the mention of the angel in Hosea 12:5, seems to be directed towards negating the role of an angel as Jacob's deliverer.[116] This situation accords well with the antiangelological trend occurring in some biblical books. Deuteronomy and the Deuteronomistic literature view the prophets as the sole messengers of God: there are no angels, no dreams, no priestly divinations with the Urim and Tummim (Deut 18:9ff). Deut 6–7 quotes Exod 23:20–33 in full, but for the portrayal of the angel who led Israel through the desert and into the Holy Land, a prominent figure in Exodus, which has been omitted in Deuteronomy. All acts are performed by God Himself, who accompanies Israel's camp. This is also the opinion of the Priestly source. In Exod 12:13, P quotes an earlier source still preserved in Exod 12:23, but omits the destroying angel: "I will pass over you, so that no plague will destroy you (ולא יהיה בכם נגף למשחית) when I strike the land of Egypt," instead of "The Lord will pass over the door and not let the Destroyer enter and plague your home (ולא יתן המשחית לבא אל בתיכם לנגף)." The plague (נגף) sent directly by God replaces the Destroyer (משחית), an independent agent.

---

115 In the longer Hebrew version of this psalm found at Qumran, Samuel is named, and called God's prophet נביאו not his angel / messenger. See J. A. Sanders, *The Psalms Scroll of Qumran Cave 11 (11QPsa.)* [*DJD* IV] (Oxford, 1965), pp. 49, 54–64.

116 See the discussion and literature cited in my book (above, n. 86), pp. 239–254, and the summary below of its conclusions.

It seems, therefore, that in the episode at Bethel, as elsewhere in the Bible, the prophet – the Man of God – replaces the angel and takes over his characteristics, thus negating the existence of heavenly angels and letting the prophets assume their role. Such an assumption contributes greatly to our understanding of the story. Only once in the story is there a reference to an angelic revelation; it is made by the old prophet from Bethel in his seduction of the Man of God: "I am a prophet, too, and an angel said to me by command of the Lord" (v 18)! If we are not mistaken in attributing antiangelological tendencies to the author of this story, then the old prophet's speech could be understood as a falsehood not only because of its message, but also because of its wording. The Man of God should have perceived this immediately. The fact that he allowed himself to be enticed to return to Bethel, to eat and drink there, admits of no extenuating circumstances. The Man of God was guilty of mortal sin.

As for the old prophet of Bethel: the author, who allows him prophetic revelation (vv 20–22), does not consider him a false prophet.[117] It is also difficult to maintain that the prophet intended to undermine the mission. Though it is twice mentioned that the Man of God flouted the command of God (vv 21, 26), there is no hint that in doing so he also confounded God's planned punishment for Bethel. If our assumptions regarding the antiangelological tendencies of the story are correct, we can understand the character of the old prophet. He was a simple man, a naive believer in primitive ideas, such as heavenly angels, and thus on a much lower level than the Man of God, who was a true believer according to the concepts held by the author of the story. The old man, however, has no malicious intent; he merely wants to host his honored colleague in accordance with proper convention. His pursuit of the Man of God is a quest for the honor

---

117 If such a concept existed at all in biblical times; contra Josephus, *Ant. Jud.* 8:236; Targum (נבי שקרא); yMoed Katan 3:5; Seder Eliyahu Rabba 12; Song Rab. 2:16; and later I. Benzinger, *Die Bücher der Könige erklärt* [KHAT] (Freiburg i.B., etc., 1899); K. Barth, *Exegese von 1. Könige 13* [Biblische Studien, Heft 10] (Neukirchen, 1955), pp. 15,17. Barth carried this line of thought much further than his predecessors. But this view had been convincingly rejected by Don Isaac Abarbanel in his commentary, *ad loc.*, later followed by Ehrlich מקרא כפשוטו, Vol. II (Berlin, 1900). *ad loc.*, and H. Gressmann, *Die älteste Geschichtsschreibung und Prophetie Israels* [SATA²] (Göttingen, 1922), *ad loc.*

which will accrue to him as the host of he who has brought the Word of God to Bethel. This can be recognized in his statement to the Man of God: "I am a prophet, too . . ." (v 18) – he compares himself with the Man of God almost by chance. The Man of God, furthermore, had demonstrated that his prayer was efficacious (v 6), thus his presence had become desirable, as he might benefit his host. These three qualities – hospitality, pursuit of honor, and hope of blessing – explain why the old prophet is so anxious to receive the Man of God, why he pursues him, and why he lies to him about an angel who never existed and certainly never appeared to him. But this lie in itself was not a sin; the Bible is replete with small lies told for accepted reasons, even by prophets or important personalities.[118] Thus the old prophet was not punished, yet the Man of God, who sinned by trusting the prophet, was. By ignoring the crude, common lie about the angel, he violated his trust as a priveleged true believer and messenger of the Lord.

The lesson taught by this parable is, therefore, that the Man of God owes his Master blind obedience, total subjugation of will and self-abnegation.[119] But even more, it stresses the fundamental difference between the prophet and other people: he is an angel of God; he must recognize this distinction and act in accordance with it.

So far for the moral of the story. But apart from the message, the parable has its own postulates which, once recognized, promote its understanding. Such a presupposition we have identified in the opposition to belief in angels. This opposition helps understand the character of the old prophet and the nature of the sin committed by the Man of God. With time, however, belief in angels became a tenet of Pharisaic and Essenic Judaism; the antiangelological assumptions of this author were forgotten; an important aspect of the parable could no longer be understood.

* * *

118 David to Ahimelekh (1Sam 21:1–9); Elisha to the army of Aram (2Kgs 6:19); Jeremiah to the nobles (Jer 38:26–27).
119 Thenius (above, n. 94), p. 191, writes: "Die Erzählung sollte nach der Abisicht ihres Verf. die Nothwendigkeit des unbedingten, durch nichts sich irren lassenden, Gehorsams der Propheten gegen J.s. Gebot... darthun..."

The prophetic paradigm and parable reflect the grappling of both early and later disciples of the classical prophets with the central issue of prophecy and prophets. Our examination has shown that these included the manner of prophetic inspiration, the fulfillment of the Word of God, and the status of the prophet. It is not surprising that interest in such issues heightened toward the end of the era of prophecy. It was the impact of the great classical prophets which inspired the later discussion of issues relating to prophecy. The evidence indicates that these stories should be attributed to the sixth-fifth centuries BCE. Though this date detracts from the value of these narratives as historical sources for the political study of the Judean and Israelite kingdoms, it restores to them their original status as important documents for the study of biblical religious thought. It is in this light that they must be read and understood.

Chapter Nine

THE EPIC – ELIJAH AND THE LORD'S STRUGGLE AGAINST BAAL

Our discussion so far may have created the impression that the authors of the prophetic *legenda* were completely free to edit the transmitted material they received as they saw fit. A political incident in which a prophet was involved, for example, might be presented in a number of different ways: as a political *legenda,* an ethical *legenda,* a prophetic biography or prophetic historiography. This impression, however, is only partially true. There is no doubt that the manner in which the stories were handed down as well as the ideas of the authors greatly influenced the finished composition. But the principal factor in shaping the story and its focal point was the prophet. By virtue of an extraordinary personality, he made a deep impact on his contemporaries which provided the impetus for the literary creation. Moreover, the ideas of the holy man found acceptance among people who later recorded them together with his activities. Thus the literary category of the story focusing on the prophet was sometimes determined by personality – his ideas and actions – no less than by his words.

It is in this manner that we can understand the lengthy account presented in 1 Kgs 16:29-19:18, of the struggle of the Lord and his prophet Elijah against the Tyrian Baal and Queen Jezebel.[1] The mentioned cir-

---

1 For an excellent treatment of a major part of this narrative (chaps. 17 and 18) employing the "close reading" method, see U. Simon, "Elijah's War on Baal Worship – Unity and Structure of the Story (1 Kgs 17–18)", in *Studies in Bible and Exegesis Arie Toeg in Memoriam* (Heb.), (Ramat Gan, 1980), pp. 51–118. For the principles governing the use of this method, see M. Weiss, "Die Methode der 'Total-Interpretation'," *SVT* 22 [*Congress Volume Uppsala, 1971*] (Leiden, 1972), pp. 88–112; idem, *The Bible from Within,* (Jerusalem, 1984).

cumscription of the section seems to be appropriate. The introduction, 16:29–17:1, presents the main characters – Ahab, Jezebel, and Elijah – as well as the crux of the matter, the introduction into Israel of Baal worship in the wake of the marriage of Ahab and Jezebel. Without the introduction of these elements in 16:29–33, Elijah's statement in 17:1 makes no sense, nor do the subsequent events. The author of the introductory section, who made use of earlier sources, afforded this section a message of stylistic unity: Ahab vexed *the Lord, God of Israel* more than all the kings of Israel who came *before* him (16:33, cf. 16:30b); Elijah opens his message proclaiming: "By the life of *the Lord, God of Israel, before* whom I stood" (17:1). On the other hand, 16:34, which describes the rebuilding of Jericho, is wholly out of context and disrupts the continuity. This verse, which is lacking in the Lucianic recension of the Septuagint, was transferred here at a later date from the end of Joshua, chap. 6, where it still appears in all the major manuscripts of the Septuagint.[2]

The *legenda* (17:17–24) which relates the resurrection of the Zarephathite widow's son is not an integral part of the narrative, as has been demonstrated above in the discussion of the ethical *legenda*.[3]

The story ends in 19:18 with God's announcement that the struggle against Baal would continue into the next generation. This proclamation is in perfect accord with the preceding story, and presents a fitting conclusion to the account of Elijah's activity. Verses 19:19–21, in contrast, do not belong to this composition. Taking Elisha from his oxen was not done in fulfillment of God's command to Elijah to appoint a prophetic successor (v 16). Here Elisha was taken to be Elijah's servant, nothing more. His transition from servant to prophet will occur only after Elijah's ascension, and without the latter's intervention (2Kgs

---

2   See above, chap. 5, n. 43 and cf. S. Holmes, *Joshua: the Hebrew and Greek Texts* (Cambridge, 1914), p. 37.

3   Above, chap. 7, sect. 3. Simon (above, n. 1) strongly defended the view that this section was an integral part of the larger story. I cannot accept this contention. On p. 75, for example, he explained 1Kgs 17:24: "And the word of the Lord in your mouth is *true*" as "stable and enduring, harmonious and peaceful, good and merciful" in order to harmonize this declaration of the widow with the previous story (17:8–16). But these characteristics of the word of the Lord were already known to the widow from the miracle of the flour and the oil. What then is the meaning of her statement that "*Now* I know" these things?

2:9–10); thus 1 Kgs 19:19–21, together with 2 Kgs 2, evidently belong to the cycle of the Elisha stories.[4]

The unity of the composition is demonstrated to some extent by its chronological framework, as we have already noted.[5] After having proclaimed that a drought, lasting a number of years would strike the land (17:1), Elijah hides for one year in Wadi Cherith (17:7), during the second year he takes refuge with the widow at Zarephath (17:15), and in the third year he goes to confront Ahab so that rain would be sent upon the earth (18:1). The remainder of the story is a continuous narrative which describes the third year, and does not need further chronological indications.

The real proof of the story's unity, however, is reflected in the interrelation between its components. As we have noted, the introduction presents the three protagonists and the issue around which the story revolves – the worship of Baal and the drought proclaimed as consequence. The first act (17:2–16) describes how Elijah hides and how he sustains himself during the famine. In the second act (chap 18) Elijah, at the command of God, abandons his hiding place and appears in public so as to put a stop to the drought thus proving, through the fire brought down from heaven, that the Lord and not Baal is God. This act ends with what appears to be a major victory for God and Elijah. Fire descends from the heavens in the presence of the assembled nation to decide the contest. In holy awe, the people proclaim that the Lord is God; the prophets of Baal are slaughtered; Ahab, a passive participant of the entire scene, meekly submits to Elijah's orders (18:41–45).

The third act, however, turns the tables on the hopeful situation. The people disperse, and Elijah is left alone, a classic example of the popular leader who succeeds in momentarily capturing the crowd, only to be left without support and forced to face the authorities alone.[6] Jezebel plots to kill him, compelling him to flee and seek refuge again. His fear of apprehension is now increased by despair and by the sense that his mission has failed(19:4). At the end, he appears

---

4   See A. Alt, "Die literariche Herkunft von I Reg 19:19–21," *ZAW* 32 (1912), pp. 123–125.

5   Above, chap. 7, sect. 3.

6   *Pace* Gunkel and others who distinguish chap. 19 from the preceding chapters; see, for example, H. Gunkel, *Elias, Jah. und Baal* (Tübingen, 1906).

before God and explains the circumstances. God's response serves as a conclusion to the entire drama, and presents a parallel to the introduction: Elijah's efforts have failed because they were not sufficiently radical. Three new characters will now step on stage instead of the present ones: a prophet – Elisha, to replace Elijah; a king of Israel – Jehu, to replace Ahab; and a new foreign ruler – Hazael of Damascus, who takes the place of Jezebel daughter of Ethbaal king of the Sidonians. All three will be appointed by Elijah and will continue his work: leading Israel through a refining process, out of which only seven thousand persons loyal to the Lord will survive.

This lengthy literary work includes much diverse material. Relatively short *legenda* with an ethical twist (17:2–16) are introduced in the account of the period of drought to serve as a link between Elijah's inaugural proclamation and his meeting with Ahab. The episode on the Carmel comprises two clearly distinguishable elements: the bringing of rain and the confrontation with the prophets of Baal through fire. Rain is the major theme of 18:1–18 (see vv 1, 5, 17–18; the term "troubler of Israel" is an apt expression describing Elijah's responsibility for the drought and belongs here) and of 41–45. There is no mention of it in vv 19–40, which contain the confrontation theme only, with no hint of the culmination of the drought. This indicates that two originally disparate stories have been interwoven here. The story also displays discordant religio-historical ideas and perspectives: at times Ahab is blamed for the idolatry and the persecution of Elijah (16:30–33; 18:10–12, 17), at times it is Jezebel (18:4, 13, 19; 19:1–2), with Ahab portrayed sympathetically (18:41–46). In some verses the nation is depicted as being neutral (18:21–26, 36–40) while in others it is portrayed as actively sinning (19:10, 14, 18).[7] Similarly, the religious terminology employed here is not uniform. Through most of the narrative Elijah acts in accordance with the Word of God, which simultaneously instructs the prophet (17:2, 5, 8; 18:1; 19:15) and gives him power to perform miracles

---

7   Cf. O. H. Steck, *Überlieferung und Zeitgeschichte in den Elia-Erzählungen* (WMANT 26) (Neukirchen-Vluyn, 1968).

8   Cf. R. A. Carlson, "Élie à l'Horeb," *VT* 19 (1969), pp. 416–439, ad pp. 425–426; R. Smend, "Das Wort Jahwes an Elia," *VT* 25 (1975), pp. 525–543. The existence of this stratum was also noted by Z. Weissman, "On the Character of Elijah in the Biblical Legends" (Heb.), מבפנים 23 (1961), pp. 398–403.

(17:14–16; 18:36).[8] In 17:1, however, Elijah announces that the drought will end only "at my bidding," as the servant of God.[9] For this reason Ahab searches so assiduously for Elijah, to force him to wield his power to end the drought (18:10). And it is by means of Elijah's efforts that rain finally falls (18:41–45); he employs his own knowledge, independent of God's Word, to inform Ahab that "there is a rumbling of (approaching) rain." Accordingly, Elijah is described as crouching on the ground, listening for the sound of the coming rain. The prophet apparently had the ability of hearing distant sounds that was not dependent on information received by the Word of God.

A number of motifs from older biblical stories can be distinguished in this story. The last scene, 19:1–18, contains motifs reminiscent of the story of Hagar (Gen 21:14–19) as well as of the account of God's revelation to Moses at Horeb (Exod 33:18–34:8).

The entire opus is preceded by an introduction composed of material taken from the Royal Chronicle of Northern Israel and includes an account of Ahab's regnal years, and the report of his political marriage to Jezebel, the daughter of Ethbaal the King of the Sidonians.[10] A brief statement at the end of the story: "I will leave in Israel only seven thousand" recalls another item from the Royal Chronicle – Hazael's oppression of Israel during the reign of Jehoahaz: "In fact, Jehoahaz was left with a force of only fifty horsemen, ten chariots, and ten thousand foot soldiers" (2Kgs 13:7).[11] A further echo of this situation is found in 1Kgs 20:15: "And then he mustered all the troops – all the Israelites – seven thousand strong."[12] In the light of this

---

9 עמדתי לפניו means "whom I serve"; cf. 1Kgs 10:8. Later, in 18:36–37, Elijah similarly describes himself as the servant of the Lord, who acted in accordance with His word, i.e., at his command. But here Elijah does not proclaim the word of the Lord. This inconsistency was noted long ago by Don Isaac Abarbanel in his commentary (ed. Jerusalem, 1956), pp. תקעג-ד.

10 For the background of this event see H. J. Katzenstein, *The History of Tyre* (Jerusalem, 1973), pp. 144–154.

11 Seven and ten are interchangeable typological numbers, as in the account of the plagues of Egypt; see S. E. Loewenstamm, *The Tradition of the Exodus in its Development* (Heb.), (Jerusalem, 1965), pp. 30–42.

12 1Kgs 20 originally described the beginning of Joash's reign; when the Aramean pressure subsided; see E. Lipinski, "Le Ben-Hadad II de la Bible et l'histoire," *Proceedings of the Fifth World Congress of Jewish Studies* (Jerusalem, n.d.), pp. 157–173.

evidence, we can conclude that the Elijah cycle was based on a great many different literary sources and its present form attests to a long prehistory.

These observations also aid in dating the composition. Though it describes events which occurred during the reign of Ahab (873 –852 BCE), it is not necessary to conclude that the story is contemporaneous with its subject matter. In fact, some aspects of this story indicate that it should be dated considerably later. God's word to Elijah on Horeb (1 Kgs 19:15–18) contains details of Aramean oppression at the end of Jehoahaz's reign (817–800 BCE), so the story could not have been written before the end of the ninth century BCE. This was the period in which the Elisha *legenda* flourished. We have seen that one of them (2 Kgs 4:1–7) made its way into the Elijah cycle, in the form of an ethical *legenda* skillfully woven into the context (1 Kgs 17:8–16). This indicates that the date must be lowered by another generation or two, until after the composition of the Elisha cycle, in other words, to the first half of the eighth century BCE. An even later date is attested by the fact that Elisha is depicted here unhistorically as Elijah's successor in his struggle against Baal (1 Kgs 19:17–18). This indicates that the author had no first hand information of Elisha's personality or career, from which we may assume that there was another gap of at least two generations which would take us down to the middle of the eighth century. An even later date is indicated by the introduction to the story, which includes material taken from the Royal Chronicles of Northern Israel. This material was not easily accessible, and it was generally out of reach for the disciples of the prophets. The "democratization" which allowed official documents to become public domain could have occurred only after the fall of Northern Israel in 722 BCE. Furthermore, the mention of Ahab's worship of Baal (16:31–33) portrays that sin as an amplification of the "sins of Jeroboam" for which all the Kings of Israel are indicted. This standard vilification is built on theological foundations which were laid down, as we have seen above, by the prophet Hosea.[13] A date following the destruction of Samaria is thus indicated by this consideration as well. The story, on the other hand, displays no knowledge of the prohibition of the altars nor of the unification of worship in Jerusalem (18:30; 19:10, 14), which

---

13   See above, chap. 5, sect. 5.

became law in Judah in the wake of Josiah's reform (621 BCE). Thus the story must have been composed sometime during the course of the hundred years between the fall of Samaria and Josiah's reform.

There is a possibility of narrowing down the date of composition of this narrative even further. During the reign of Manasseh (698–643 BCE) idolatry once again became a crucial issue in Judah. The king "rebuilt the shrines which his father Hezekiah had destroyed; he erected altars for Baal and made a sacred post, as King Ahab of Israel had done" (2Kgs 21:3).[14] Once again, prophets were sent to warn of impending doom (vv 10–15). One of the statements attributed to them: "I will apply to Jerusalem the measuring line of Samaria and the weights of the House of Ahab" (v 13), indicates that an analogy between Manasseh and Ahab was clear to the people at the time of Menasseh and had found its way into the sources of the Book of Kings. The prophet Micah similarly accuses the people of Judah, at the end of the eighth century BCE, of following "the laws of Omri and all the practices of the House of Ahab" (Mic 6:16). All this indicates that the days of Manasseh were the most plausible period to which we can attribute the composition of the story of God, Elijah and Baal.[15]

This chronological conclusion can help explain one of the most difficult aspects of this story: the scattered references to the slaughter of the prophets by Jezebel (1Kgs 18:4, 13, 22) and by Israel in general (19:10, 14). This tradition, which was an integral part of post-exilic Jewish literature and was considered as the general policy of the entire pre-exilic period,[16] seems by all evidence to lack historical foundation. During most of the ancient period Israelite prophets enjoyed immunity, not because of the righteousness of the people but because the prophets were feared by the population. Who dared lay a hand on God's Holy Men? Amos, accused of plotting against Jeroboam II, was

---

14 As result of an extensive study of idolatry as practised in Judah during the reigns of Ahaz and Manasseh, M. Cogan concluded that it was of Canaanite and Aramean, rather than Assyrian, origin. See M. Cogan, *Imperialism and Religion: Assyria, Judah and Israel in the Eighth and Seventh Centuries B.C.E.* [SBLMS 19] (Missoula, MO 1974), pp. 65–96.

15 This suggestion was made long ago but has never received due attention. See J.C. Todd, *Politics and Religion in Ancient Israel* (London, 1904), pp. 195–196.

16 See our discussion below, chap. 10.

exiled to Judah (if he indeed obeyed the orders of Amaziah of Bethel) but not slain or even jailed; Micah, who prophesied the destruction of the Temple (3:12), was cited by the elders one hundred years later as proof that a prophet should never be harmed (Jer 26:18–19). A change occurred only at the end of the seventh century, when Jehoiakim slayed Uriah son of Shemaiah (Jer 26:20–23) and Jeremiah himself was persecuted by the priests, the prophets (Jer 26:7–16) and the king (36:26). This is consistent with the fact that the Book of Deuteronomy, whose composition was undertaken in the mid-seventh century BCE, prescribed a death penalty for the false prophet (Deut 18:20) and for the prophet who preached idolatry (13:2–6). This change in attitude may have begun with Manasseh, for the reference to the prophets' preaching during his reign is immediately followed by the mention of the innocent blood shed by him (2Kgs 21:10–16). In any event the turning point in the appraisal of the prophetic *persona* came in the mid-seventh century, when according to all indications prophets were no longer considered holy men and people lost their fear of causing them bodily harm. If, as we contend, the Elijah epic was indeed written during Manasseh's reign, this would explain the otherwise incomprehensible references to the murder of prophets, as an anachronism reflecting the realities and religious conceptions current in Judah in the late monarchial period.

Despite the relatively late date of the story – more than two hundred years after the events described – and the presence of anachronistic elements, one should not conclude that the story is completely unreliable as a historical source for Elijah's personality and activities. It is true that the details of Elijah's career cannot be reconstructed from this story. Miracles are phenomena beyond history, belonging to the realm of belief, not of science. For the historian a miracle is an indicator of the intensity of the faith of a religious group at a given period, or of the extent to which a community of believers was influenced by the unique personality of a leader. Elijah was without doubt such a unique person. He is portrayed as a fearless man who dared to provoke the wrath of princes and kings. He reprimanded the king for his worship of Baal (18:18) and commanded him to assemble all of Israel on Mt. Carmel; he reprimanded the people for their inconstancy and commanded them to slay the prophets of Baal. His whole being speaks spiritual power of an other worldly nature, an impression which is strongly reinforced by Elijah's mysterious habit of sudden appearances and disappearances. Elijah's contemporaries thus believed that the prophet divided his time between the earthly and the heavenly spheres. Not without cause was Elijah the only prophet who is twice described as receiving miraculous divine sustenance (17:2–7; 19:5–8). All his energy was directed to a single end: zeal on behalf of the Lord, first and foremost against the worship of the Tyrian Baal imported by Jezebel, next against Ahab's arrogant and imperious rule, in the Phoenician spirit, which violated the ancient and hallowed rights of family inheritance (1Kgs 21).

This description of Elijah and his activities should not be considered as being entirely without historical basis. For one thing, it is unique in its portrayal of Elijah, who is presented as unlike any of the other prophets of the Monarchy period, and especially Elisha. No admiring "sons of the prophets" accompany Elijah.[17] He is not portrayed as a "wonder worker" who engages in the performance of minor miracles to benefit the common man. He had no close relations with the king and court nor was he a savior of the people in times of oppression or war. Moreover, there is no reason to doubt the historical background of his career – Jezebel's introduction of the worship of the Tyrian Baal, which was later abolished during the reign of Jehu. And similarly, there is no reason to judge as unreliable the story of a prophet coming from Transjordan, where worship of the Tyrian Baal had not yet taken hold, to zealously advocate the exclusive worship of the Lord of Hosts.

Scholars differ as to Elijah's religious views and the nature of his acts. Some have claimed that Elijah represented a monolatrous faith which had not yet reached the level of monotheism. Others have maintained that the sacrifice on Mt. Carmel was no more than an act of analogical magic, in which the pouring of water on the altar was intended to bring about the granting of rain by God.[18] In my opinion, such views stem from the failure to differentiate between the various

---

17 See above, chap. 3, sect. 1.
18 This strange claim – that the water poured on the sacrifice and wood was analogical magic intended to induce rain – appears frequently in scholarly articles. D. R. Ap-Thomas, "Elijah on Mount Carmel," *PEQ* 92 (1960), pp. 146–155, went so far as to explain all of Elijah's actions on Mt. Carmel as magical.

theological and literary strata contained in the prophetic stories. Though there are undoubtedly many prophetic *legenda* that are alien to a monotheistic belief as represented, for example, in the Book of Deuteronomy, the story under discussion belongs to a different category. The whole struggle between Baal and God is based on the assumption that only one of them exists, a single God, whose identity needs to be established: "How long will you keep hopping between two opinions? If the Lord is God, follow Him; and if Baal, follow him!" (18:21). The portrayal of the prophets of Baal calling out to him, Baal's failure to answer them, and Elijah mocking them in consequence is meant to express unequivocally the futility of belief in a non-existent god and the folly of accepting all the myths about him.[19] This story is purely monotheistic in its outlook. The suggestion advanced above that this story was written by the faithful of the Lord during the period of Manasseh's reign confirms this. In this period monotheistic belief struggled with idolatry for the last time, a struggle in which it emerged the victor. After the cessation of the persecutions associated with Manasseh, the faithful were able to implement the ultimate logical consequences of the belief in one God – a centralized worship at the chosen sanctuary in Jerusalem. This was the reform instituted by Josiah in 621 BCE.

Along the same lines, the claim that the sacrifice on Mt. Carmel was a magical act designed to induce rain is without foundation. First of all, we have already seen that the story of the sacrifice was originally unconnected to the story of the rain. Viewing them as a single unit ignores the conclusions of historico-literary criticism. Secondly, it also ignores the context of the account of the sacrifice, in which the wetting of the offering and firewood was done in order to amplify the miracle and to emphasize to all that the fire was of divine origin (18:23, 25). And indeed, fire descended from heaven and consumed "the burnt offering, the wood, the stones, and the earth; and it licked up the water that was in the trench . . ." (18:38). This fire descended not as a result of any magical activity, but in response to Elijah's prayer: "O Lord, God of Abraham, Isaac, and Israel! Let it be known

---

19 Searching for hints of monolatry in this story will therefore result in distortion of its interpretation. For a particularly extreme example of this see H. H. Rowley, "Elijah on Mount Carmel," *BJRL* 43 (1960–61), pp. 190–219 (= *Men of God* [London], pp. 37–65).

today that You are God in Israel and that I am Your servant, and that I have done all these things at Your bidding. Answer me, O Lord, answer me, that this people may know that You, O Lord, are God . . ." There is no magic in Elijah's miracle, just as there is none in the ethical *legenda.* And as in the *legenda,* here too the miracle has a purpose: it testifies. The people see, fall on their faces and proclaim: "The Lord alone is God! The Lord alone is God!"

We may summarize our conclusions as follows: the story in itself expresses an unquestionable monotheistic view and portrays the miracles as occurring not through magic but through the sovereign will of God, for the purpose of proving His divine power. As for the personality of the historical Elijah, his beliefs and actions, it is difficult to reconstruct them on the basis of a story written some two hundred years after his demise. It seems that the historical Elijah was known both as a miracle worker who possessed the ability of arresting rain and of hearing distant sounds as well as a zealous fighter against Baal. While we should not deny the primitive elements in his portrayal, we should also not attempt to diminish his towering stature and the greatness of his mission by a primitivistic interpretation of his deeds.[20]

The present story of Elijah on Mt. Carmel, in all events, is far superior to the primitivism of the miracle-worker *legenda* and bears the strong impress of an "idea." In this sense it is closely related to the ethical *legenda,* though it cannot be defined as such. Firstly, because the idea expressed in the story is not a creation of the author, who reshaped his story by it (cf. the above comparison of 1Kgs 17:8–16 with 2Kgs 4:1–7) or integrated it into the existing narrative components (as in 2Kgs 20:1–11). Here the idea is central to Elijah's entire life conception; it is the mission entrusted him by the Lord. Without this Elijah is nothing. In contrast to the prophets of the *exempla* (Jonah and 1Kgs 13), the prophet in this case fully identifies with his mission. Secondly, the story is of much greater length than the ethical *legenda.* Extending from 1Kgs 16:29 to 19:18 (with the exception of 16:34 and 17:17–24), the story is recounted in eighty-five verses and forms one of the longest units of prophetic narrative.

---

20 This claim is also advanced, on the basis of interesting observations from comparative religion, by C. A. Keller, "Wer war Elia," *ThZ* 16 (1960), pp. 298–313.

Besides its length, its time scope is also extensive. It covers the events of at least two years and foretells various events which will take place in the following generation (19:16–18). As we noted above, the story is composed of numerous components. Elijah appears in a multi-faceted role: as a forceful servant of God, as a saintly individual enjoying His favor and supported by Him, as a refugee in Sidon bringing blessings to the faithful, as a master of the king's officers and of the king himself, as a ruthless warrior slaying the prophets of Baal, as a miracle worker who halts the rains and predicts their return, as an enthusiast running before the king's chariot, as a fugitive pursued by the royal powers, abandoned by all, and finally as the messenger of God returning in despair from his mission. Thus in its artistic complexity, the story is richer even than the *legenda,* not to mention the ethical *legenda* which are so lacking in literary detail.

The concluding scene of the story, though alluding to past events contained in the introduction, points mainly to the future, to events yet to come: the anointment of Hazael, Jehu and Elisha, in which the continuation of the epic can be witnessed. The meeting of God and Elijah on Mt. Horeb marks the end of the tale, but not the end of the struggle, which will continue even after Elijah's death. This is the decisive point for the understanding of the story. Though Elijah is its most active character, the story does not in fact revolve around a description of his life and accomplishments; its concern with the prophet's biography is minimal. The true subject of this narrative is the struggle between God and His followers and Baal and his worshippers.[21] In the present act, Elijah served as God's champion; in later acts other champions and other heroes will undertake that role.

We thus have here a Battle of the Gods. The Lord and Baal struggle for control over the Israelite kingdom, a mighty battle with no quarter given. Each side conducts massacres – Jezebel slays the prophets of God and Elijah slaughters the priests of Baal in quick succession. These acts are accompanied by accounts of miraculous flights, to Wadi Cherith, to Zarephath in Sidon, to Beersheba in Judah and from there to Horeb. This total war leaves its stamp on nature as well: a severe drought decreed by the Lord decimates man and beast; it ends

21   See Keller (previous note).

in a great rain storm. At Elijah's initiative, the Gods duel; whoever answers with fire is the winner. Though the Lord proves the stronger, Jezebel refuses to surrender and prepares her revenge.

There is, however, one significant difference between this and a true Battle of the Gods . . . Here there is only one participant: the Lord. The other combatant, Baal, exists only in the imagination of his worshippers. Thus the battle is not fought along lines generally followed in theomachies. There is no mythic struggle between divine beings who employ weapons, strategems, and monsters to aid their causes.[22] This battle is fought in the human sphere. It is a struggle for men's minds, to convince them that the Lord is real and that Baal is an illusion. Even when the Lord seals the skies, it is at Elijah's command, intended to punish those who had left God and followed the Baals (18:18). The theomachy here is thus a historico-cultural crisis in Israelite history.

Despite the theological distinction, the sense of grandeur of the classical Battle of the Gods (and their champions) is preserved in our tale. Of the characters involved, Jezebel is certainly a worthy opponent for Elijah. After the slaughter of the prophets of Baal at the foot of Mt. Carmel, she sends a message to Elijah: "If you are Elijah, I am Jezebel;[23] thus and more may the gods do to me if by this time tomorrow I have not made you like one of them" (1 Kgs 19:2). She is just as zealous, just as dedicated to her beliefs and gods as the prophet is to his; she exudes power and confidence in her right to command.

Aside from the characters, the subject of the tale itself is an expression of its grand scope. It depicts Israel at a crossroads in its history – a point at which it will be determined whether Israel follows the Lord or Baal. Despite Elijah's prodding, the people are unable to choose. Heavenly intervention, in the form of miracles, makes them choose the Lord.[24] The majestic ambience of this story, expressed in

22 Cf. Y. Kaufmann, *The Religion of Israel,* trans. M. Greenberg (Chicago, 1960), pp. 60–67.

23 This reading is reflected in most mss. of LXX, and its authenticity is in my opinion unquestionable. The name Jezebel איזבל was probably understood as the antithesis of Elijah יהו - אלי. Its second element זבל, is one of the epithets of Baal at Ugarit. The first element probably was אלי or אבי. The two names indicated the archetypal conflict between the Tyrian queen and the prophet from Gilead.

24 Indeed, even among those scholars who limit the true meaning of 1 Kgs 18 to the ethno-political struggle between the Canaanites and Israelites over control of Mt.

both its theme and characterization, provides a clue as to its genre: the story of God, Elijah and Baal is an *epic,* a broad, sweeping and rich canvas of images, places and people interacting over a long period of time, which recounts the mighty battle that determined for all times the fate of the entire nation.

Carmel, some maintain that Elijah was responsible for a fundamental turning point in the nature of Israelite belief; i.e. he was the first to assert that the Lord controlled the forces of nature, a claim which led to His recognition as the Creator of the universe. See G. Fohrer, *Elia* (Zürich, 1957), pp. 80–89.

Chapter Ten

THE RISE OF MARTYROLOGY

1. *The Literary Genre, Its Character and History*

Martyrology is a type of narrative in which a believer, at the risk of his life, testifies to the existence of God before those who do not know or recognize Him. The name is derived from the Greek word μάρτυς meaning witness.[1] The analogous Hebrew term is קידוש השם the sanctification of the [Divine] Name. But the Hebrew expression has wider connotations, being used to describe all acts which demonstrate the sanctity of God, His power and justice, and the complete allegiance of the faithful to Him and to His law. Sanctifying God's name reveals His holiness and proclaims His immanence. Thus there is a great deal of semantic and theological overlapping between the two concepts. In our discussion we employ the Greek-derived term martyrology, because of its more restricted meaning, since *kiddush hashem* may include acts performed in private, day-to-day moral conduct, daily prayer, as well as divine intervention in the course of affairs intended to sanctify the Name.[2]

---

1 For the history of this term, see H. Strathmann, "μάρτυς κτλ ." *Theological Dictionary of the NT,* ed. G. Kittel, Eng. trans. G. W. Bromiley, Vol. IV (Grand Rapids, MI, 1969), pp. 464–512, esp. pp. 489–508. Originally martyrology referred to *lists* of martyrs – Christian witnesses who died for their faith. We use the term here in its prevalent sense of a story about a martyr.

2 See M. D. Herr, "Decrees of Persecution and Sanctification of the Name in Hadrian's Time" (Heb.), in: *Holy War and Martyrology; City and Community; Proceedings of the Eleventh and Twelfth Annual Conferences of Historical Society* (Heb.), (Jerusalem, 1968), pp. 43–92, ad p. 83; H. H. Ben-Sasson, "Kiddush Ha-Shem etc.," *Encyclopaedia Judaica* (Jerusalem, 1972), Vol. 10, cols. 977–986.

In listing the characteristics of martyrology[3] we should first note that, fundamentally, it assumes the existence of two opposing camps – the believers, usually few in number and weak, and the more numerous and stronger forces of infidelity. In the course of the struggle between them, the heretics overpower the faithful and attempt to convert them forcibly to their own position, or at least to silence their opposition and assume an outward appearance of submission. The believers resist to their last breath, strongly declaring their faith while reviling their conquerors and oppressors. At this point events reach a climax – the believers are led away to be tortured or slaughtered, certain to die a horrible death unless saved by a miraculous last minute divine intervention. Invariably the believers' dedication makes a powerful impression on the enemy, who recognize and acknowledge the power of a God whose faithful display such a readiness on His behalf. Often the impression made by their self-sacrifice induces a change of heart or even conversion of the non-believers and they or their children become enthusiastic followers of the faith in their own right.

Martyrology is thus composed of six basic components: conflict, struggle, declaration of faith, provocation, torture, conversion. Obviously, not every martyrological story will contain all, or even most of these elements. The variations can be innumerable. But even if only one or two of these factors appear in a story, it can, in my opinion, still be identified as a martyrology if they dominate the story.

Moreover, martyrology is not simply a folk-legend, the product of casual fancy, but springs from a concrete set of historical circumstances in which a religious minority adheres firmly to its faith and therefore is the object of persecution.[4] For this reason martyrology was a constant companion of the Jews during their long years of exile. Martyrological stories, though literary compositions, are indubitably grounded in con-

---

3 Much material on Jewish martyrology of the Second Commonwealth and later periods has been collected by H. A. Fischel, "Martyr and Prophet," *JQR* 37 (1947), pp. 265–280, 363–386. For a collection of ancient Christian martyrologies, see H. Musurillo, *The Acts of the Christian Martyrs* (Oxford, 1972).

4 For a comprehensive study of the history of Christian martyrdom and its Jewish roots, see W. H. C. Frend, *Martyrdom and Persecution in the Early Church* (Oxford, 1965).

crete historical realities.[5] Obviously, the presence or absence of the
martyrology in each individual case is dependent on the historical circumstances underlying the story. For example, conversion of heretics
is to be expected in stories recounting the activities of religious groups
who attempted to spread their faith among their antagonists; it is therefore a widespread element in stories from the periods of the Second
Commonwealth[6] and early Christianity, but is almost completely lacking in stories which originated among medieval Franco-German Jews.[7]

In view of this it is not surprising that martyrology is completely
absent from early biblical historiography, and especially from the
prophetic stories – the historical circumstances of those times simply
did not lend themselves to the development of this type of literature.
Firstly, the religious polarization and consequent dissention which
produced religious persecution, the essential requirements for a
martyrological scenario, are totally lacking.[8] Secondly, because of the
people's attitude of veneration towards the prophets, these could not
be viewed as suffering martyrs. As Holy Men of God, in constant
contact with God who sickens and heals, revives and kills at a word,
they were feared and revered even by kings. Their word was law, their
remonstrances honored, and of course their person sacred. If kings
responded to the prophets in this fashion, how much more so would
the common people. During the entire First Commonwealth, up to the
eve of the Exile, no historical evidence of the slaying of a prophet can
be found.[9] The clash between Amos and Amaziah, the priest at Bethel

---

5   A rather conservative attempt to distinguish between historical elements and their
literary development is made by H. Délehaye, *Les passions des martyrs et les
genres littéraires* (Brussels, 1921).

6   Some extreme examples of this are: the story of the "repentance" of Antiochus
Epiphanes in 2Macc 2:9 and the story of the executioner of R. Hanina b. Teradyon
who cast himself into his victim's pyre (b'Abod Zar 18a). The motif recurs in
Paul's participation in Stephen's execution and the revelation to him in Acts
7:58–9:9.

7   See A. M. Haberman, ספר גזירות אשכנז וצרפת (Jerusalem, 1946). Only in R. Ephraim
b. Ya'acov of Bonn's story about the immolation of Jews during the blood libel
in Blois: "the uncircumsized ones saw and exclaimed to their fellows: 'truly these
are holy ones'" (*ibid*, קבד).

8   Faint traces of this trend may be found in the story of Gideon's destruction of the
altar of Baal (Judg 7:25–32), but when is this story to be dated?

9   On the reported slaughter of the prophets mentioned in 1Kgs 18–19, see above,
chap. 9.

(Amos 7:10–17), is an excellent example of this situation. Despite the serious crimes of which Amos is accused – conspiracy against King Jeroboam – he is neither sentenced to death nor imprisoned. Amaziah merely tells him to flee (back?) to Judah. It is not clear whether this is a request or an order. In any event it results in Amaziah being personally cursed by Amos in the name of God. Even if this testifies to Amos's courage, at the same time it demonstrates that he enjoyed prophetic immunity.

Only at the end of the monarchy, in the seventh century BCE, does this situation change. The Book of Deuteronomy contains a four-paragraph law prescribing the death penalty for idol worshippers (17:2–7; 13:2–19), which includes a special injunction dealing with a prophet who preaches idolatry (13:2–6).[10] Another law decreed death for a prophet who speaks in the name of foreign gods or who presents his own views as the words of God, in other words, a false prophet (18:20). While the first two provisions demonstrate the author's zealousness, the third attests to a secularized conception of the prophet's person. From this time onwards, the nation's leaders received the right to criticise a prophet's statements and to decide, on the basis of their own judgment, whether they were true or false prophets.[11] It is during this period, on the eve of the discovery of the Book of Deuteronomy and the cultic reforms of Josiah, that the young Jeremiah hurled a harsh accusation against the nation for the first time: "Your sword has devoured your prophets like a ravening lion" (Jer 2:30). It therefore seems that the juxtaposition in 2Kgs 21:10–16 of accounts of the prophets' castigations and the statement: "Menasseh put so many innocent persons to death that he filled Jerusalem (with blood) from end to end" attests that the idolatrous king was responsible for the murder of prophets. In any event, only several years later, at the beginning of Jehoiakim's reign (from all indications prior to his subjugation by the Babylonians in 605 BCE), the king ordered the assassination of Uriah son of Shemaiah of Kiriath-jearim (Jer 26:20–23).[12] Jeremiah himself was in mortal

---

10 This and the following paragraph (13:7–12) state that even if the idolatrous preacher is a prophet, relative, or friend, one is still required to slay him like any other idolator.

11 The criterion to be used to distinguish between them presented in Deut 18:21–22 is a later addition; see above, chap. 5, sect. 5 and n. 59 there.

12 Uriah son of Shemaiah was evidently extradited by the Egyptians to Jehoiakim.

danger because of his preaching, and was saved only through the intervention of the ministers. The "elders of the land," probably elders from the outlying districts, produce a hundred-year-old precedent – an incident which occurred before the change in attitude towards the prophets (26:17–19) – to prove that a prophet who preaches the destruction of the temple should not be put to death. Jeremiah's treatment by the ministers during the siege of Jerusalem (Jer 37–38) attests to the clash between the old and the new attitudes; while desiring Jeremiah's death, they dared not cause direct violence to his person. Instead, they cast him into prison to die of starvation (or into a mud pit to drown, according to the anecdotal version of the story).[13]

Any reservations the Judean authorities may have had in their treatment of the prophets were surely not shared by their Babylonian counterparts. In Jer 29:9–9, 15, 21–23, we find a harsh prophecy concerning Ahab son of Kolaiah and Zedekiah son of Maaseiah, prophets in Babylon, who will be consigned to the flames by the king of Babylon. This incident seems to have been a result of prophecies which these and other prophets preached to their compatriots in exile: predictions of salvation, oracles of doom regarding Babylon (as in Jer 50–51), and derision and contempt for the Chaldean gods (as in Isa 40–47). The same situation prevailed in the Persian period when accusations such as: "You have also set up prophets in Jerusalem to proclaim about you, 'There is a king in Judah!'" when made before the king, were interpreted as rebellion against Persian rule (Neh 6:6–7). From this period there is historical evidence of an outbreak of anti-Jewish violence by the inhabitants of a district in which the Jews were a minority. In Elephantine, the Egyptian masses rose up against the Jewish colony, attacked its residents, and razed the sanctuary of Yahu which was in the citadel.[14] All the essential conditions necessary for the creation of a martyrology were therefore present in this period: religious and political polarization of Jews and non-Jews living under common rule and the appearance of prophets (such as Haggai and

---

This would indicate that Jehoiakim at the time was still an Egyptian vassal, which would place the incident between 609 and 605 BCE.

13 Cf. above, chap. 6, sect. 2, end.

14 See A. E. Cowley, ed., *Aramaic Papyri of the 5th Century BC* (Oxford, 1923), nn. 38, 34 + 56, 27, 30, 31, 32, 33, new trans. by B. Porten and J.C. Greenfield, *Jews of Elephantine and Arameans of Syene* (Jerusalem, 1974), pp. 83–101.

Trito Isaiah) who represented Jewish aspirations for political liberation as well as others who promulgated monotheism among the foreign nations (Jer 10; Isa 40–48).

The political developments during this period had an important influence on the reformulation of religious ideas.[15] Dispersal and foreign domination are the two characteristic features of the Second Temple period. Of the 657 years between the destructions of the First and Second Temples, only the 79 years of the Hasmonean interlude were years of Jewish independence. The signers of Nehemiah's pledge already sense the humiliation of foreign rule, and express their feelings openly.[16] Subjugation demanded theological justification, and it was interpreted as being God's just punishment for Israel's sinfulness which had persisted, from the time of its enslavement in Egypt until the fall of Jerusalem (Neh 9:16–37). This theodicy recurs in many late prayers, such as Jer 32:17–25; Ezra 9:6–15; Neh 1:5–11; Dan 9:9–14 and Ps 106.[17] The guilt feeling led to a *generalization* of blame. This is clearly attested in Neh 9:26: "Then, defying You, they rebelled; they cast Your teaching behind their back. They killed Your prophets who admonished them to turn back to You; they committed great impieties." Elijah's words of accusation at Horeb: "The Israelites have forsaken Your covenant, torn down Your altars and put Your prophets to the sword" (1Kgs 19:10, 14) is here applied to all generations. Thus in the spirit of guilt and repentance, Israel came to portray itself as a nation which devoured its prophets.

During the period of independence under the Hasmonean rulers there was an intensification of this trend, as it provided new reasons and circumstances for martyrological conceptions. No sooner was the revived Jewish commonwealth established than it was torn asunder by bitter controversy.[18] The religious sects which arose at that

---

15 This problem was extensively studied by O.H. Steck, *Israel und das gewaltsame Geschick der Propheten* [WMANT 23] (Neukirchen-Vluyn, 1967).

16 "Today we are slaves, and the land that you gave our fathers to enjoy its fruit and bounty – here we are slaves on it! On account of our sins it yields abundant crops to kings whom You have set over us. They rule our bodies and our beasts as they please, and we are in great distress," Neh 9:36–37.

17 Other biblical and extra-biblical texts are discussed at length by Steck (above, n. 15).

18 Josephus first mentions the emergence of sectarian groups in his account of the rule of Jonathan the Hasmonean (153–142 BCE); see Ant. Jud. 13:171–173. The

time turned the state into a battlefield in their attempt to achieve dominion and to exploit the political institutions as instruments for the coercion of religious belief and practice. The Pharisees rebelled against Alexander Jannaeus and were persecuted by him.[19] They in turn persecuted the Sadducees during the reign of Salome Alexandra.[20] Both groups persecuted the Qumran sectarians on the eve of Pompey's conquest of the country.[21] From that time there was no end to religious-civil strife, through the uprising of the Zealots in the Great Revolt of 66–70 CE. This situation lent support to the belief that religious persecutions had occurred in pre-exilic times as well. The sufferers of persecution, irrespective of their sectarian affiliation, as well as the opponents of civil strife and religious intolerance,[22] could therefore take consolation in the ancient stories about the prophet's trials and tribulations, and draw from them the strength and inspiration needed to overcome their own trying circumstances. Thus, for example, the Book of Jubilees, which was composed in proto-Qumranian circles at the beginning of the Hasmonean era,[23] describes the history of the institution of prophecy as follows: "And I will send witnesses unto them, that I may witness against them, but they will not hear, and will slay the witnesses also, and they will

rift between the Hasmoneans and Pharisees occurred in the time of John Hyrcanus, and resulted in the ethnarch's joining the Sadducee party; see Ant. Jud. 13:288–298.

19   Bel. Jud. 1:90–106; Ant. Jud. 13:372–383; bSota 47a; bSanh 107b (ms. Munich). The story in b.Kid 66a combines the beginning of the split during the days of John Hyrcanus with the persecution of the Pharisees by Alexander Jannaeus.

20   Bel.Jud. 1:110–116; Ant. Jud. 13:408–418.

21   See 4QpPs37 2:15–20: "'The wicked have drawn the sword and bent their bow to cast down the poor and needy and to slay the upright of way. Their sword shall penetrate their own heart and their bows shall be broken.' Its interpretation concerns the wicked ones of Ephraim and Manasseh who will seek to put forth a hand against the Priest and the men of his counsel in the time of trial that is coming upon them. But God will redeem them from their hand and afterwards they will be given into the hands of the ruthless Gentiles for judgement." (Trans. J. M. Allegro. *Qumran Cave 4 I (4Q 158 - 4Q 186)* [DJD V] (Oxford, 1986), p. 46. See also D. Flusser, *The Dead Sea Scrolls²* (Heb.), (Jerusalem, 1968), pp. 88 – 100.

22   Like Honi, who refused to place a curse upon the priests of Aristobulus' faction and was stoned by Hyrcanus' men: Ant. Jud. 14:19–24.

23   J. C. VanderKam, *Textual and Historical Studies in the Book of Jubilees* [HSM 14] (Missoula, MO, 1977).

persecute those who seek the law ...(1:13).[24] The bias of this view of
the fate of the prophets can be best appreciated against the
background of comparable statements found in the Bible. According to 2Kgs 17:13–14: "The Lord warned Israel ... by every
prophet ... But they did not obey; they stiffened their necks"; and in
2Chr 36:15:–16: "The Lord ...had sent word to them through his
messengers daily without fail ... But they mocked the messengers of
God and disdained His words and taunted His prophets ..." Initially
the attitude of the people towards the prophets was said to have been
negative; later it was portrayed as blasphemous; and finally it was
described as murderous! The end of the above-cited verse from
Jubilees emphasizes how strong the notion of propheticide had
become. The description of the persecution of "those who seek the
law," (the Hebrew original probably had דורשי התורה) indicates that
this verse addresses the past to comment upon contemporary events:
דורש התורה was the title of one of the founders of the Qumran sect (CD
6:7; 7:18–19 and מדרש התורה was the characteristic form of its Torah
study 1QS 6:6; 8:15, 25–26). Here one clearly sees how the
Qumranians likened the fate of their persecuted leaders to the fate of
the ancient prophets; the past is being viewed in the light of the
present.

The four stages in Israelite history and in the development of
Israelite religio-historical consciousness which we have described
contribute to explain the rise of martyrology in the late biblical and
apocryphal literature. In these writings too, the history of martyrology
can be divided into four separate stages. The struggle against
Manasseh's idolatry and the incidents of the murder of the prophets
in the seventh century BCE left their mark on the epic of Elijah, God,
and Baal (1Kgs 16:29–19:18) which, according to all indications, was
composed at this time. Persecution of the prophets is a recurrent
theme throughout the story. Elijah was forced to hide during the
drought and famine (17:3); Ahab searched for him in every nation and
kingdom (18:10); Jezebel decimated the prophets of the Lord and the
remainder hid in caves (18:4, 13; 2Kgs 9:7). In a slightly different
version, Elijah blames the people for putting the prophets to the sword

---

24 Trans. R. H. Charles, ed, *The Apocrypha and Pseudoepigrapha of the OT*, Vol. II
(Oxford, 1913), p. 12. Cf. also the Ethiopic Enoch 89:51–53.

(19:10, 14).[25] Elijah pays the prophets of Baal in the same coin (18:40), and Jezebel attempts to retaliate (19:2). This description is of a full-scale religious war, with the prophets presented as the chief representatives of the faith for which they are slain. The first martyrological element – the prophet who sacrifices his life for his beliefs – entered Israelite literature at this point.

This element was expanded and developed by the historical sense of guilt and sin prevalent in the Second Temple period. This process can be detected in the prophetic stories appearing in the Book of Chronicles. Hanani the seer is put into the stocks by Asa because of a prophecy he had delivered (2 Chr 16:7–10); Micaiah son of Imlah is imprisoned (2 Chr 18:26–31; it is not a coincidence that this is the only prophetic story from the Book of Kings also included in Chronicles); the life of an anonymous prophet who admonished Amaziah for his idolatry is threatened, the threat being serious enough to silence the prophet (2 Chr 25:15–16); and most significant of all Zechariah son of Jehoiada is stoned "by the order of the King, in the court of the House of the Lord" (2 Chr 24:20–22). Even if ancient traditions underlie these stories, there is no doubt that the martyrological element of a prophet being slain for his faith has entered them, exemplifying the principle: "They killed Your prophets who admonished them to turn them back to You" (Neh 9:26).

The midrashic reworking of the prophetic stories during and after the Second Temple period accepted this idea and developed it. It made sense, in light of the historical experience of mutual intolerance and persecution by the various sects from the Hasmonean era through the destruction of Jerusalem in 70 CE. The prophets of the Bible were transformed into martyrs in both apocryphal and rabbinic literature. According to the Babylonian Talmud (b Yeb 49b), Manasseh slew Isaiah, who had hidden in a cedar, when in the tree.[26] Hur was slain by the worshippers of the golden calf (b Sanh 7a). Aaron, too, feared for his life, and was concerned that in killing him, the people would have committed the act denounced in Lam 2:20: "Alas, priest and prophet are slain in the Sanctuary of the Lord!" a sin for which there

---

25 O. H. Steck, *Überlieferung und Zeitgeschichte in Elia-Erzählungen* [WMANT 26] (Neukirchen-Vluyn, 1986), pp. 5–31.

26 A similar legend is told in *The Ascension of Isaiah*, chap. 5. See Charles (above, n. 24), pp. 155–162.

is no penance. He, therefore, made the calf. Since Aaron was a priest, the prophet mentioned in the verse must have been Hur. *The Lives of the Prophets*[27] tells of the deaths as martyrs of Isaiah, Jeremiah, Ezekiel, Micah of Moreshet (slain by Joram son of Ahab), Amos (slain by the son of Amaziah, the priest at Bethel), and Zechariah son of Jehoiada. A late midrash claims that the Jews in Egypt slew Jeremiah, the worshippers of the golden calf killed Hur, Baasha murdered Shemaiah, Abijah killed Ahijah the Shilonite, Joash killed Zechariah son of Jehoiada, and Manasseh killed Isaiah.[28] The accusation voiced by Jesus: "Oh Jerusalem, Jerusalem, killing the prophets and stoning those who are sent to you" (Matt 23:37),[29] was not, then, a Christian invention, but passed on to them from the Jewish Aggadah.

It was, however, during Israel's subjugation to the Babylonian and Persian empires that martyrology evolved into its classical form: the testimony of monotheistic belief against the pagan religions. Hatred of the Jews as a religious minority and the exclusive nature of their faith incited the authorities to repressive acts. The prosaic description of Ahab son of Kolaiah and Zedekiah son of Maaseiah being consigned to the flames by the king of Babylon is reflected by a more poetic version in the story of Hananiah, Mishael, and Azariah (Dan 3).[30] Similar in character is the tale of Daniel in the lions' den (Dan 6). These stories did not originate during the times of the Antiochean persecutions of 168 BCE but prior to them.[31] Though the oracles contained in Daniel (chaps. 7–12) were redacted during these very persecutions, before the Hasmonean victories, the stories, which represent a totally different literary genre, are earlier. In neither story (chaps. 3 and 6) is a blanket persecution of the Jews as a religio-national group implied, but rather of individuals who served as royal officials. The attacks on these Jews were not the result of official royal policy but of the hatred of court rivals. The king is not

---

27 C. C. Torrey, *The Lives of the Prophets* [JBLMS 1] (Philadelphia, PA, 1946).

28 S. Buber, ed., מדרש אגדה על חמשה חמשי תורה (Vienna, 1894), on Num 30:15.

29 See also Matt 5:12; 23:19–35; Luke 6:23; 11:47–51.

30 See J. A. Montgomery, *Commentary on the Book of Daniel* [ICC] (Edinburgh, 1927), p. 93.

31 See G. Hölscher, "Die Entstehung des Buches Daniel," *ThSK* 92, 2(1919), pp. 113–138; C. Kuhl, *Die drei Männer im Feuer (Daniel Kapitel 3 und seine Zusätze)* [BZAW 55] (Giessen, 1930), pp. 77–84; Y. Kaufmann, *History of the Religion of Israel*, Vol. IV, trans. C. W. Efroymson (N.Y. 1977), pp. 496–500.

protrayed as an arch-enemy, as was Antiochus Epiphanes, but as a neutral personality (Nebuchadnezzar) or even a friendly one (Darius). Moreover, even if the Book of Daniel received its final form during the Antiochean persecutions, it was compiled from older sources, as is demonstrated by the independent character of its individual stories: Daniel himself is not mentioned even once in the story about Hananiah, Mishael, and Azariah.

These stories contain all the characteristic elements of martyrology: tension between Jewish and gentile officials leading to a confrontation, with the gentiles informing against the Jews. The Jews affirm their belief (in Dan 6:17 the king himself makes the declaration for Daniel!) and defy the authorities (in Dan 6:16 the ministers urge the king to take action against Daniel). In consequence the Jews are condemned to a violent death; when they are miraculously delivered, the king proclaims his belief in the God of Israel. It should be noted that the martyr in these stories is not a prophetic figure, thus indicating that the Israelite religion had undergone a process of "democratization." Any Jew who believed and cleaved unto God had the ability to withstand trials such as these.

In one of these elements – a heathen ruler's proclamation of belief – we can observe how the Midrash reworked biblical stories to imbue them with a martyrological content which they lacked. In b Sanh 96b, it is related that Nebuzaradan, after having slain 940,000 Jerusalemites to assuage the boiling blood of Zechariah, "considered repentance. He said to himself: 'If [so many of them were slain] who only destroyed one life, what will happen to me?' He deserted, disposed of his estate, and converted." This arch-enemy, destroyer and murderer, recognized the God of Israel because of a bloodbath he himself had perpetrated, and accepted the faith of the slaughtered. As is recounted in a *Baraita (loc. cit.)*: "Naaman was a righteous gentile; Nebuzaradan was a proselyte; the grandchildren of Sisera studied Torah in Jerusalem; the grandchildren of Sennacherib taught Torah in public, and who are they? Shemiah and Abtalyon. The grandchildren of Haman learned Torah in Bene Brak." Only the repentance of the descendants of Nebuchadnezzar was refused by God, because of the protests of the ministering angels. The martyrological tendency transforms the sworn enemies and destroyers of Israel, or their descendants, into proselytes and sages. Paradoxically, Naaman, who never harmed Israel, became merely a "resident alien," while the descendants of Sennacherib, who blasphemed God, were among the greatest Pharisees of the Second Temple period. The greater the enemy, the greater and more convincing would his conversion be.

2. Jeremiah and Nebuzaradan

The recognition of the martyrological character of these midrashic interpretations sheds light on the literary history of the account of Jeremiah's liberation from prison.

This story is contained in Jer 38:28b – "When Jerusalem was captured" – and continues in Jer 39:3, 11–14; 40:1–6. Two other episodes are intermingled in the story: part of the chronicle of the fall of Jerusalem (39:1–2, 4–10), of which a more lengthy version is presented in 2Kgs 25 and Jeremiah 52, and a prophecy concerning Ebed-melech the Ethiopian, who rescued Jeremiah from the pit (39:15–18).[32] But even the remainder, the brief account of Jeremiah's liberation, is not consistent, as is clear from the duplications contained in it. As will be immediately evident, this tale is in fact composed of two separate and different versions.[33]

One version relates that when Jerusalem was conquered (38:28b), the officers of the king of Babylon came and sat in the city gate (39:3), that is, they assembled to judge the people who remained in the city, to decide who should be freed, who detained, who exiled, and who executed. They then took Jeremiah from the prison compound, where he had been confined, freed him, and gave him into the keeping of Gedaliah son of Ahikam, who had been appointed governor of the conquered land by the Chaldeans (39:14). The reason for Jeremiah's release is clear. During their interrogation of the people of the city, the Babylonian officials discovered that Jeremiah had been imprisoned for preaching surrender, and they therefore decided to

---

32 See Y. Zuckerbram, "Variants in Editing" (Heb.), *Melilah* (Manchester) III–IV (1950), pp. 1–54. His conclusions regarding the story of the release itself differ from ours.

33 See B. Duhm, *Das Buch Jeremia, erklärt* [KHAT] (Tübingen and Leipzig, 1901), *ad loc.*

spare him from punishment, and attach him to the circle of loyalists to Babylon gathering around Gedaliah.

The second version relates that Nebuchadnezzar himself, in the course of his instructions of Nebuzaradan, gave special orders regarding Jeremiah – to protect him and fulfill all his requests (39:11-12). Nebuzaradan discovered Jeremiah at the very last minute, in a column of chained exiles at Ramah, making their way to Babylon (40:1).[34] He took the prophet, made a short speech (40:2-3), unchained him and allowed him the free choice to decide where he wanted to go (40:4). When Jeremiah hesitated, Nebuzaradan advised him to join Gedaliah, giving him provisions and a royal gift (40:5).[35] Jeremiah took his advice and made his way to Mizpah, where he found Gedaliah (40:6).

Both versions conclude with an identical description of Jeremiah's life: "So he dwelt among the people" (39:14; 40:6), those who were "left in the land." A minor attempt at harmonizing the two accounts is made in 39:13. The verse repeating part of the list of the Babylonian officials from the first story (39:3) adds Nebuzaradan, commander of the Babylonian expeditionary force, who was responsible for freeing Jeremiah in the second story. A further attempt to combine the stories may be found in the resumptive repetition in 40:6 of 39:14, and in 39:13 of 39:3.[36]

Additional attempts at harmonization were made by various biblical commentators.[37] Most of these are based on the claim (not

---

34 The present text of Jer 40:1 is in itself problematic: what was "the word that came to Jeremiah from the Lord," if the prophet first speaks in 42:7? It seems that this title was composed by a late editor from materials available to him, and that it was intended to introduce a new "book." The preceding book contained the prophecies which occurred until "Jerusalem went into exile in the fifth month" (Jer 1:3); the new book presents the post-exilic prophecies. A differing opinion is held by S. Zalewsky, "The Caption to the Book of Jeremiah" (Heb.), *Beth Mikra* 20 (1975), pp. 26–62.

35 This is the meaning of ארחה ומשאת.

36 The absence of 39:4–13 from the Septuagint is a result of a homoeoteleuton, in which the copyist's eye skipped from שרי מלך בבל appearing in one column of his Vorlage to רבי מלך בבל written in a parallel line in the following column. Cf. A. Rofé, "The Composition of Deuteronomy 31" (Heb.), *Shnaton: An Annual for Biblical and Ancient Near Eastern Studies* 3 (1979), pp. 59–76.

37 See M. Z. Segal, "Jeremiah the Prophet During the Days of the Destruction" (Heb.), in *The Biram Volume* (Heb.), (Jerusalem, 1956), pp. 100–105 [= מסורת וביקורת (Jerusalem, 1957), pp. 149–159]; W. Rudolph, *Jeremia²* [HbzAT]

incorrect in itself) that the existence of two reports of Jeremiah's release need not be two versions of the same account. In the turmoil prevailing in Jerusalem following the flight of Zedekiah and his army and the capture of the city, Jeremiah may indeed have been released and again detained by the Chaldeans several times. Moreover, Jeremiah had already demonstrated that in situations of this kind – false or mistaken arrests – he was quite incapable of taking care of himself (37:12–15).[38] However, the question here is not what *could* have happened, but what is *reported* to have happened. And in this regard the indisputable fact remains that we are twice told of Jeremiah's release, but we are never told how Jeremiah came to be recaptured by the Chaldeans after his first release from the prison courtyard.

Moreover, we cannot separate this case from its analogies in biblical literature as a whole. The phenomenon of duplicate accounts of the same incident is characteristic of biblical narrative and historiography.[39] It appears that when Israelite authors and editors had at their disposal two oral or written traditions of one story, they endeavored to avoid choosing between them, preferring to include them both one after the other for the value inherent in each of them; an example of this process is the two accounts of Jeremiah's release.

This conclusion can be confirmed when we examine the character of these two stories. The first (38:28b, 39:3, 14) is a very brief and factual rendering of the events. The Babylonian officials sit in judgment on the rebellious city in the course of which they also decide the fate of the political prisoner Jeremiah; they release him and entrust him to the good offices of their man in Judah, Gedaliah son of Ahikam. The reliability of this description is open to question. Whereas the list of Chaldean officers is historical and has been partially confirmed (with minor emendations) by a Babylonian list of

---

(Tübingen, 1968); O. Eissfeldt, "Baruchs Anteil an Jeremia 38²⁸ᵇ, 40⁶," *OrAn* 4 (1965), pp. 31–34; [= *Kleine Schriften* IV (Tübingen, 1968), pp. 176–180].

38 Even less plausible is the view that Jeremiah went into exile willingly; see S. Spiegel, "Gedaliah, the Head of the Household" (Heb.), in עין יעלי: *The S. Z. Schocken Volume* (Heb.), (Jerusalem, 1948–1952), pp. 9–16. If this had been the prophet's intention, he would have chosen to accompany the exiles without shackles upon his wrists, as Nebuzaradan had suggested.

39 See, e.g., A. Kuenen, *The Origin and Composition of the Hexateuch* (London, 1886), pp. 38–41.

officials,[40] the "trial" in the middle gate seems to be a conscious fulfillment of the prophecy in Jer 1:15: "And each shall set up a throne before the gates of Jerusalem." The results of their deliberation – the handing over of Jeremiah to Gedaliah – is also doubtful, because Jeremiah is neither seen nor heard of again until after Gedaliah's assassination and the flight of Ishmael son of Nethaniah to Ammon (chap. 42). It is thus possible that this account of Jeremiah's release is not based entirely on historical events, but was subsequently created in an attempt to bridge the gap between the story of Jeremiah in the prison courtyard and that of the consultation with him in Geruth Chimham (41:17). In any event, there is no doubt that this account attempts to deal briefly with the progress of Jeremiah's life in the simplest, most natural fashion that the author could conceive.

The second story (39:11–12; 40:1–6), on the other hand, falls into an altogether different category. It is complex, richer in detail, and comprises far more than the dry facts. Here Jeremiah is portrayed as a well-known figure with an international reputation. The ruler of the mighty Babylonian empire, King Nebuchadnezzar himself, has given explicit orders to Nebuzaradan, chief of the guards, regarding the prophet's treatment (39:11–12). Jeremiah is not freed from prison after the fall of Jerusalem, but is shackled with chains and led off in a column of exiles. He participates in the people's suffering in their time of tragedy. But, at the last moment, when the convoy is about to depart from Ramah, Nebuzaradan recognizes Jeremiah and dramatically sets him free, confirming to Jeremiah that the fall of Jerusalem brought about by the people's sins, was a fulfillment of the Word of God. This implies that Jerusalem was not subdued by the Chaldean arms, but by the intervention of the Lord, God of Israel (cf. Jer 21:4–7). Nebuzaradan treats Jeremiah with great honor. He offers the prophet his patronage in Babylon, or alternatively advice on where in Judea he should go. In the end he dismisses him and presents him with a generous gift (40:1–5). This story unquestionably adds dignity

---

40 See E. Unger, "Namen im Hofstaate Nebukadnezars II," *ThLZ* 50 (1925), pp. 481–486; J. A. Bewer, "Nergalsharezer Samgar in Jer 39:3," *AJSL* 42 (1925/6), p. 130. So also S.I. Feigin, "The Babylonian Officials during the Days of the Destruction (Jer 39:3, 13)" (Heb.), מסתרי העבר (New York, 1943), pp.118–130. Nebuzaradan, however, should not be sought in v 39:3, as Feigin does. See now W. Rudolph's comments on this verse (in his commentary cited above, n. 37).

and honor to the reputation and standing of the unassuming prophet from Benjamin.

The naive attribution of international repute to Jeremiah indicates that this second account was a later one, written by an author who could not conceive that the historical Jeremiah had not played an important part in the main events of his time. In the exact same manner the author of the Book of Chronicles rewrote the account of the fall of Judah which he found in the Book of Kings, inserting Jeremiah's name three times into the narrative (2 Chr 35:25; 36:12, 21). But the main indication of the story's late date is the martyrological tendencies it displays. The Jewish prophet is freed from his chains, and the foreign oppressor, the destroyer of Jerusalem and the Temple, wholeheartedly proclaims the greatness and power of the God of Israel. If there is no more than this – if the prophet is not first cast into a fiery furnace or a lions' den and the foreign oppressor does not become a convert – it is because this legend is not a mere product of the imagination, but attempts to integrate itself into an existing historical framework. The tendency of the story however, the portrayal of the prophet as suffering in the struggle between the Lord and the unbelievers, his depiction as an international figure whose speeches deeply moved even gentile kings, and above all, the acknowledgement of the greatness of the Lord of Israel by the enemy and destroyer – this tendency already denotes a characteristic feature of martyrology, the new legendary creation of Judaism in the Second Commonwealth.

These first appearances of martyrology have been integrated into Jeremiah's biography. This is an instructive example of how legend "corrects" history. The lone prophet, despised and tortured, depicted in numerous stories as one whose admonitions fall on deaf ears, here becomes an authoritative figure for "many lands" and "great nations." In this manner the later author has corrected the wrongs perpetrated by the prophet's contemporaries. Moreover, here the martyrological legend conceals a prophetic truth. In days to come, all will be forgotten: Nebuchadnezzar, with his great armies and his glorious kingdom, Zedekiah, with his nobles and servants, and all the people of the land. Only one remains: he through whom God spoke "concerning this place for disaster." Jeremiah, prophet of Anathoth, in time became the hero of the fall of Jerusalem for generations of Jews and Christians, for the whole of Western civilization.

INDICES

2. Subjects
(selected items in historico-literary criticism)